www.wadsworth.com

www.wadsworth.com is the World Wide Web site for Thomson Wadsworth and is your direct source to dozens of online resources.

At *www.wadsworth.com* you can find out about supplements, demonstration software, and student resources. You can also send email to many of our authors and preview new publications and exciting new technologies.

www.wadsworth.com
Changing the way the world learns®

THE MACRO PRACTITIONER'S WORKBOOK

A Step-by-Step Guide to Effectiveness with Organizations and Communities

RODNEY A. ELLIS
University of Tennessee

KIMBERLY CRANE MALLORY
Vanderbilt University

MISTY Y. GOULD
Vanderbilt University

SUZANNE L. SHATILA
Tennessee Department of Children's Services

THOMSON
BROOKS/COLE

Australia • Canada • Mexico • Singapore • Spain
United Kingdom • United States

THOMSON
BROOKS/COLE

The Macro Practitioner's Workbook:
A Step-by-Step Guide to Effectiveness with Organizations and Communities

Rodney A. Ellis, Kimberly Crane Mallory, Misty Y. Gould, Suzanne L. Shatila

Executive Editor: *Lisa Gebo*
Assistant Editor: *Monica Arvin*
Editorial Assistant: *Sheila Walsh*
Technology Project Manager: *Barry Connolly*
Executive Marketing Manager: *Caroline Concilla*
Marketing Assistant: *Rebecca Weisman*
Senior Marketing Communications Manager: *Tami Strang*
Project Manager, Editorial Production: *Christine Sosa*
Art Director: *Vernon Boes*

Print Buyer: *Rebecca Cross*
Permissions Editor: *Sarah Harkrader*
Production Service: *Peggy Francomb, Shepherd, Inc.*
Copy Editor: *Amy Freitag*
Cover Designer: *Paula Goldstein*
Cover Image: *People Around Globe*
Cover Printer: *Thomson West*
Compositor: *Cadmus Professional Communications*
Printer: *Thomson West*

For more information about our products, contact us at:
Thomson Learning Academic Resource Center
1-800-423-0563

For permission to use material from this text or product, submit a request online at
http://www.thomsonrights.com

Any additional questions about permissions can be submitted by email to
thomsonrights@thomson.com

Library of Congress Control Number: 2005926911

ISBN 0-534-63311-0

Thomson Higher Education
10 Davis Drive
Belmont, CA 94002-3098
USA

Asia (including India)
Thomson Learning
5 Shenton Way
#01-01 UIC Building
Singapore 068808

Australia/New Zealand
Thomson Learning Australia
102 Dodds Street
Southbank, Victoria 3006
Australia

Canada
Thomson Nelson
1120 Birchmount Road
Toronto, Ontario M1K 5G4
Canada

UK/Europe/Middle East/Africa
Thomson Learning
High Holborn House
50/51 Bedford Row
London WC1R 4LR
United Kingdom

Latin America
Thomson Learning
Seneca, 53
Colonia Polanco
11560 Mexico
D.F. Mexico

Spain (including Portugal)
Thomson Paraninfo
Calle Magallanes, 25
28015 Madrid, Spain

We dedicate this book to the practitioners who have blazed the trail before us, who have developed the principles and practices described in this book; as well as to those who will follow, who will use and refine those principles and practices and pass them on to the next generation.

TABLE OF CONTENTS

Preface   ix

Unit 1: Assessment, Planning, and Preparation
    for Organizations and Communities

Introduction   1

Assessment, Planning, and Preparation for Organizations and
    Communities Case Study   2

Chapter 1 Techniques of Organizational and Community
    Assessment   7

Chapter 2 Strategic Planning   29

Chapter 3 Contingency Planning   50

Chapter 4 Recruiting Collaborative Partners   68

Chapter 5 Gaining Support and Minimizing Opposition   83

Chapter 6 Developing a Public Relations Plan   100

Unit 2: Effective Communication for Agencies,
    Groups, and Communities

Introduction   121

Effective Communication for Agencies, Groups, and Communities
Case Study   122

Chapter 7 Effective Communication in Agencies, Groups,
    and Communities   125

Chapter 8 Forming a Task Force or Committee   144

Chapter 9 Working with a Board of Directors   156

Unit 3: Effective Recruiting and Hiring

Introduction   169

Effective Recruiting and Hiring Case Study   170

Chapter 10 Creating Job Descriptions and Classified Ads   172

Chapter 11 The Hiring Process   181

Chapter 12 Conducting Interviews   196

Unit 4: Effective Financial Management and Fundraising

Introduction   207

Effective Financial Management and Fundraising Case Study   208

Chapter 13 Basics of Financial Management   211

Chapter 14 Writing a Government Grant Proposal   224

Chapter 15 Writing a Foundation Inquiry Letter   242

Chapter 16 Planning a Fundraising Event   253

Chapter 17 Writing a Fundraising Letter   266

Index   277

PREFACE

Although the majority of all social workers are direct practitioners, many engage in some form of macro practice at various points during their careers. Some, for instance, may be called upon to lead task groups or participate in grant writing and program development. Others are promoted to supervisory levels at which they continue to work directly with clients and also assume supervisory responsibilities. Still others take on roles that are almost entirely oriented toward program management or agency administration.

Regardless of the path they follow into macro roles, practitioners are often confronted with tasks with which they are unfamiliar. They may be asked to engage in strategic planning, develop an agenda, write a funding proposal, or help build a coalition. Such tasks can be daunting when practitioners lack the knowledge of how to perform these tasks. Although many texts provide background theory and general practice guidelines, unfortunately few resources provide step-by-step guidelines that practitioners can follow in order to complete specific macro tasks.

WHY DID WE WRITE THIS TEXT?

This text was written to meet the need for step-by-step, task-related guidelines. As such, it is a working text in which the theory and principles involved in the completion of each task are described in narrative form and then followed by worksheets that guide the practitioner to the successful completion of the tasks. It should not be regarded as a survey text of macro practice. It will not, for example, help the reader understand bureaucracies or grasp the intricacies of management theory. It will, however, ensure that its users can perform many of the critical tasks required for successful macro practice.

FOR WHOM WAS THE TEXT WRITTEN?

The text is written for students, faculty, and practitioners. Students will find it helpful in classes that range from introductory macro courses to advanced leadership and management courses. Where curriculums are designed with fields of practice as concentrations, its guidelines are sufficiently broad enough to allow it to be used within virtually any field.

Faculty will find the text useful in a number of ways. The narrative section of each chapter provides important background material that can supplement and further develop principles identified in other resources. For instance, where other texts discuss the principles of position analysis, the narrative in this text explains the principles while the worksheets lead the reader to translate those principles into action: a job description, a classified advertisement, and an interviewing plan to fill the position. The worksheets can be used either in class or as take-home assignments. For example, after discussing organizational charts in class, an instructor might provide a case study (most chapters contain case studies) and assign students to use the case study to develop a chart before the next class session. In addition, each chapter contains exercises and discussion questions that can be used as assignments to help students develop a greater understanding of the tasks of macro practice.

As the title suggests, the text focuses on organizational and community practice. Policy practice, program development, and program evaluation are complex topics worthy of entire texts of their own. This cannot, therefore, be regarded as a primary text for a macro practice survey course, but should be seen as a supplemental course suitable for survey classes or for leadership courses where instructors wish to prepare students to perform real-world tasks.

Practitioners will also find the text beneficial. Those who have not learned to complete these tasks in classwork or posteducational training programs will be able to follow the clear guidelines to successful practice.

HOW DOES THE TEXT MEET THE NEEDS OF CURRENT AND FUTURE PRACTITIONERS?

This text meets the needs of practitioners in several ways. First, it provides a practical and effective tool for learning in the classroom or in the field practicum. Further, it constitutes a resource that can be accessed after students have graduated when they are called upon to complete one of the tasks of macro practice. For those already in the field, it provides a workbook to facilitate effective practice. For those who are already skilled in the tasks it contains, the book can be a guide for instructing and mentoring others.

WHAT ARE THE BENEFITS OF THIS TEXT?

The most fundamental benefit of this text is the way in which it provides practical instructions with guided activity, allowing students and practitioners alike to complete vital practice tasks in an effective, efficient manner. The recommended activities included with each chapter add further insight into the application of the chapter's task and increase the likelihood that readers will be able to apply that task in the real world.

IN SUMMARY

We believe this book can greatly improve both the academic and practice lives of its readers. In today's increasingly turbulent task agency environment, it is critical that those performing macro tasks do so with optimal effectiveness. This book can play a key role in generating that effectiveness.

THE MACRO
PRACTITIONER'S
WORKBOOK

ASSESSMENT, PLANNING,

AND PREPARATION

FOR ORGANIZATIONS

AND COMMUNITIES

INTRODUCTION

Although there are certainly differences in the work done by macro practitioners who function primarily in agencies and those who engage in activities such as community organizing, there are many similarities as well. In fact, many agency administrators are called upon to participate in community activities, and community organizers sometimes run small programs or agencies. In each case there are activities in which the practitioner must engage that involve assessment, planning, and preparation. Even when practitioners work only in an agency or operate alone in the community, most still must engage in these processes. Their activities are sufficiently similar to allow them to be treated together in unit 1.

In the first chapter, "Techniques of Organizational and Community Assessment," the basic processes and strategies of macro-level assessment are identified and explained. Many of the steps of assessment for organizations and communities are similar. These similarities form a framework for the chapter. Where the processes differ, those differences are noted and discussed. Assessment forms the foundation for many of the processes in this book and is particularly key to successful planning, intervention, and management.

Chapter 2, "Strategic Planning," uses an organizational context to illustrate the principles of long-term planning. However, strategic planning can and should be used within the context of community interventions. The chapter uses references within the text and illustrative boxes to help the reader understand how the principles can be applied in community practice.

"Contingency Planning," the third chapter, is similar to chapter 2 in that it illustrates the process within the context of an organization, then uses break-out boxes to explain how it would be used in a community. In truth, there are few differences in planning between agencies and communities, although the stakeholders, allies, and opposition are likely to vary.

The fourth chapter, "Recruiting Collaborative Partners," explains the procedures that should be used in assessing, recruiting, and working with partners in either agencies or communities. In this chapter, the strong similarities between practice in both settings make it possible to discuss them simultaneously. In any kind of macro practice, collaboration is essential for success. This chapter will provide the basic knowledge required to form cooperative partnerships.

Chapter 5, "Gaining Support and Minimizing Opposition," applies to both agencies and communities. The differences are, as with other chapters, discussed in the boxes. The chapter focuses on methods of identifying and classifying various groups with different perspectives on an agency's initiative, as well as on the strategies that might be employed to address those groups.

Chapter 6, "Developing a Public Relations Plan," describes the essential processes involved in presenting an organization to the public in a planned, organized manner. It is written primarily using references to organizations because an organized campaign like the one described is used much more often by agencies than by individual community practitioners. Where groups or coalitions involved in community work find a need for public relations planning, the principles discussed in this chapter can be used with minimal adjustment.

In each of the chapters, the general format of the book is followed. First, a narrative is provided that explains how the task to which the chapter is dedicated should be performed. The narratives include boxes that either explain how the process might differ for other forms of macro practice or illustrate some idea that is critical to both organizational and community practice. Each chapter is followed by worksheets that walk the reader through the completion of each task. Students should use the case study on the following pages to complete the worksheets.

CASE STUDY

You have recently been appointed to the position of a middle-level administrator with a human services agency, the Department of Human Endeavors (DHE). Although the agency has a broad range of responsibilities, yours fall primarily into two areas: (a) operating a region for the child abuse and neglect division of the department and (b) a community mobilization project in two communities within your region. The first of these areas of responsibility is the essence of your job description. The second is an assignment by your state office as a part of its collaborative effort with local government.

As a result, you find yourself directly involved in two forms of macro practice: administration and community organization.

Your work as an agency administrator requires that you manage the department budget and oversee a network of 400 employees, 450 foster homes, and approximately 25 outside contract service providers. Your assignment as head of the Disadvantaged Communities Subcommittee (DCS) of the Council of Communities (CC) for your area requires that you assess conditions in two communities and, working with a task force of approximately 20 agency designees and community volunteers ("approximately" because many of the task force members attend erratically), develop and implement interventions to improve the standard of living for residents of the communities. The council is composed of 30 high-ranking community leaders from a variety of social service agencies including health, mental health, substance abuse, law enforcement, education, and similar groups, as well as from funding organizations such as a local community foundation and the United Way.

Organizational Practice Information

Your first day on the job is an eye-opening experience. You ask for an organizational chart (OC, a document containing a diagram of the structure of the organization) and job descriptions for your employees and are told that there is no OC and that the job descriptions have not been updated in over ten years. You ask for any kind of documentation that explains what your employees do. You are told that there is nothing current to document the role of any employee. You ask for any kind of document that may offer insight as to the strengths and weaknesses of your organization. You are told that no such document exists. You realize that you must gain some kind of understanding about how your organization operates before you can make any administrative decisions.

You begin the second day of your employment by standing at the door of your office. Every time someone passes, you stop them and introduce yourself. You ask them, "Who are you? Do you work for me?" If they respond in the affirmative, you ask them, "Then who works for you. Who works for the persons who work for you?" After three days you have a reasonably complete diagram of the organization you supervise and a list of the job expectations for each position. It becomes clear to you during the first week of your employment that assessment and planning are in order.

When you meet the person who handles your budget, you discover that your organization is funded in large part by federal dollars passed through the state office. In addition, some state and local dollars are added, as well as contributions from local and national foundations. The total amount of funding you receive sounds like a great deal of money ($67,000,000.00) until you learn of the cost of your yearly operation ($98,000,000.00). You also learn that there are children who have been taken into custody who have no place to sleep at night, that you need additional foster homes, and that your adoptions unit is lagging behind federal standards. You also discover that not only your employees but also the press and members of the region you manage are also aware of these things. You decide that you need an assessment, some very intensive planning, and a strong public relations campaign.

The organization you operate has a number of strengths and weaknesses. Of primary concern is the fact that a recent reorganization has left vacant the two main administrative operational positions that answer to you. Each of these positions supervises five Program Operations Specialists (POS), who in turn supervise the five field offices. Each office has ten supervisors who handle small case loads in addition to overseeing four to seven direct service workers. The grouping of one supervisor plus her employees is termed a "unit." Each office has units that specialize in some aspect of child welfare: protective investigations, foster care, adoptions, independent living, and supportive services. Each office also has a support staff that includes one office manager and three secretaries. In addition to the vacancies at the top of your organization you have one unfilled position at the POS level, three vacancies at the supervisory level, and 15 vacancies at the direct service worker level.

Two of the current Program Operations Specialists, Ms. Brown and Ms. Woodward, have sufficiently strong backgrounds to allow them to be considered for your top two administrative positions (called "Associate Administrators") . There is also one very strong applicant from outside your organization. Five other applicants have enough experience to allow them to be considered at the POS level or at the supervisor level. No recent applications for the direct service level have been sought or obtained.

You have a clear need for additional foster homes because many are already housing in excess of the permissible three children. You also see the need for additional residential facilities, shelters, psychiatric facilities, and therapeutic homes. Most of these specialized services are acquired through contracts with private agencies.

In addition to our employees and contract providers, three other groups play important roles in the services you provide. One of those groups is the Child Welfare Advisory Council, a group of agency heads and private citizens who have no authority, but who serve in an advisory capacity to your organization. The second is composed of three private foundations who provide funding for special programs you operate. The third is the local Human Services Department for the municipal government in the area you serve.

Your organization faces a number of problems, most of which are visible in the area of service delivery. Many of the investigations of abuse and neglect are not investigated within the legally allocated time period. As mentioned before, there are too many children in many foster homes, and some of the homes are substandard in terms of both resources and facilities. The adoption process is lagging for many children so that an excess number of federal exceptions are being filed. The Independent Living Program seems to be going well, although too few children are aware of it and do not utilize its services. Overall, there are problems with many children in custody failing to receive adequate educational, medical, dental, and mental health care.

You have strong support in your work from members of the community and from local agencies. Your contractors provide high-quality services, and the local school system is anxious to work more closely together to assure that foster children receive a good education. Your advisory board has excellent members with a wealth of experience that can benefit you. Two are capable of providing substantial financial support to your organization, while two others have strong contacts in the business community where support might be obtained.

Some of the factors that have perpetuated your organization's problems include drastic underfunding by the state legislature, a lack of innovative partnering with other organizations, a history of hiring direct service workers with few or none of the skills required for the job, and a poor perception of your agency by the community at large. Recently, the local newspaper has initiated a series of articles criticizing your agency and its services. Nearly everyone at both the state and local levels expressed strong concerns about the problem, but few have made any practical suggestions for improvement.

A number of past attempts have been made to try to improve conditions. These include appeals to the state legislature for additional funding, attempted partnerships with the local Human Services Department, and one approach to a national foundation for technical assistance in establishing an effective Independent Living Program. In addition, a partnership with a group of local churches is being explored to determine whether they might be able to provide additional foster homes.

There are additional resources in the community on which you may draw to improve conditions within your organization. Two local universities have Schools of Social Work and Departments of Public Administration. They have faculty with both practical experience and academic training in assessment, management, organizational change, and evaluation. Two of your advisory council members have direct experience in these areas and one has done consulting work in facilitating various types of task groups. In addition, a local business persons organization has expressed a desire to help you in your work.

Community Practice Information

In your capacity as community organizer you have two group members in place. The first, Leila, a former community worker from the 1960s, is very knowledgeable about the processes used in those days, but is unfamiliar with the conditions in modern communities, current methods of intervention, and any form of program evaluation. The second, Delores, is a wealthy retired woman who lives off her investments and volunteers more than 40 hours of her time each week to various community organizations. She sits on a number of local boards and advisory councils and knows a great deal about the local power structure, funding sources, effective intervention, and quasi-experimental program evaluation. You can also add your administrative assistant, Diana, to the group, who can bring the administrative support you need. One problem you face is that the composition of both communities is predominantly Hispanic and African American, while the current four members are Caucasian. You also need to evaluate the group for current strengths and weaknesses as you compose the balance of it.

You decide to focus on the Addiesburg community before proceeding to the second community. You know that several organizations are based in or serve the community. There is an active block watch, a strong Parent-Teacher Organization in the schools, and an effective Community Development Corporation operating there. All are likely to participate in both the assessment and the intervention processes. Other agencies that do not have offices in the community but who are active in the community include the local law enforcement agency, the State Department of Juvenile Justice Services, two mental health and substance abuse agencies, a medical/dental clinic, and an income maintenance distribution center (TANIF service center). There are also three local universities with departments that might be willing to offer assistance. There are also a number of local churches that are interested in improving community conditions, but lack the expertise or power to direct an initiative.

You will be able to offer about 25% of the funding you will need from federal funds distributed through your own organizations. The United Way is also excited about the project and may be willing to contribute as much as another 25%. Other possible funding sources include the county Department of Human Services, two local foundations, wealthy persons in the community, and the possibility of writing a grant for federal funding. The Department of Human Services has offered to supply office space, telephones, computer access, and office supplies.

The community has a number of problems, including a low median income, a high level of transience, an elevated crime rate, a high unemployment rate, an excessive level of truancy, and a high presence of prostitutes and drug users on the streets. The elementary and middle schools are old and crumbling, with inadequate libraries and computer systems. High schoolers are bussed to a distant community. Most return to Addiesburg immediately after school because they must use public school transportation. There are few after-school programs for any age group.

The community is isolated, accessible through only two streets that contain numerous potholes. During the summer season these potholes fill with water and become a breeding ground for mosquitos that are both a nuisance and, in the local subtropical climate, a threat which may spread disease. Infant mortality is high, and the rate of an assortment of diseases and medical conditions among older children is also elevated.

Although all residents of the community experience these problems, they tend to affect the various subgroups differently. The Hispanic population, primarily recent immigrants, appears to have fewer problems securing jobs, often displacing African American workers because of their willingness to work for lower wages. Although the willingness of these Hispanic workers to accept substandard pay does provide some income, it is insufficient for families to live on and does not even approach poverty wages. The displaced African Americans are often unable to secure other employment, resulting in even lower levels of poverty. There is a good deal of animosity between the Hispanic and African American groups as a result of this dynamic.

Older people are isolated and often unable to readily secure food, medication, and access to services. Most grocers and drug stores have left the community, and those who remain charge exorbitant prices. No public transportation currently runs into the community.

Attempts to improve community conditions in the past have failed due to either discouragement among well-intentioned advocates or loss of funding. As a result, both community members and local power brokers have become skeptical about the likelihood of any intervention's effectiveness. It is clear that whatever interventions are selected early in the process will need to show rapid and noticeable success to gain the confidence of both groups. It is equally clear that funding sources must be either stable or readily replaceable to assure the stability of the project.

The problem is seen as significant by local decision makers, but, until the creation of this new initiative, their skepticism has caused them to be reluctant to address it. It appears that they are now more willing to proceed. Further information should be available from the upper administration of the Department of Human Services who were around for many of the earlier attempts at intervention, from local law enforcement which has maintained the only consistent community advocacy presence over the last 15 years, and from some of the current community leaders and residents.

TECHNIQUES OF ORGANIZATIONAL AND COMMUNITY ASSESSMENT

CHAPTER I

CHAPTER OUTLINE

Why Conduct Macro Assessments?

Steps in Macro Assessment

Preparing a Report

Obtaining Feedback and Making Final Revisions

Using the Macro Practitioner's Workbook

Summary

One of the primary roles of most social workers is that of **change agent.** In this role, macro practitioners plan and implement strategies to improve the conditions and the level of functioning within organizations and communities. An initial step in any incident of planned change is an assessment. Through assessment, practitioners can assure that problems are thoroughly understood, resources have been effectively identified, and plans can be strategically developed.

There are many similarities between assessments conducted by professionals in direct practice and those who work in the macro arena. In each case, the problems experienced by the client or client group must be understood. This involves a thorough examination of not only the presenting problem but other psychological or social conditions that may contribute to it. In micropractice this might mean that, in addition to determining the level of depression experienced by an older client, a social worker might seek information about his living environment, social support, and economic circumstances. When working with a community task group to try to reduce the crime rate, a practitioner might examine the degree of police activity in the area, but might also work to determine whether sufficient programs such as block watches and after-school programs for youth were in existence. Both micro and macro practitioners also seek to identify resources among their clients or client groups. For example, a child welfare worker hoping to assure the safety of a child following an allegation of neglect might call upon relatives or neighbors to provide care when the parent is overly stressed or unable to provide adequate care. An agency administrator hoping to bolster the cultural competence of her agency might look at the current budget to determine whether additional dollars might be available for hiring and might also explore the possibility of outside funding from a community foundation or a branch of local government.

Effective assessment forms the foundation for effective intervention which can, in turn, lead to effective change. But inadequate assessment can undermine the best intentions and lead to the failure of the intervention. In the example of the older client suffering from depression, this might mean that a practitioner failed to understand the lack of social support his client experienced. Despite effective counseling, medical services, and nutritional counseling, the client's level of depression might never change because of her loneliness and isolation. The macro worker attempting to establish after-school programs might underestimate the amount of funding needed or the degree of resistance among local school board members. Either could lead to inadequate or nonexistent programming.

It is clear, then, that many of the processes involved in assessment are similar at all levels of practice. It is equally clear that these processes must be understood and mastered, and that the differences that do exist at various levels of assessment are thoroughly understood. Competent assessment is a primary tool in the repertoire of the macro practitioner leading to the process of planned change. Netting, Kettner, and McMurtry (1998) correctly point out that professional change is carefully planned and executed. Change occurs, they assert, without any intervention by professionals. Change is driven by social forces that are likely to bring communities and agencies to ruin if interventions such as planning, collaboration, effective hiring, and proactive public relations campaigns are not undertaken. Assessment provides the foundation for these and other important activities.

This chapter discusses macro assessment, focusing specifically on working with organizations and communities. The similarities of the two methods permit them to be treated in a single chapter, with important differences either described in the body of the text or highlighted in boxes. The chapter's sections include a discussion of the purposes of assessment, a summary of the steps involved in assessment, and a narrative on how to prepare findings for presentation. The chapter concludes with the first worksheets from the Macro Practitioner's Workbook. Worksheets 1.1 through 1.6 will walk you through the process of macro-level assessment for the case study for unit 1.

WHY CONDUCT MACRO ASSESSMENTS?

There are many reasons for conducting organizational or community assessments. The first, discussed briefly in the previous section, is to deal with specific problems that exist or are about to arise. In a community this might reflect a need for better transportation or medical services. In an organization it might be the result of sudden mass departures of the clinical staff resulting in a need to cover the client load in the short run while hiring competent replacements in the long run.

A good assessment can also provide the groundwork for effective planning. The examples offered in the next two chapters of this book are strategic planning and contingency planning. By knowing what the conditions are within an agency or community, it is possible to plan for the things that need to be. Either of these types of planning might be used in either organizational

BOX I.I	REASONS FOR CONDUCTING ORGANIZATIONAL OR COMMUNITY ASSESSMENT

1. To deal with specific problems that exist or are about to arise
2. To lay the groundwork for planning
3. To establish a basis for successful coalition building
4. To allow for effective organizational management
5. To promote effective management of personnel
6. To provide the basis for effective fiscal management

BOX I.2	STEPS IN MACRO ASSESSMENT

1. Create a work group
2. Understand the problem
3. Understand supportive conditions
4. Understand the participants
5. Understand the available resources
6. Understand supportive and oppositional forces

or community practice. In fact, a thorough assessment may provide the information that would have been gathered in the internal and external scanning processes (see chapters 2 and 3). The assessment can prepare a community or agency to fully understand both the challenges it faces and the opportunities it will have. This, in turn, can prepare the agency to decide what it hopes to accomplish in the long term as well as the contingencies that it must be prepared for in the near future.

Effective assessment can also establish a basis for building successful coalitions and overcoming resistance, the topics of chapters 4 and 5. A good assessment should identify other agencies or community groups that are allies, competitors, and opponents in the community. It should also help practitioners recognize both the assets they can offer to a coalition and the needs it can have met by others in the group. Further, the assessment can help an agency or community group determine how it is perceived by others, allowing it to shape its public relations campaign.

An organization cannot be effectively managed if the conditions under which it operates are not understood. Assessment should provide leaders with the kind of information they need. For example, a residential facility that has relied on food donations from a local grocery store will need to know how reliable that source is likely to be in the future. Similarly, community practitioners must often manage small offices or coalitions. A coalition could be strengthened by the arrival of a new philanthropic organization in the community if that organization were supportive of the community worker's cause. Conditions such as these should be discovered during an assessment. Assessment can also help an agency shape its public relations program by providing information about how it is perceived in the community. This is the subject of chapter 6.

Similarly, assessment can provide the information necessary for effective personnel management. This is particularly true in organizations, where there are likely to be at least several employees. It may also be true for communities, where part-time personnel or volunteers may do much of the work. For instance, in the case of a mental health agency, it would be important to know whether the standards for employee licensure might be changing. In community practice, those seeking to improve transportation for a community by developing a fleet of jitney taxies would need to know about the requirements for licensing such a company, as well as its vehicles and drivers.

Assessment also provides a basis for effective fiscal management in both organizational and community settings. Both agency and community workers need to know the financial demands that will be placed upon their budgets and the resources they will have available to meet those demands. Effective assessment can answer these questions.

Assessment has many purposes and provides many benefits to agency and community workers who engage in its processes. It is equally important to remember that, although practitioners may designate a specific period of time during which a formal assessment is to be conducted, assessment should be an ongoing process. This suggests that a part of the formal process should be setting up ongoing feedback mechanisms, both formal and informal. This would keep the agency or community worker abreast of important changes in the community that might affect operations.

STEPS IN MACRO ASSESSMENT

As stated earlier, the assessment processes for communities and organizations have many similarities. The degree to which they differ depends, to a large extent, on the individual settings. For example, both an organizational administrator and a community practitioner are likely to be involved in some forms of internal and external assessment activities. In a large agency, the internal aspects of the process may require more attention. When engaging in community assessment, the focus is likely to be external to any community organization or task force. In both cases, however, it is vital to understand the conditions both inside and outside the groups that conduct and implement the assessment.

Creating a Work Group

In any episode of macro assessment the first step involves creating a work group. The work group should consist of no more than eight to ten people and should contain some mixture of persons with the skill, expertise, and motivation to accomplish the task. (See chapter 8 on composing a task force for additional information.) It should also include, if not be, entirely composed of, stakeholders who have various types of involvement in the project. Additional information is available in chapters 2 and 3 under the headings of "Composing a Work Group."

It will be important to try to recruit persons with a number of different special skills into the work group. For example, both organizational and community assessment are likely to require extensive literature review and telephone work. The group will also benefit from the leadership of an experienced facilitator, that is, someone who has experience in macro assessment processes and can provide leadership and direction to the group. Some situations may call for professional assistance in the form of a hired consultant. In other cases, the group may have adequate expertise and resources to be able to complete the assessment on its own. In addition, both agency and community work groups will probably need a group member or members with strong organizational skills. This may be accomplished by including a member with those skills or by having the facilitator recruit an administrative assistant from within his organization. Box 1.3 describes special concerns for organizations that are putting together an assessment work group. Box 1.4 describes issues peculiar to communities.

BOX 1.3 | CONSTITUTING AN ASSESSMENT WORK GROUP: SPECIAL CONCERNS FOR ORGANIZATIONS

1. Find a way to include group members from every level of the organization.
2. Be sure to include experts in the field from outside the agency.
3. Include representatives from as many stakeholder groups as possible.

4. Be sure to include someone with each of the special skills needed for the analysis.
5. Be sure to include both "detail" people and those who are particularly strong in dealing with issues related to the "big picture" and future planning.

BOX 1.4 | CONSTITUTING AN ASSESSMENT WORK GROUP: SPECIAL CONCERNS FOR COMMUNITIES

1. Be sure to include people who understand the community's strengths and needs.
2. Be sure to include people with the power, expertise, and motivation to complete the assessment.
3. Group members should be motivated to participate, as should others who have control over their participation (such as agency administrators).

4. Be sure that the group is composed of members who will try to understand the community's needs from its perspective, not just from a top-down perspective.
5. Be sure to involve community members in the process from the very beginning. They should help select the assessment work group members.

Understanding the Problem

The second vital component of macro assessment is understanding the problem. Understanding the problem involves several steps that include: (a) knowing the nature of the problem and how it affects those who experience it, (b) knowing what forces act to create or sustain the problem, (c) knowing what attempts have been made to understand and address the problem within the organization or community in the past, (d) knowing what attempts have been made to address similar problems in other agencies or communities, and (e) knowing the degree of significance to which the problem is regarded by agency or community leaders. After this information has been gathered, practitioners should develop a **problem statement,** that is a concise but comprehensive description of the problem.

Knowing the nature of the problem and how it affects those who experience it means that a concise expression should be identified that describes both the type of problem that is being experienced and the way in which it impacts the affected group. In Box 1.5, the central problem is housing instability. Its effects include disruption of income or employment preparation and homelessness.

Several forces operate to create or sustain the problem and its effects. The initial problem was created by the lack of opportunity for immigrants who were professionals in their countries of origin. It is further complicated by the influx of higher-income people and probably by the encouragement of

| HOUSING NEEDS IN AN IMMIGRANT COMMUNITY

The East Oceanside community in southeast Florida has been known for many years as an area composed of people of lower socioeconomic status who were also of primarily African American descent. Over the last ten years its population has changed. Its current residents are still predominantly lower income, but are now primarily of Hispanic descent rather than African American. Many are refugees and are legal residents but are unable to pursue the careers they left behind in the countries they fled. As a result, these former attorneys, physicians, teachers, and other professionals struggle to support their families as they learn new trades or obtain a license or certificate that will allow them to be compensated for the work they once performed in other countries.

Although the business portion of East Oceanside is booming with trendy shops and a long strip of beachside bars that boast a hustling nightlife, the housing areas are poor and in disrepair. A third area contains warehouses and assorted businesses such as repair centers. Many of these buildings are empty. In recent years, the housing and warehouse areas have begun to experience gentrification, that is, young upwardly mobile professionals have been purchasing dilapidated housing, repairing it, and moving into the area. Although this has benefitted the community in a number of ways, it has caused the former Hispanic population to lose their homes. The challenges they already faced in attempting to establish sufficient and stable income are becoming compounded by a lack of acceptable housing.

community leaders who are anxious to see the community revitalized. Further assessment would reveal the degree to which these conditions are present as well as help determine whether other contributing factors exist.

Practitioners would also want to know what attempts have been made to understand and address the problem within the organization or community in the past. Should such efforts have been made, it would be important to either avoid such efforts or to learn from them. If the efforts were abject failures with no possibility of success, repetition of those efforts should be avoided. If the efforts had promise but were thwarted by problematic conditions, it might be possible to renew the efforts while avoiding the problems of the past. In Box 1.5 it seems likely that given the short period of the problem of unstable housing, no concerted effort may have been made to solve it. It is likely, however, that efforts may have been made to deal with poverty in the neighborhood or to help the recent immigrants find ways to find employment more consistent with their background and training. Lessons learned from these efforts might be used to further the proposed initiative.

Understanding the problem would also require that the work group be aware of attempts that have been made to address similar problems in other agencies or communities. This could be accomplished in a number of ways, including reviews of the professional literature, calls to similar communities in other areas, and contact with state and federal agencies. Although it cannot be assumed that initiatives effective in some areas may necessarily be effectively replicated elsewhere, much can be learned from studying these efforts. If, in fact, the communities are similar, it may be that an initiative that succeeded elsewhere can be used in the target community. In other situations the conditions between communities may vary substantially, but some facets may be sufficiently similar to warrant the incorporation of some aspects of the intervention.

Another important step is developing an understanding of the degree to which the problem is seen as significant by agency or community leaders. In the case in Box 1.5, community leaders may be more concerned about increasing property values in the community than with maintaining housing for immigrants. In other cases the leaders may be unaware of the problem. If leaders are either unconcerned about or unaware of the problem, the assessment group will need to determine whether the problem will need to be officially recognized in order to have it addressed. In the example of the immigrants in East Oceanside, some level of support and participation by community leaders will almost certainly be required. In order to obtain their official participation, it will be necessary for them to make some sort of official, public recognition that the problem exists. Netting, Kettner, and McMurtry (1998) refer to this process as moving from a condition (in which the difficulties of the disadvantaged group are not officially recognized) to a problem (in which the existence of the condition has been officially recognized). The assessment group should make a determination as to whether this step will be necessary and develop basic information about how the recognition might be obtained.

Ultimately, the process of understanding the problem should lead to the development of a problem statement. The statement should include information about the nature, size, and scope of the problem (Netting, Kettner, & McMurtry, 1998). If it is linked to or affected by current social policy, it might also be beneficial to identify that policy within the statement (Ellis, 2002). For the community described in Box 1.5, a problem statement might read as follows:

Increasing numbers of Hispanic families within the East Oceanside area are being displaced through the process of gentrification. As many as 30% have been forced to relocate within the last three years and approximately 12% have become homeless, at least temporarily. Those who have not become homeless have experienced extreme disruption to their processes of reestablishing or acquiring careers that will allow their breadwinners to earn an adequate income.

When working with communities, the process of understanding the problem may be particularly sensitive. A careful approach is particularly important when the assessment is being initiated by someone from outside the community, such as a social worker designated by an agency that serves the area. Members of disadvantaged communities often express anger at the way they have been treated by researchers and community activists in the past. They feel that they have been exploited by researchers who came and took what they needed, then left without benefitting the community. Some also feel that they have been victimized by community activists who have brought enthusiasm and expertise to their community, only to abandon them when frustration set in or resources ran out.

In addition to recalling past experiences of the community, community members can offer their own perspective on the problem, providing insights that would be missed by the work group alone. To fail to elicit community input would not only predispose the initiative to failure, it would also constitute a violation of the Social Work Code of Ethics. Because the Code of Ethics requires that practitioners support the self-determination of their clients, it is critical that community members be included in every aspect of assessment and intervention.

The process described here has been set in a community context. Some differences might exist for organizational assessment. Some of these are listed in Box 1.6. This example also assumes that the assessment was being conducted for the purpose of addressing the problem. If the assessment was being conducted for some other purpose, the group should develop a purpose statement, which would clearly define the task the group hopes to accomplish.

BOX 1.6 | SPECIAL CONSIDERATIONS FOR UNDERSTANDING THE PROBLEM IN AN ORGANIZATIONAL ASSESSMENT

1. Remember that there are many sources of power within an organization. Informal sources, such as relationships based on friendship or loyalty, can be difficult to detect, yet very powerful in their capacity to undermine an intervention.

2. Be sure to include participants from every level of the organization.

3. Be sure to include participants from every stakeholder group.

Understanding the Participants

Once the problem has been understood and described, it is necessary to understand the participants. Participants refer to any individuals or groups that may have some sort of involvement in the entire episode of change, not just in the assessment. Clearly, this would be a much broader group including, for example, persons and groups that might benefit from the change despite not being a part of the target group or a participant in the intervention. The participant groups have been identified as the initiator system, the change agent system, the client system, the support system, the controlling system, the host system, the implementing system, the target system, and the action system (Kettner, Daley, & Nichols, 1985; Netting, Kettner, & McMurtry, 1998).

The *initiator system* is composed of those who first recognize the problem's presence and effects and who bring it to the attention of those who can provide a potential solution. In the scenario in Box 1.5, the initiator system might be a social worker at an employment agency or training facility who works with some of the people who have immigrated to the area. Alternatively, it might be a parent whose children attend school with the children who are losing their homes or a teacher in one of those schools. In any case, this person would recognize the problem and either bring it to the attention of those who have the expertise to address it or organize a group that would be capable of addressing it. In an agency, the initiator might be a case manager who discovers that many clients who do not show up for one appointment are never rescheduled and who brings this problem up at a staff meeting.

Those who take the lead for the initial stages of change are referred to as the *change agent system*. Members of this group receive information about the problem from the initiator system and begin the process of organizing to address it. For the community in Box 1.5, this might be a Community Development Corporation, a local human rights group, or a human services agency in the area. This group might convene a task force or committee to determine how the problem should be addressed. It might conduct the assessment or pass that responsibility to others, perhaps those who will actually implement the intervention. The change agent system might also assume the responsibility of getting an issue recognized as a condition elevated to the status of a problem. It is important to remember that, as suggested in the section above, persons who actually experience the problem should be included at this stage. In our example, this would mean that some of the Hispanic immigrants who have lost their homes or are in danger of losing their homes would be a part of the change agent system.

The third group to be identified and understood is the *client system*. The client system is constituted of those who experience the problem and who are directly intended to benefit from the change. In the current example this would include the immigrant families in East Oceanside, as well as some others who might benefit indirectly, such as other community members who experience similar problems. This underscores the importance of understanding differences in perspective or culture within the client system and between the client system and other participant groups. For example, some East Oceanside African American families might also benefit from the initiative. There might, however, be cultural differences that could cause the responsiveness of the two groups to vary. These would need to be anticipated in the assessment. Differences due to race, ethnicity, culture, gender, age, sexual orientation, disability, and other conditions must be considered and included in the assessment (Atkinson, Morton, & Sue, 1998; Green, 1982). Only if they are considered at this point are they likely to be incorporated into the intervention. Within the organizational example we have mentioned, the client group not being rescheduled would be the direct recipient and therefore within the client system.

The *support system* refers to those outside the client system who may experience some benefit from the proposed change. Examples from East Oceanside might include social service agencies that work in the community, Spanish language newspapers, colleges and schools of social work, and similar groups. It is important to remember that the groups identified in this section may not be exclusive. For instance, a Hispanic immigrant in East Oceanside (client system) might be active in bringing attention to the problem (initiating system) and might go on to be a part of the change agent system and the support system.

The *controlling system* includes those with the authority to make the change. This may include agency heads, government officials, and private citizens or groups that hold power because of their financial and political connections. (See the discussion in chapter 4 about political alliances.) In the example in Box 1.5, this might include local or state government officials, local real estate firms, local groups of attorneys, and local government bureaucrats.

The group responsible for seeing that the change happens is referred to as the *host system*. Although the assessment work group will probably not be able to identify exactly which agency or agencies will constitute this group, it should be able to identify a number of alternative possibilities. This system is referred to as "host" because it includes the members on the persons who do the day-to-day work to make change happen, the implementation system.

The *implementing system* includes portions of the host system and is likely to include people outside the host. These are the individuals or small groups that provide the hands-on work to implement the intervention. Although identification of all the members is likely to be beyond the capacity of the assessment work group, some of the potential participants should be recognized during the assessment.

The *target system* is composed of the individuals and groups that must be changed in order for the intervention to be successful. They are the people, groups, policies, or practices whom the intervention targets rather than those whom it seeks to benefit. In the case of East Oceanside, the target group might include local government officials, local government structure, and local real estate professionals. If, for example, community residents could be organized into a cooperative group that would purchase an abandoned property using public housing funds and agree to build that property into a cooperative housing arrangement to be sold by local Realtors and would pay the customary taxes to local government, the target system might agree to the initiative.

The group that is responsible for planning the change and seeing that it is implemented is known as the *action system*. This group is typically composed of members of some of the other systems. In fact, it is likely to function best if it includes someone from each of the systems. The assessment group is unlikely to be able to identify all members of the action system, but should be able to make some recommendations about its members.

Understanding the Available Resources

After developing an understanding of the problem and the participants, the assessment work group must determine what resources will be available to support the change. Resources might include funding, personnel, office space, computer equipment, and similar items. Funding may be obtained from a variety of sources. These include foundations, local units of government, and philanthropic groups and individuals. Personnel may be employees assigned by agencies, volunteers, or members of the community. Office space, office supplies, telephones, computer equipment, and similar resources can be paid for by funders or supplied by participating agencies. It is important, however, that the assessment work group identify as many sources as possible and report those sources to those who will implement the intervention.

Understanding Resistance to Change

It is also important that the assessment work group identify and report the likely sources and reasons for resistance to change. Information about resistence can be obtained from a number of sources. These include the media, key informants, publications, and personal interviews.

Perhaps the most important source of information about possible resistance to an initiative is **key informants.** Key informants are people who have information based on experience, training, or some other reliable source that will allow them to predict the way in which influential people or groups may be likely to respond to the proposed initiative. They may be community leaders, community activists, members of the press, or others who have been politically active. Key informants are most often effectively approached through a scheduled appointment and a structured, or semistructured, interview. This requires preparing a script and an interview guide. Script preparation is described in chapter 4. An interview guide is prepared by thinking through and writing down the questions you want to ask in such a way that you have space on a piece of paper to record answers. For example, you might ask, "What people or groups might you expect to support this initiative?" "What persons or groups might you expect to oppose it?"

Newspaper or magazine articles are yet another source of information about possible sources of resistance. By reviewing the archives of a variety of media sources, it may be possible to determine who has opposed similar efforts in the past, as well as to obtain some information about the reason for their opposition.

Government records may also be helpful. County commissions and state legislatures typically maintain records about the way their members have voted. Governmental units may have position papers or drafts of legislation that can help practitioners anticipate the position its employees are likely to take.

PREPARING A REPORT

After the assessment information has been gathered, it should organized and prepared as a written report or summary. The summary should be thorough, but concise. It can be written in a format that follows the narrative in this chapter. The presence of a written summary of the group's findings will help in a number of ways. First, it will help to assure that the group is in agreement regarding their results and recommendations. Second, it will allow the members to clearly communicate their results to others. Third, it will create a record which will assure that, over time, the results of the group's work are not confused or forgotten. The following suggestions should be helpful in report preparation.

The first page should be a title page including the name of the project, the authority who commissioned it, and the names of the group members. The second page should contain an executive summary, a short paragraph that summarizes the activities and findings of the work group.

The third page should begin the actual narrative. It should include a brief statement of the purpose for the assessment and a discussion of forces that brought about its existence. The introduction should be followed by a section entitled "The Composition of the Assessment Work Group." This section should include a brief description of the members of the group, the organizations they represent, and any special contributions they made.

Next the report summary should contain information about the problem or purpose the assessment was intended to address. It might be entitled simply, "The Purpose of the Assessment." In keeping with the format suggested above, the report should include subsections entitled: (a) the nature and effects of the problem, (b) the forces that create or sustain the problem, (c) past attempts to address the problem locally, (d) past attempts to address similar problems in other settings, and (e) perceptions of community leaders. The report should conclude with the problem or purpose statement developed by the group.

The next section of the report should include a summary of the potential participants identified by the work group. The taxonomy described above could be used so participants would be designated as the initiator system, the change agent system, the client system, the support system, the controlling system, the host system, the implementing system, the target system, and the action system (Kettner, Daley, & Nichols, 1985; Netting, Kettner, & McMurtry, 1998). Each group would need to be defined, and the potential for participation by each of its members described.

The fourth section of the report should describe the resources identified by the work group. It would simply be called "Potential Resources." They should be organized by category, such as funding, personnel, office space, computer equipment, and similar items. Potential sources of support should be noted and contact persons identified.

BOX 1.7 | SPECIAL CONSIDERATIONS FOR UNDERSTANDING THE PROBLEM IN A COMMUNITY ASSESSMENT

1. Knowing the degree to which the problem is regarded as significant by community leaders.

2. It is vital to obtain community input and participation at the most fundamental levels of the process.

The fifth section might be entitled, "Potential Resistance to Change." In this section, those who are likely to oppose the initiative should be identified and the source of the group's expectation revealed. If, for example, the group is told that a county commissioner is likely to be oppositional, the source of the information as well as the logic that supports the assumption should be described. If the information has been given anonymously, every caution should be taken to preserve the identity of the source while assuring that members of the action system will have enough information to objectively evaluate the opinion.

The final section should be a summary (and should be included under that heading). The summary should simply recap the contents of the report. The report should be thorough but concise. It is very important that its recommendations are clear and that no misunderstanding is likely to arise regarding its proposals.

OBTAINING FEEDBACK AND MAKING FINAL REVISIONS

After the report is written, the work group should review it and submit it to any other contributors for review. Revisions should be considered before providing the final draft. Others from the participant groups who were unable to participate in the assessment may be able to add additional insight. The assessment work group might also consider preparing a short overview of the report to provide orally to interested parties.

USING THE MACRO PRACTITIONER'S WORKBOOK

As mentioned in the introduction, each chapter contains several worksheets that compose the Macro Practitioner's Workbook for that task. For this chapter they are included on Worksheets 1.1 through 1.6. For each worksheet, use the information included in the case study for unit 1. In some cases you may need to be creative, but the basic information you need should be supplied.

SUMMARY

In this chapter, the assessment of communities and organizations were discussed. First, the purposes of assessment were reviewed and then recruiting a work group was discussed. Then the steps to effective assessment were examined and one way in which a report might be prepared was discussed. In the remaining two chapters of this unit, two of the processes for which assessment is sometimes conducted will be looked at: strategic planning and contingency planning.

Activities for Learning

1. Working with a group of your classmates, volunteer to help a community organizer conduct a community assessment. Produce a report that follows the guidelines in this book.
2. Ask local agencies to allow you to examine copies of past assessments of their organizations. How were the assessments conducted? How were the reports prepared? Were their recommendations followed? Why or why not?
3. Consider a disadvantaged community in your area. What problems exist there? Prepare problem statements describing at least three of them.

Questions for Discussion

1. Why are so many problems in communities interconnected? How can assessment groups decide which are the most important? How can they decide which problem should be concentrated on with an intervention?
2. Under what circumstances might an organization wish to conduct an assessment? What are some of the ways it might be used?
3. Consider the characterization of participants offered in this chapter. What are its strengths? What are its weaknesses? How would you change the characterization in order to improve it?

Key Terms

Change agent—a person or people who play a key role in the change process for an organization or community.

Key informant—a person or people who have information based on experience, training, or some other reliable source that will allow them to predict the way in which influential persons or groups may be likely to respond to the proposed initiative.

Problem statement—a clear, concise statement that describes a problem in terms of its nature, size, and scope.

References

Atkinson, D. R., Morten, G., & Sue, D. W. (1998). *Counseling American minorities.* New York: McGraw-Hill.

Ellis, R. A. (2002). *Impacting social policy: A practitioner's guide to analysis and action.* Pacific Grove, CA: Thompson/Brooks Cole.

Green, J. W. (1982). *Cultural awareness in the human services.* Englewood Cliffs, NJ: Prentice-Hall.

Kettner, P. M., Daley, J. M., & Nichols, A. W. (1985). *Initiating change in organizations and communities.* Monterey, CA: Brooks/Cole.

Netting, F. E., Kettner, P. M., & McMurtry, S. L. (1998). *Social work macro practice* (2nd ed.). New York: Longman.

WORKSHEET I.I │ STEPS IN MACRO ASSESSMENT: COMPOSING
A WORK GROUP

(8-10 people)

1. What groups need to be represented in the assessment work group? (If you are assessing a community, be sure to review the list of participant groups in the "Understanding the Participants" section of this chapter. (If you are assessing an organization, think in terms of including all stakeholder groups as well as each level of the organization.)

    1. Child Welfare Advisory Council = 1
    2. Human Services Dept.
    3. Hispanic Community leader
    4. African-American Community lead.
    5. University Reprensative
    6. Community Development Org.
    7. United Way
    8. Rep. from private foundation
    9. Delores (community volunteer)
    10. Diane (admin. Assist)

2. Who can bring special talents and abilities to the work group? Who will provide motivation? Who will provide expertise? Who will provide power?

    Diane - admin Assist - note taking Sending ect..
    Delores - has power w/in community
    HSD + CWAC - expertise
    Com. Delvep.
    Unted way - Power (finanal)
    Private foundatuns (Power) finanial
    2 Communty leaders (could? provide motenation

3. - Whom will you choose to facilitate the group?
    your self plus, Someone from Child welfare Advisory Committee

4. If you hire a consultant, how will you identify that consultant? How will the consultant be compensated?

    If hired the consltant should be neutral in opionion. Through negitation a contract should be drawn-up. Compensation could come through a private donation or grant.

5. Who will provide the work group with organizational and administrative support?

    You who are putthe org. together. Using your in house staff

WORKSHEET 1.2 | STEPS IN MACRO ASSESSMENT: UNDERSTANDING THE PROBLEM

1. What is the nature of the problem?

    Underfunding by state legislature
    lack of innovative partnerships w/ other organizations
    poor perception of overall agancy to community at large
    poor hiring practices
    Commo

2. Who experiences the problem?

    Everyone involved in community

3. What groups experience the problem (race, ethnicity, gender, age, sexual orientation, disability) and how do those groups experience or perceive the problem?

    Hispanic - Poor paying jobs, but will work
    African American -
    Seniors - Isocaled
    School age - no school programs, due to no transportation after
            School
    There is anamosity amongest different ethnicity groups

4. What barriers to solving the problem may exist within the mindset of the majority population?

    That they have been through this before, loosing the
    Stepfialm about the likihood of any interventions being
    Successful

5. What forces act to create or sustain the problem?

    none or Poor communibtion between communty leader, and
    the poor perception of the agency that the communty
    has

6. What attempts have been made to understand and address the problem or situation in the past?

1) appeals to STATE legisature for additional funding
2) partnership w/ HSD

7. What attempts have been made to address similar problems or situations in other agencies or communities?

Contacting local agencies
But other than that None

8. To what degree is the problem or situation regarded as significant by agency or community leaders?

I believe the degree is regarded as important, because thier
are many years (15+) of information available, and that
thier are many agencies wanting to "buy in" to changing things

9. Prepare a purpose or problem statement based on the guidelines offered earlier in this chapter.

For what?
case study

WORKSHEET 1.3 | STEPS IN MACRO ASSESSMENT: UNDERSTANDING
THE PARTICIPANTS

1. Who are the members of the initiator system? What role(s) might they be able to play in the episode of change? *You, who work for DHE, initial research into problem, your admin. Assist.*

2. Who are the members of the change agent system? What role(s) might they be able to play in the episode of change?
Community Development Committee - design the change
United way
Local leaders

3. Who are the members of the client system? What role(s) might they be able to play in the episode of change?
Local churches *⟩ offer information about the*
School officals *wheres, whats, how, who's of*
Local leadership *the community.*

4. Who are the members of the support system? What role(s) might they be able to play in the episode of change?
Local officals + leadership ⟩
Churchs
Schools
Community advocates.
Newspaper
Social Service agencies who work in community

5. Who are the members of the controlling system? What role(s) might they be able to play in the episode of change?
agency heads *They have authority*
goverment officals ⟩ to make change
private citizans
groups that hold power.

6. Who are the members of the host system? What role(s) might they be able to play in the episode of change? *these are the people who can make day to day changes, and might not be idenified but will implement the changes*

7. Who are the members of the implementing system? What role(s) might they be able to play in the episode of change?

Include members of the host systemm

8. Who are the members of the target system? What role(s) might they be able to play in the episode of change?

Local goverment, or the groups ,policies, proceduces practices whom the implementation will target

9. Who are the members of the action system? What role(s) might they be able to play in the episode of change?

This group would consist of members from all the combined groups , They are incharge of planning the change and seeing it through.

WORKSHEET 1.4 | STEPS IN MACRO ASSESSMENT: UNDERSTANDING
THE RESOURCES

1. What types of funding resources might be available to the initiative? How would those resources be
    accessed? If the resources became available, what would be the timing of their availability?

    Funding may be found through a varity of resources.
    foundations. local units of government, philanthopic
    groups and individuals. They could be assessed by the
    priority needs, and by thier timely availability. There
    would be immed needs, short team & long team.

2. What types of personnel resources might be available to the initiative? How would those resources
    be accessed? What kind of training or preparation would be necessary to allow these people to be
    successful?

    Employess assigned by agencies
    Volunteees
    members of the community

    TRainng should always be provided, a defined description
    of thier needs. Typing, filling ect... Timing to have
    these people in place is important.

3. What types of physical resources and materials (office space, telephones, computer equipment, trans-
    portation, etc.) might be available to the initiative? How would those resources be accessed? If the
    resources became available, what would be the timing of their availability?

    Office space, office supplies, telephones, computer equpmert
    and similar resourses can be paid for by funders
    or supplied by partisipating agenqes. Must idenify
    as many resources as possible and make sure the
    who is going to implement the intervention knows ASAP

4. What other kinds of resources might be available for the initiative? How would they be accessed? When
    might they be available?

    document information from agencies
    Newspaper achieves
    Personal interviews
    goverment records

    - All public record and should be available upon
      request

WORKSHEET I.5 | STEPS IN MACRO ASSESSMENT: UNDERSTANDING
                 RESISTANCE

1. Whom should you approach as key informants to ask about potential sources of resistance to change?
    What will you ask them? Develop a script and an interview guide for each one.

    Media, Key informents, personal interviews, publications
    Who might you think will buy into idea?
    who might you think will resist.

2. What media sources might provide you with information about possible sources of resistance? Who will
    access those sources? How will they access them? What kinds of information will they look for in those
    sources?

    Newspaper and magizine articles. anyone can access this
    Information. Computers, orgoing to libary archives or contacting
    person who wrote article.
    who has opposed similar efforts in the past, reasons for
    thier opposition.

3. What government records might be helpful in discovering potential sources of resistance? Who will
    access those sources? How will they access them? What kinds of information will they look for in those
    sources?

    Government records from County commissioners and
    state legislatures, typically keep records on how people
    voted. Thee might be papers on thier position, or
    even drafts of legislation, that can be used to know how
    someone might feel or vote on a particular matter.

WORKSHEET I.6 | PREPARING A REPORT

1. Prepare a title page including the name of the project, the authority who commissioned it, and the names of the group members.

(name) Community Mobilazation Project
(authority) Department of Human Endeavors
(group) Disaduantaged Commitees SubComittes
Council of Communities.

2. On the second page, write a brief summary outlining the activities and findings of the work group. The paragraph should be entitled, "Executive Summary" and should not be more than 150–200 words.

3. On the third page begin the narrative. Start with an introduction that includes an explanation of why the assessment was done and a discussion of the events that caused it to happen.

4. Follow the introduction with a centered heading, "The Composition of the Assessment Work Group." Within it include a brief description of the members of the group, the organizations they represent, and any special contributions they made.

5. Head the next section with the title "The Purpose of the Assessment." It should include subsections entitled: (a) the nature and effects of the problem, (b) the forces that create or sustain the problem, (c) past attempts to address the problem locally, (d) past attempts to address similar problems in other settings, and (e) perceptions of community leaders. It should end with the problem or purpose statement developed by the group.

6. Begin the next section with the heading, "Understanding the Participants." Describe each participant as they fit into the following groups: the initiator system, the change agent system, the client system, the support system, the controlling system, the host system, the implementing system, the target system, and the action system.

7. "Understanding Available Resources" should head the next section, in which potential sources of funding, personnel, office space, computer equipment, and similar items are described.

8. The next section should be entitled, "Potential Resistance to Change." In this section, those who are likely to oppose the initiative should be identified and the source of the group's expectation revealed.

9. End the report with a summary (headed with that word as a title). Include a summary of both findings and recommendations.

STRATEGIC PLANNING

CHAPTER 2

CHAPTER OUTLINE

What Is Strategic Planning?

Why Develop a Strategic Plan?

Composing a Work Group

Writing or Revising the Mission Statement

Values, Vision, and Goals

Internal and External Scanning

Developing Objectives, Tasks, and Strategies

Committing the Plan to Writing

Using the Macro Practitioner's Workbook

Summary

In today's turbulent task environment, strategic planning is crucial to the success of virtually every agency. Yet many practitioners lack the knowledge and skill to be able to develop and execute this type of plan. In this chapter, the theory of strategic planning, the essential processes involved in developing a plan, as well as the basics of plan execution will be presented.

WHAT IS STRATEGIC PLANNING?

Strategic planning has been described as "a systematic process through which an organization agrees on and builds commitment among key stakeholders to priorities which are essential to its mission and responsive to its operating environment" (Allison & Kaye, 1997, p. 3). In other words, it is a process through which an organization develops a road map to success. The process involves the development, review, or revision of a mission statement and the identification of **goals**, objectives, and tasks that will allow the agency to accomplish that mission. With a strategic plan in place, an organization can move confidently along the road toward its purpose. Without a plan, the same organization is likely to become diverted, squander its resources, and fail to adequately serve the population it intends to help.

Strategic planning is not a solitary task to be conducted by agency leaders. It should involve a variety of stakeholders and, ideally, should include input from all the constituencies involved in or affected by the agency. Further, it must be taken seriously. Effective strategic planning affects and is affected by the very core of an agency's purpose, philosophies, and ethics. According to Edwards, Yankley, and Altpeter (1998) the process involves: (a) examining, defining, and redefining an organization's mission, (b) clarifying the values and **vision** of an organization, (c) undertaking internal and external scanning, (d) identifying and selecting strategic issues, and (e) forming strategies to address these issues. Clearly, such a significant and important undertaking must have the full support and participation of agency administration, the board of directors, and every other stakeholder group.

WHY DEVELOP A STRATEGIC PLAN?

The need for strategic planning by social service agencies has become increasingly evident over the last several years. In the not too distant past, many not-for-profit organizations did not engage in such formal processes. In recent years, however, several forces have converged to make it an absolute necessity. These factors include: (a) increasingly unstable task environments, (b) increasing emphasis on accountability, and (c) increasing conservatism among both elected officials and the general public.

The first factor that has contributed to the need for strategic planning is that the **task environments** in which the agencies operate have become increasingly unstable. Instability refers to a variety of conditions, including decreasing funding, proliferating competition, changing needs among the populations served, and service alterations required by new information gained through social science research. This instability can create problems for agencies in a number of ways. For example, when state budgets are cut, allocations to social service agencies are often negatively affected. In agencies where budgets are tight, these cuts may represent the difference between survival and failure. Strategic planning enables agencies to anticipate these types of changes in their task environments and assure's that the appropriate measures will be put in place to address them.

| BOX 2.1 | A PARTIAL LIST OF REASONS FOR ENGAGING IN STRATEGIC PLANNING |

- To address the forces that have compelled agencies to initiate strategic planning
- To build a sense of community among shareholders
- To enhance communication between all interested parties
- To clarify and focus the mission of the agency
- To ensure that all tasks are assigned and accountability mechanisms are in place
- To help define goals
- To communicate goals to stakeholders
- To create a sense of ownership of the plan
- To provide the basis for determining the degree to which progress is achieved
- To improve staff communication
- To increase staff investment in the organization
- To help anticipate problems
- To create a framework for daily decision making
- To create an occasion for examining agency values and beliefs

| BOX 2.2 | TIPS FOR COMPOSING A WORK GROUP |

- Determine what expenses will be incurred and where resources will be obtained to meet those expenses
- Generate a budget for the project
- Identify members for the work group from various stakeholder groups
- Include participants from every level of an organization
- Consider an outside consultant or experienced staff member to facilitate the group
- Keep the group size down to eight or ten people
- Include people who will be involved in the implementation of the plan
- Recruit people who enjoy being involved, but who are not overextended
- Define the roles of group members
- Explain the group's goals
- Describe the strategic planning process
- Outline the time frame for the project's completion

A second factor that has contributed to the need for strategic planning is increased attention to accountability by funders and accrediting or monitoring institutions. In the past, agencies were often allowed to operate under the assumption that the services they were providing were effective and efficient. Today, both funders and organizations that monitor the activities of agencies expect them to have clear, measurable goals and objectives and to provide evidence that those goals and objectives are being met. The goals must be derived from the agency's mission, which must, in turn, be consistent with the goals of the funder. Strategic planning provides an opportunity for agencies to assure that their services are needed, that they remain consistent with the goals of their funders, and that they are achieving an adequate level of success in meeting their goals.

The third factor that has caused strategic planning to become essential to social service agencies is a move toward political conservatism and reduced confidence in social services. Both politicians and the general public have become increasingly skeptical about the role and effectiveness of social services. There has been an increasing tendency over the last several years to hold vulnerable and oppressed populations responsible for their plight and to expect them to use their own resources to better their condition. This attitude has been accompanied by increased levels of skepticism about the unbusinesslike manner in which some agencies have operated in the past. Strategic planning, an activity long utilized by for-profit agencies outside the social services, helps bring established business mechanisms into the social service arena. This can build confidence among skeptics, helping to assure the survival of essential services.

In addition to addressing the forces that have compelled agencies to initiate strategic planning, the process has several other advantages. It helps build a sense of community among shareholders, enhances communication between all interested parties, helps to clarify and focus the mission of the agency, and assures that all relevant tasks are assigned and accountability mechanisms are in place. McNamara (1999) adds that it (a) helps to define goals realistically, (b) communicates those goals to stakeholders, (c) helps to create a sense of ownership of the plan, and (d) provides the basis for determining the degree to which progress is achieved. Lehman and Zimmerman (1999) note that strategic planning improves staff communication, increases staff investment in the organization, helps an organization to anticipate problems, creates a framework for daily decision making, and causes the organization to examine and align its values and beliefs.

COMPOSING A WORK GROUP

Strategic planning is typically done by a committee, but before the committee can be formed, agency administrators and board members must determine what expenses will be incurred and where resources will be obtained to meet those expenses. For example, an agency may apply for a grant that will support its efforts. Alternatively, funds may be made available from an agency's budget. Although strategic planning is not usually a costly undertaking, certain kinds of expenses may arise and should be planned for. For example, funds might be used to pay the travel expenses of committee members, to cover the expenses generated by supportive research such as a literature review, or to hire a consultant who has the necessary expertise to help the agency through the process. Where expenses are anticipated, agency leaders should generate a budget for the project in which they set aside the necessary funds. Guidelines for budgeting are included in chapter 13.

After costs and resources have been considered, members of the work group can be identified. Strategic planning work groups should be composed of several individuals representing as many of the stakeholder groups as possible. Where multiple levels within a single group exist, efforts should be made to represent each of those levels. For example, the various levels of personnel from the agency (upper administration through direct service worker) should participate. This will both assure that the perspectives of all stakeholders are represented and help promote buy-in from all stakeholder groups. In addition to stakeholders, some agencies choose to hire an outside consultant or to recruit a member of the staff who has experience with the strategic planning process. Other factors that should be considered in the recruitment of a work group include:

- Keep the group size down to eight or ten people. Too many people can prevent the group from reaching consensus and may limit the potential for participation by all members.
- Include people who will be involved in the implementation of the plan.
- Recruit people who enjoy being involved in the agency, but who are not overextended in their commitments to other activities.

Once the work group has been constituted, the roles of the members must be defined, the group's goals explained, the process that will be followed described, and the time frame for the project's completion outlined. "Role" refers to the function each member will fulfill in the group. Some may have been recruited specifically because of a special set of skills they bring to the group. For example, the **facilitator** should be someone who is familiar with the strategic planning process and should be clearly identified as the one responsible for directing the overall process. In other instances, persons who are particularly skilled in literature review or who have strong contacts in the community may have been included. The roles these members are expected to play should be thoroughly explained so that both they and the other members understand what they are to do.

The initial meeting of the work group should include an explanation of the group's goals, that is, why strategic planning is important and what it is intended to do. The relationship between the mission statement, the vision statement, goals, objectives, and tasks should be clearly explicated. It might be helpful to show group members an example of a good plan completed at another agency. This could enhance their understanding of what they need to accomplish.

The first meeting should also include a description of the process the group will follow. This would include a schedule of meetings, the likely format for those meetings, the protocol that will be used for developing the various components of the plan, and a proposed schedule for the completion of each component. Although an executive director or board chair may want to introduce the facilitator and the other group members, the facilitator should conduct the rest of the initial meeting. This will help to establish leadership and will enhance communication between members.

WRITING OR REVISING THE MISSION STATEMENT

The foundation of any strategic plan is that agency's **mission statement.** It is the initial step in the development of a matrix that lists one or more goals the agency must accomplish. Each goal is accompanied by the objectives and tasks that will be required to reach it, as well as the date by which each must be accomplished and a list of those who will accomplish them.

The foundational role of the mission statement makes it clear that it must be well written and must comprehensively and accurately express the purpose for the agency's existence. If no mission statement exists, a good one must be written. If the current mission statement needs revision, the work group should draft a new one before continuing its work. The finished product should be truly expressive of what the agency does and intends to do. The following questions should be answered during these processes:

1. Is the mission statement outdated?
2. Does it truly embody what an agency hopes to convey to those reading it?
3. Are staff and board members committed to the current statement?
4. Is the mission statement used to guide policy and practice?

A good mission statement has several characteristics. It should reflect what the agency does in a succinct manner. Rarely does a mission statement need to exceed two sentences. It should include the agency's name, profit status, target population, and a summary of the services it provides to that population. Read the example in Box 2.3.

The mission statement for Hope for Teens might be "Hope for Teens is a not-for-profit agency serving adolescent offenders through education, advocacy, treatment, and case management." While a mission statement does not have to include every specific service an agency provides, it must capture the core service areas and convey this to anyone who reads it.

VALUES, VISION, AND GOALS

After the mission statement has been prepared, the work group must clearly identify the values, vision, and goals of the agency. **Values** refers to the ideas the agency and its personnel hold about what is good and important. Vision

---

| BOX 2.3 | SERVICES TO JUVENILE OFFENDERS |

Hope for Teens (HFT) is a small not-for-profit agency that specializes in delivering services to juvenile offenders. In addition to operating a residential facility for young men and women who have been released from the detention center but are not ready to return to their homes or have no home to return to, the organization also provides advocacy in the schools, outpatient drug treatment services, mentoring, tutoring, GED classes, and intensive case management. In short, the agency provides wraparound services to juveniles and their families who have avoided incarceration due to their involvement in this program and those who have been released as part of their probation. Recently, staff members have started to complain that they are being stretched too thin. They lack a clear focus in their work, and because they are responsible for so many aspects of program activities, they no longer feel effective in their roles. In response to this, the executive director has decided to develop a strategic plan in order to focus program staff and other resources on aspects of the program that are most important.

refers to what the agency sees itself doing, both currently and in the future. Its goals are the things it hopes to accomplish. The process of articulating values, vision, and goals is often neglected, yet is critical to an agency's success. Over a period of years these important concepts can be lost or abandoned, often without anyone in the agency being aware of it. This "drift" from foundational principles can result in confusion, frustration, and, ultimately, burnout among agency staff. By clearly identifying vision, values, and goals, the work group can help refocus the agency's efforts, soothing the confusion and frustration among staff. The process also helps assure that client well-being remains the primary purpose of the agency, and that all its resources are directed toward that purpose.

Exercises that identify the core values of the agency can be incorporated into staff retreats and staff meetings. An exercise may be as simple as having everyone in the room record and report the things they value and the things they think the agency should value. It is important to seek the input of agency employees from outside the work group. It is particularly important to not restrict these discussions to upper-level administration. This is true for at least two reasons. First, direct service workers and support staff often have a perspective on agency operations that upper-level administration lacks. In addition, exclusion of these groups sends a message that they are unimportant, perhaps alienating them from both the process and the agency. Including direct service workers and support staff in the development of value statements can bolster agency cohesion and help to assure a buy-in to the process at all levels of the organization.

After identifying core values, the next step for the work group is to create a vision statement. A vision statement is similar to a mission statement in that the mission statement describes what the agency intends to do, while the vision statement describes what things will look like if the mission is successful (Allison & Kaye, 1997). While mission statements are concise, vision statements do not have to be limited and can encompass a wide array of ideas.

In developing a vision statement, it is once again important to include ideas from all levels of the agency and from people outside the work group. This can be accomplished through informal conversations, through structured interviews, or through a retreat or staff meeting. The work group should take the results of these conversations into consideration when developing the final product.

Identification of values and the development of a mission statement should be followed by the preparation of goal statements. The goal statements should be expressions of the things that must be accomplished in order to make the vision a reality. If, for example, the agency has included the development of cultural diversity and competence among its clinical staff as a part of its vision, it may have goals that identify the number of minority clinicians to be hired by a given date or to have all staff attain a given score on some measure of cultural competence. Goal statements should be succinct, very specific, attainable, and measurable. They may, however, be fairly broad, and should be such that the steps to attaining them can be clearly designated.

INTERNAL AND EXTERNAL SCANNING

After establishing the values, visions, and goals of an agency, the work group must undertake the next step, *internal and external scanning* (Edwards, Yankley, & Altpeter, 1998). During these processes the work group assesses the internal and external environment of the agency, considering such characteristics as resources, threats, funding sources, service, competitors, and staff strengths and weaknesses. The results of this step will prove useful in other aspects of management as well, such as in contingency planning. (For a more in-depth discussion on internal and external scanning, please refer to chapter 3.)

Internal scanning involves taking a look at the internal operations of the agency. It entails assessing what resources, opportunities, and potential threats exist within the agency. The work group must consider patterns of funding, staff strengths and weaknesses, staffing patterns, professional development opportunities, and the roles of the key stakeholders. It must also look at the quantity and quality of service provided to clients and consider ways it might be improved.

External scanning requires examination of conditions outside the agency. It involves looking at several factors including: (a) the current political and social climate; (b) the competition; (c) the economic condition of the community, the state, and the country; (d) the level of need in the community; (e) and any other factors that could impact service delivery or other agency functions.

DEVELOPING OBJECTIVES, TASKS, AND STRATEGIES

After goals have been developed and both agency and environmental conditions have been assessed, it is time to identify the objectives that will enable the agency to reach its goals. Objectives are statements of the things that must be accomplished in order for the goals to be met. If, for example, the agency has stated a goal of having all clinical staff score at least a 25 on the Clinical Competence Rating Scale by January 1, 2007, its objectives might include things like holding one in-service training in cultural issues per month for the next two years. Each objective would be written as a brief, clear, time-limited, and measurable statement. For example, "The agency will hold one in-service training per month for its clinical staff dealing with issues relevant to culturally sensitive counseling."

Just as objectives are the steps that lead to goals, tasks are the steps that lead to objectives. Once a sufficient number of objectives have been developed for each goal to assure that it can be reached, an adequate group of tasks must be developed to assure that each objective will be reached. Tasks are specific activities that can be completed within a relatively short period of time by an individual or a small group of individuals. Tasks for the cultural competence objective, for instance, might include: (a) reserve one day per month on the agency calendar for in-service training, (b) prepare a list of potential speakers and activities to use for the in-service training, (c) contact each potential speaker and schedule a date on which they can present.

Tasks are very specific and time limited. They are often lockstep in nature, that is, they must be completed in a specific order because the ability to complete the next task is dependent on successful completion of the one before it. As tasks are identified, each should be assigned to a person or persons and both a due date and a mechanism for reporting the results to the work group should be established. In the cultural competence example, one member of the work group might be assigned to schedule the training sessions and another to prepare a list of possible speakers. Both might be asked to provide a written summary of the results at the next work group meeting.

During the process of identifying tasks and objectives it may be clear that certain barriers exist, which may stand in the way of their successful completion. When such barriers are recognized, it is important that the work group develop strategies for overcoming them. The strategies should also be stated as objectives and broken down into assigned tasks. A strategy to achieve the cultural competence example would be that the agency increase salaries in order to make it a more attractive employer for persons of minority cultures. Tasks might include approaching the executive director and the board of directors with the idea, consulting with the finance director regarding the way those increases would be structured, and developing a list of potential sources for funding the raises.

COMMITTING THE PLAN TO WRITING

The final stage of strategic planning prior to the actual execution of the plan is to commit the plan to writing. This may be done in one of several ways. Two of the most common are strategic planning narrative and strategic planning matrix.

Strategic Planning Narrative

A strategic planning narrative is a written summary of all the products of the work group. It should include the mission statement; a summary of the values identified; the vision statement; a summary of the results of the internal and external scans; and the goals, objectives, and tasks. It should also specify who will complete each task and the way in which the results will be reported. Tasks are grouped with the objectives to which they relate and objectives are grouped with the goal to which they lead. Other portions of the narrative may be arranged in different ways. An example of a way a narrative might be laid out follows. It uses the cultural competence example mentioned previously assuming that the plan has been done for the Safe Haven Mental Health Center.

Strategic Plan—Safe Haven Mental Health Center

Mission Statement: Safe Haven Mental Health Center is a not-for-profit human service agency dedicated to the provision of comprehensive mental health services to persons of all ages in Imaginaryville, Tennessee.

Values: The staff at Safe Haven Mental Health Center value cultural diversity and are committed to the provision of effective services to people of all cultures.

Vision: The staff at Safe Haven Mental Health Center envision an agency to which people of any culture can come to experience effective, culturally sensitive interaction and intervention.

Resources and Challenges: Resources available to enhance cultural competence in the agency include an open and willing attitude on the part of all staff, funding available from Imaginaryville's metropolitan government, and a variety of people available in the community who are willing and able to teach about various cultures and cultural competence. Challenges include the broad range of cultures present in Imaginaryville and the current lack of diversity among staff.

Goal: To have all clinical staff score at least a 25 on the Clinical Competence Rating Scale by January 1, 2007.

Objective 1: The agency will hold one in-service training per month for its clinical staff dealing with issues relevant to culturally sensitive counseling.

Task 1a: Reserve one day per month on the agency calendar for in-service training. This will be done by Mr. Jones, who will provide a list of those dates at the next work group meeting.

STRATEGIC PLANNING MATRIX

Goal: *To have all clinical staff score at least a 25 on the Clinical Competence Rating Scale by January 1, 2007.*

Objective 1: *The agency will hold one in-service training per month for its clinical staff dealing with issues relevant to cultural counseling.*

Task	Person Responsible	Accountability Method and Date
1a: Reserve one day per month on the agency calendar for in-service training.	Mr. Jones	Report at the next work group meeting.
1b: Prepare a list of potential speakers and activities to use for the in-service training.	Ms. Smith	Report at the next work group meeting.
1c: Contact each potential speaker and schedule a date on which they can present.	Ms. Smith and Mr. Jones	Report at meeting on September 30.

Task 1b: Prepare a list of potential speakers and activities to use for the in-service training. This will be done by Ms. Smith who will provide a list of those dates at the next work group meeting.

Task 1c: Contact each potential speaker and schedule a date on which they can present. This will be done by Ms. Smith and Mr. Jones by September 30. They will provide a list of speakers and dates at the work group meeting scheduled on that date.

It is important to note that the goal of all clinical staff scoring a 25 on a measure of cultural competence is unlikely to be met using only the objective listed in the narrative. In fact, each goal is likely to have several related objectives with each objective having a number of related tasks. Had we included a second objective in this example it would have been listed as Objective 2, with related tasks identified as 2a, 2b, and 2c.

Strategic Planning Matrix

An alternative way of presenting the strategic plan is to develop a **matrix** in which goals, objectives, tasks, assignments, and accountability methods are displayed in tabular form. An example of a matrix for the Safe Haven Mental Health Center is included in Box 2.4. The mission statement, values, resources, and challenges would be included in a section above the matrix.

USING THE MACRO PRACTITIONER'S WORKBOOK

Worksheets 2.1 through 2.8 constitute part of the Macro Practitioner's Workbook. They are designed to be used in conjunction with the case study included in the introduction to unit 1, but are equally relevant to real life experience. By following the step-by-step instructions and answering the questions, you will be able to complete a strategic plan for Hope for Teens as well as for your own agency. If you experience problems, refer to this chapter and study the examples.

SUMMARY

In this chapter the theory and processes of strategic planning have been discussed, including the purpose of this planning method, the processes involved in completing it, and two alternative methods of putting the plan into writing. In chapter 3 we will look at a second type of planning: contingency planning.

Activities for Learning

1. Obtain the mission statements for five local agencies. Examine them critically. Do they meet the criteria for a good statement? Do they appear to reflect what the agency actually does? If the statements should be revised, how would you choose to revise them?
2. Follow a major political issue in the news for several days. Working in a small group, discuss the following questions. What values do the opposing sides hold that appear to be in conflict? What values do they have in common? How do your own values compare to those on each side? Develop a statement or statements of values for both groups and for yourself.
3. Think about an agency that serves the target population in which you have the greatest interest. Write answers to the following questions. What goals does the agency appear to have with regard to its target population? What goals do you believe it should have? Write goal statements as though you were a part of the work group for that agency.

Questions for Discussion

1. What are the most important characteristics of members to consider when you are putting together a strategic planning work group? What are some characteristics that you would want to avoid? How would you assure that all stakeholder groups are represented?
2. How do you determine when a barrier to a goal is so great that the goal should not be included in a strategic plan? What would the characteristics of such a barrier be? How might you convince a work group not to include that goal?
3. How do you decide whether to use a strategic plan narrative or a strategic plan matrix for your report? What are the advantages and disadvantages of each?

Key Terms

External scan—the process of reviewing every aspect of an organization's task environment to identify strengths, weaknesses, problems, and opportunities.

Facilitator—a person who is responsible for directing the activities of a group.

Goals—the things an agency hopes to achieve in order to achieve its mission.

Internal scan—the process of reviewing every aspect of an organization's operation to identify strengths, weaknesses, problems, and opportunities.

Matrix—a tabular presentation of data or information.

Mission statement—a summary statement of the reason for an agency's existence.

Stakeholders—those who have some sort of interest in a program or initiative.

Task environment—the world in which an agency functions, including its client base, it's funding sources, its role and place in the community at large, and its interactions with private and public agencies.

Values—the ideas the agency and its personnel hold about what is good and important.

Vision—what the agency sees itself doing in the future, the way things will look when the agency's goals have been met.

References

Allison, M., & Kaye, J. (1997). *Strategic planning for nonprofit organizations: A practical guide and workbook*. New York: John Wiley and Sons, Inc.

Brody, R., & Nair, M. D. (2000). *Macro practice: A generalist approach* (5th ed.). Wheaton, IL: Gregory Publishing Co.

Bryson, J. M. (1995). *Strategic planning for public and nonprofit organizations: A guide to strengthening and sustaining organizational achievement*. San Francisco, CA: Jossey-Bass.

Bryson, J. M., & Alston, F. K. (1995). *Creating and implementing your strategic plan: A workbook for public and nonprofit organizations*. San Francisco, CA: Jossey-Bass.

Edwards, R. L., Yankley, J. A., & Altpeter, M. A. (1998). *Skills for effective management of nonprofit organizations*. Washington, D.C.: NASW Press.

Howe, F. (1997). *The board members guide to strategic planning: A practical approach to strengthening nonprofit organizations*. San Francisco, CA: Jossey-Bass.

Lehman, A., & Zimmerman, R. (2000). *How to develop a strategic plan*. Available online: www.zimmerman-lehman.com

McNamara, C. (2004). *Strategic planning (in non-profit or for-profit organizations*. Available online: http://www.managemathelp.org/plan_dec/str_plan.htm

WORKSHEET 2.1 | COLLECTING BASIC INFORMATION

1.   What is the name of your agency?

Better Decisions

2.   What population do you serve?

Incarcerated women

3.   What is your staff size?

One / part-time

4.   What programs and services are offered by your agency?

An 8-wk structed course teaching life planning
and problem-solving skills

5.   What are your sources of funding?

State of Tennessee
Local congregations
Vanderbilt University
United Way Com. Owing Camp.
The Memorial Foundation

Individual donors
registration fees from volunteers

6.   Where are you located? Where do you provide services?

Services are provided at TPW and
Woodland Hills Youth Develop Center

WORKSHEET 2.2 | COMPOSING A WORK GROUP

1. Who are the stakeholders for your agency? List them by category, for instance, members of the board, administration, direct service workers, support staff, volunteers, clients, and so on.

Director - Kathy Masulis
Chief fundraiser - Kathy Masulis
   Volunteers
   Inmates
   Board members (ex-volunteers who were mentors and teachers)

2. Which people from each group will you ask to be a part of the work group? Why will you choose that person? (Remember to limit the group to eight to ten people.)

The work group would be composed of reprentives from St of TN, Local orgainzations, United way, Induidval donor, volunteers Vanderbilt Univ.

3. Whom will you choose to facilitate the group?

Director - Kathy Masulis and a long term volunteer

WORKSHEET 2.3 | WRITING OR REVISING THE MISSION STATEMENT

1.   Does your agency have a mission statement? If so, what is it?

To teach + Foster life skills among women and
teenage girls who are incarcerated and others
expressing an interest, by means of a structed
cirriculum delivered by trained volunteers,
Name: Better Decesions
          incorparted as a 501(c)(3)

2.   If your agency has a mission statement:
   a.   Is it succinct? (borreft conceise)
          yes.

   b.   Does it include the agency's name and profit status?
          yes

   c.   Does it identify the agency's target population?
          yes

   d.   Does it provide a summary of the services the agency provides?
          yes

3. If you do not have a mission statement:
    a. What are your agency's name and profit status?

    b. What is your agency's target population?

    c. What services does your agency provide?

4. In the space below write or revise the mission statement for your agency.

WORKSHEET 2.4 | VALUES, VISION, AND GOALS

1. What are the values of the staff at the agency?

Director is overall the person who runs agency, and also does all major fundraising.
There is one part-time paid staff member who is responsible for all administrative work

2. . What are the values of the other stakeholders?

Volunteers - teach the programs
Inmates - receive the services
Board members - Continued success of program

3. How do the values of the groups vary?

don't think there is much difference, all are working towards same goal.
Volunteers - to be the best teachers
Inmates - to graduate from program and learn new skills
Bd. members - the combination of both

4. How should the similarities and differences be expressed in the work group's statement of values?

Appropriate authority and information passed along with responsibility and decisions are made by concesus in a manner where volunteers feel valued. There is minimal conflict, but diffences do arise, and are discussed calmly and rationally

5. In the space below write a statement of the values of the agency.

WORKSHEET 2.5 | THE VISION STATEMENT

1. How do the stakeholders visualize the clients being different as a result of the agency having fulfilled its mission?

The Better descriesions program empowers women notto to be "stuck" by choices made ealier in life. It reinforces the idea of choosing today

2. How do the stakeholders visualize the community being different as a result of the agency having fulfilled its mission?

Influences that affect Better Descisions are the growth of other reentry programs. The growth of other programs gives way to both healthy competition and room to help more clients who are communty reentry programs

3. How do the stakeholders visualize the agency being different as a result of the agency having fulfilled its mission?

By its growth and particiaption of its all volunteer base.

4. How do the stakeholders visualize themselves being different as a result of the agency having fulfilled its mission?

5. Use the information gleaned from the answers above to write a vision statement for the agency.

The whole societal attitude of persons with crinninal offenses operates from a punishment perspective. but these programs are trying to model for the society is the ability to see persons as human with specific needs and rights first, before you see thier offenses

WORKSHEET 2.6 | RESULTS OF THE INTERNAL AND EXTERNAL SCANS

1.   What are the internal challenges the work group discovered?

They found that inmates tend to react, implusivily, flee difficult sihations by using alcohol or drugs or float along, letting others make decisions for them.

2.   What are the internal resources the work group discovered?

Both the Dept of Corrections and the Board of Paroles supports the program. Program graduates recommend course to other inmates.

3.   What are the external challenges the work group discovered?

Overcrowding and construction of new prisons is a growing trend that externally influences Better Discesions program and effects how they are able to serve it's clients.

4.   What are the external resources the work group discovered?

. growth of other reentry programs
. the expansion of current/past volunteers involved in individual projects.

5.   Use the information gained from answering questions 1–4 above to write a statement regarding the results of the internal and external scanning.

WORKSHEET 2.7 | GOALS, OBJECTIVES, AND TASKS

1.   What goals must the agency meet in order to fulfill its mission and vision statements?

To ~~teach~~ inmates at TPW and Woodlands Hills Youth center, life skills

2.   What objectives must be achieved in order to fulfill each goal?

- ~~enough~~ volunteers who are trained to teach program
- funding for supplies
- community awareness
- Clearence in prison
- inmates for program

3.   What tasks must be completed in order to achieve each objective?

1. Call for volunteers
2. training program for volunteers
3. forms to be filled out for prison, schedules for prisons,
4. Interviews for prisoners, to be matched w/ volunteers

4.   Who will complete each task?

1) director of Betterdesions
2) Prison staff
3) ex-volunteers

5.   What method of accountability will be used to ensure that each task is completed?

meetings and checklist

6.   Use the information from the previous five questions to complete the strategic planning matrix in Worksheet 2.8.

WORKSHEET 2.8 | COMMITTING THE PLAN TO WRITING

Name of Agency:

Mission Statement:

Agency Value Statements:

Agency Vision Statement:

Results of the Internal and External Scan:

STRATEGIC PLANNING MATRIX

Goal:

Objective 1:

_____

Task	Person Responsible	Accountability Method and Date

Objective 2:

_____

Task	Person Responsible	Accountability Method and Date

3

CONTINGENCY
PLANNING

CHAPTER OUTLINE

When Is Contingency Planning Needed?

Composing a Work Group

Identifying Processes and Trends

Internal and External Scanning

Generation and Prioritization of Alternatives

Committing the Plan to Writing

Obtaining Feedback and Making Final Revisions

Using the Macro Practitioner's Workbook

Summary

Today's social service agencies work in a turbulent environment. They face an assortment of financial, political, and organizational challenges that require constant planning and preparation. Change is the norm and, at times, seems to occur almost constantly. Those who are not able to keep pace fail. Their doors close and the clients they have served may be left without any form of support. An example can be seen in the agency described in Box 3.1, an organization forced to close its doors after 100 years of service. Although this agency was fabricated to be used as an example in this chapter, its story is not unlike that of other organizations that have struggled for survival. Some have managed to survive. Others no longer exist. In many cases, the difference was in the ability of the respective agencies to form plans and backup plans that would allow for unanticipated changes in the environment. The method of creating multifaceted plans that consider multiple possibilities, or multiple contingencies, is known as contingency planning and is the subject of this chapter.

In contingency planning, practitioners consider the range of possible conditions they may face as well as the strengths and challenges present

BOX 3.1 | VOICES FOR SOCIAL SERVICES

A small nonprofit with a staff of six (Voices for Social Services—VSS) has been in existence since the early 1900s. The agency specializes in advocacy on behalf of other nonprofits. Staff members lobby for nonprofits and causes impacting clients served by the nonprofit community. Some staff members facilitate planning and development for other nonprofits and serve as consultants. The agency produces monthly legislative bulletins and resource guides for the non-profit community. Because they provide no direct services to the larger community, they have difficulty securing funding and must rely solely on selling resource guides and agency memberships to generate income. When the staff member responsible for producing the resource guides accepts a position with another agency, the project is indefinitely delayed until the organization can fill her position. After months of not finding her replacement, agency income begins to drop as a result of its inability to produce an up-to-date resource guide. In addition, the agency begins to lose credibility as a result of its inability to provide the service its member agencies need and expect. Eventually, a replacement is hired but it is too late, the damage is already done. The agency has lost so much revenue that it is forced to consider downsizing or closing its doors. The board calls an emergency meeting to discuss alternatives. After a lengthy meeting, the executive director meets with the staff to announce that the agency will close at the end of the year.

within and around their agency. Based on this analysis, they develop a series of alternatives, Plan A being the one they consider most desirable, then additional alternatives to be utilized should Plan A fail. When contingency planning has been completed practitioners can say, "We'll try Plan A. If that doesn't work, we'll go for Plan B. Should Plan B fail, we will try Plan C."

WHEN IS CONTINGENCY PLANNING NEEDED?

Contingency planning is almost always a good idea. There are very few reasons that alternatives should not be available at virtually any point. Some situations, however, are more conducive to very thorough planning, while others call for more spontaneous thought based on available information.

Some experts would not consider the type of planning done when a rapid and spontaneous response is needed to be a true form of contingency planning. Indeed, the processes used under these circumstances are far less formal, yet the result is the same: two or more alternative plans that help practitioners deal with different contingencies that might arise. These situations might vary from a quick discussion between a supervisor and one of her case managers prior to an unexpected court hearing to a hurried conversation between agency executive staff in response to the unexpected arrival of a newspaper reporter. Either situation would call for quick assessment of strengths and challenges, the ability to anticipate possible scenarios that might develop, and the capacity to design viable alternative responses to any of those situations.

More formal contingency planning occurs when practitioners recognize a potential opportunity or challenge that is neither so immediate as to require an informal response nor so distant as to be a part of a strategic plan. Contingency planning might be used, for example, when an agency is considering expanding current space as opposed to obtaining new space on a remote site to accommodate new programs.

Contingency planning allows an agency to be proactive and to create solutions to problems before they exist, to manage crises before they actually occur. As stated previously, undertaking contingency planning can be a long and laborious process or a relatively short and easy one, depending on the situation. While some agencies have detailed plans on file, others may have a page or two. Still others may not have a plan for a given situation before it arises and may be forced to develop alternatives quickly. It is vital, however, that the planning process begin as soon as possible after the opportunity or problem is recognized. As a general rule, the more time that is available to examine the situation and create alternatives, the greater the probability that the plan will succeed.

Contingency planning is a relatively easy process once its fundamentals are understood. It can be conceptualized as an operation with several stages: (a) constituting a work group, (b) identifying processes and trends, (c) internal and external scanning, (d) identifying and prioritizing alternatives, and (e) committing the plan to writing.

COMPOSING A WORK GROUP

The first step in contingency planning is to identify a work group of capable, willing people. As with strategic planning, the group should not contain more than eight to ten people. In many cases, particularly when there is a need for quick action that will affect a limited number of people, the group can be even smaller. For example, in the situation discussed above in which a supervisor and a case manager need to prepare for a court hearing, the work group might include only them, or perhaps an agency attorney and a more experienced case manager.

Identification of potential members should begin with the primary stakeholder groups. As with board members, administrative staff, direct service workers, support staff, clients, community members, and employees from closely aligned agencies might be considered. Others might be included because they have special skills or can bring necessary political power to the table. It will be particularly important to include someone with developing contingency plans, or to have a workbook such as this one to guide the facilitator. In order to have agencywide buy-in, planning committees should be representative of all facets of agency life.

For those who are primarily macro practitioners, it is here that clinical skills, such as facilitating a group, will be useful. Alternatively, if there is someone on staff who has strong group-work skills, it may be wise to ask that person to lead the committee. Whomever becomes the facilitator, that person should possess some specific characteristics. She should be open to suggestions and should have a good working relationship with other committee members. She should also have the time and the necessary skills to effectively facilitate meetings.

After members of the committee have been chosen, the group members must decide how to proceed through the planning process. They will need to determine, for instance, whether the plan will be developed in a series of monthly meetings, or whether they will meet for a day or two in a retreat to hammer out the plan. Several factors should be considered. One is the degree to which needed information will be available to the committee. Whether the members will either have that information available or can easily access it is an intensive, short-term process that may be practical. Where much information will need to be obtained by or for the committee, it may be necessary to prolong the experience. A second consideration is the availability of work group members. Some members may have schedules that lend themselves to intensive, short-term activities. Others might find a retreat difficult to manage, but could easily arrange a day or two per month to commit to the work group. Yet another factor to consider is the culture of the agency for which the report is produced. When an agency expects or requires great detail and specificity, for example, a greater length of time may be needed to assure that the report meets expectations. If, however, the agency is accustomed to operating in a more informal manner, the report may be more conceptual, with only an outline of basic recommendations and procedures. This might allow the group to accomplish its task in fewer meetings, considerably shortening the process. Although there are steps to be followed in contingency planning, there is also substantial room for flexibility. The steps identified in this text, for example, should be viewed as a guide to the process rather than a prescription to be followed absolutely.

IDENTIFYING PROCESSES AND TRENDS

In order to devise a contingency plan, the work group will need to select tools that are appropriate for understanding both the problem or possibility they intend to address and the current and future processes that may affect it. These tools include such processes as brainstorming, focus groups, forecasting, and literature reviews (Ellis, 2003).

Brainstorming refers to soliciting opinions from experts in your field from within a group setting. It is a specific process in which members of a group respond freely to a series of questions asked by a facilitator or facilitators. Clear rules are employed regarding these interactions. The initial presentation of ideas is to be completely free, with no expression of negativity about any of the ideas that are suggested. Facilitator(s) record the group's responses on a marker board or flip chart. After the ideas for each question have been exhausted, the group normally takes a break, then comes back to sort through the ideas that have been offered. The result is hopefully a cogent answer to the question or questions that were asked.

Brainstorming can be useful for most of the processes needed for contingency planning (Osborn, 1963). It can be helpful, for example, in identifying problems, defining problems, anticipating future trends, and developing alternative responses. Whatever the group's function, members should be selected who have expertise specific to that area. The group might contain members of the contingency planning work group, but should not be limited to those individuals. A facilitator should be identified in advance and the work group should help with the preparation of a suitable group of questions.

Focus groups are another useful tool for contingency planning work groups. In focus groups, as with brainstorming, a panel of experts is assembled, and they are asked to contribute their opinions. Unlike brainstorming groups, however, focus groups utilize interaction between members throughout the process. Typically, the facilitator asks each expert a prepared set of questions. The participants are able to build on or react to the responses of other group members. Also like brainstorming, focus groups can be helpful for identifying or defining problems, anticipating future trends, and proposing alternative responses. Those who would like to conduct their own focus groups can find the basic guidelines are in Krueger (1994). Additional information on alternative group processes can also be found in Ginsberg & Keys (1995).

Forecasting is yet another tool that can be applied to contingency planning. Forecasting involves the observation of current trends while using information about other environmental forces to predict whether the trends will increase, decrease, or remain the same. The process can be as simple as asking a group of leaders (in a format such as a focus group) what they think will happen and why. It can be as complex as using computer models to predict the course of various trends. Those who wish to use the more complex methods should seek the assistance of experts. More information about this technique can be found in Patton & Sawicki (1993).

Literature reviews can also be informative to the contingency planning process. The scientific and professional literature can often provide insight into what has worked well in other settings, allowing the work group to incorporate those solutions into its own planning. Similarly, they may locate the results of forecasting, needs assessments, and other studies that can inform them about trends, challenges, and opportunities. Articles may also provide information about new funding sources, new techniques in service delivery, technological advances, computer systems, and community response to relevant conditions. Literature reviews should be reported in a written summary that offers the name of each article, its author, date, and published source followed by a short summary of what was reported in each article. Copies should then be distributed to the members of the work group.

INTERNAL AND EXTERNAL SCANNING

The next step in contingency planning is to do **internal and external scanning** of the agency (Edwards, Yankley, & Altpeter, 1998). At this stage the work group seeks to determine what conditions exist both within and outside their own agency may affect their recommendations either for better or for worse. Scanning can involve looking at funders, contributors, services, staff members, community needs, client needs, and other conditions. These areas of consideration will be referred to in this text as dimensions. Although many dimensions of scanning (particularly the ones used in this example) are consistently relevant across agencies, each agency may face individual circumstances that require examination of different dimensions. Internal and external scanning may be used to inform a variety of agency tasks. For example, the process of scanning was discussed in chapter 2 as it relates to strategic planning.

Internal Scanning

Internal scanning involves taking a close look at how an agency is run from the inside. It entails assessing what resources exist within an agency, who is served by its programs, and where funding comes from. Internal scanning is an important part of contingency planning because it allows the group to determine what resources are present and what resources may be needed to deal with future situations. It involves a comprehensive examination of many dimensions of agency functioning including funding, management, operations, public relations, and service delivery. The questions that should be asked as a part of an internal scan are listed below. Answers based on the example in Box 3.2 are also included.

1. **Who are the clients/who does the agency serve?** Low-income families, children, youth, parents, the community
2. **What services does the agency provide/what programs exist within the agency?** After-school care for school-age children, state pre-K and Head-Start, infant and toddler care, nontraditional child care, youth development, and parent education classes
3. **Where does the agency derive its funding? How secure is the funding? What is needed, if anything, to make the sources of funds more secure? What new sources of funding might be accessed?** The United Way, the state, federal programs, and to a lesser degree, contributions from community members and parent fees
4. **Who are its stakeholders?** Parents, children, youth, volunteers, staff members, board members, community members

BOX 3.2 ALTERNATIVES FOR CHILDREN

Alternatives for Children is a large nonprofit that was established in the 1960s. It began as an after school program for low-income families offering tutoring, recreation, and child care for school-age children and had a part-time staff of seven. During the 1980s, the agency expanded to two sites and established both a pre-K and Head Start program. Staff size grew to 67 full-time staff members. In the 1990s it expanded again, opening a third site with infant and toddler care, as well as overnight care to low-income families. The agency also began to offer parent education classes and sponsored community events, such as health fairs, for the neighborhoods in which they were located. Staff size grew to 194 staff members. In addition to providing needed services to three underserved communities, the staff became advocates for community members and were involved in lobbying for working parents, living wages, low-cost medical care, and other issues impacting the families they served. The agency also offered recreational activities, mentoring, and tutoring to youth in the area.

The agency has a distinct culture. The management is efficient and effective. It is supportive of agency employees, and while offering sufficient support for task completion, it allows freedom for employees to choose how assigned projects and tasks will be completed. If management can be faulted, it would be for being too loose in its supervisory style. At times, tasks assigned to employees go uncompleted for extended periods of time without intervention from administrators. Agency operations are effective and efficient. Costs are carefully controlled so that expenses never exceed the budget.

Four of the original seven staff members remain and many former students have returned to work as teachers or volunteer with the various youth programs the agency provides. Turnover is extremely low. The agency also boasts one of the few parent-controlled boards in the country, so community members and clients have a direct say as to what direction the agency takes. Because so many community members have worked for the agency, served on the board, or attended as children, the agency has strong ties to the neighborhood. The community has relied on this agency for almost 40 years, and children who grew up in the program have returned as adults to enroll their own children.

Currently, the agency relies heavily on the United Way funding and state contracts. The fees they collect monthly from parents and the few donations they receive from community members would not be enough to sustain even one program. Though the agency does have a full-time staff member who is devoted to development and fund-raising, they still primarily rely on their contracts and the United Way for funding.

The agency provides a wide variety of services to a diverse group of clients. However, it has a predominantly middle-class, Caucasian staff in a community in which low income people from a variety of ethnic backgrounds increasingly reside. Anecdotal reports and community response appear to indicate that services are effective, but no formal evaluation component is in place for any program.

---

5. **What management style does agency administration use? What are the strengths of agency administration? What are its weaknesses? What unutilized strengths exist among agency administration that could be used to deal with the anticipated opportunity or challenge?** The agency management is conducive to creativity and staff participation. It provides adequate support for assigned tasks but needs to provide closer supervision in some cases. Regular reporting mechanisms should be put in place for staff members in which progress on their tasks and projects can be assessed. Failure to install the needed feedback systems may significantly harm the agency's future efforts.

6. **What are the strengths of agency operations? What are the weaknesses? How will these strengths and weaknesses impact the anticipated opportunity or challenge? What can be done to enhance the probability of success or protect against the possibility of failure?** Agency operations are effective and efficient. Management does an excellent job of budgeting and manages the budget so that costs are effectively contained. Care must be exercised, however, to assure that the agency's expansion does not overextend its resources.

7. **What are the strengths of the agency's public relations program? What are its weaknesses? How is the agency perceived in the community? How is this likely to affect the anticipated opportunity or challenge? What can be done to enhance the probability of success or protect against the possibility of failure?** The agency has an excellent reputation in the community and with other service providers and its funders. Although its primary public relations efforts appear to be word of mouth, they have been effective to this point. Given the nature of the future challenges it faces, Alternatives for Children may wish to hire an employee or contract with an agency to provide public relations support.

8. **What are the strengths of the agency's direct service provision? What are its weaknesses? What kinds of measures are in place to assure and to evaluate program effectiveness? What changes should be made to assure effectiveness and provide evaluation? How is the direct service provision of the agency likely to affect the anticipated opportunity or challenge? What can be done to enhance the probability of success or protect against the possibility of failure?** The agency provides many different critical services to a disadvantaged community. There are at least two steps it must take to deal with future challenges. First, the agency must increase the diversity and level of cultural competence among its staff. Second, it must put formal evaluation mechanisms in place.

This list of questions and answers provides an illustration of the kinds of issues that should be examined during the process of internal scanning. In the case of some agencies, they may need to be adapted or other questions added. More information about internal and external scanning is available in Edwards, Yankley, & Altpeter (1998).

External Scanning

External scanning helps an agency focus on what exists outside itself that can either help or hinder the plan. This includes not only the world in which the agency operates but also the interaction between the agency and the world. External scanning involves looking at such dimensions as the people and organizations the agency serves, the physical location of the agency, the accessibility of the agency, the experiences of individuals and organizations in the community, relationships with individuals and organizations in the community, and threats to the existence of the agency. Possible dimensions to which external scanning might be directed by Alternatives for Children are listed. Please keep in mind that this list might have items added or deleted depending on the situation of any given agency. For Alternative's for Children (AFC) (Box 3.2), external scanning might include these questions and answers.

1. **Whom does the agency serve?** Those served include the children and families to whom AFC provides direct services, schools and school employees, and the larger community.

2. **What neighborhood/community is the agency operating in?** AFC operates in three underserved, low-income communities, zip codes 00001, 00002, and 00003.

3. **How accessible is the agency to its clients?** AFC has made strong efforts over the years to make a greater variety of services readily available to a larger number of people in its service area. The result has been good access for many clients throughout each zip code. In order to improve accessibility, the agency might consider providing services in homes or in a variety of locations throughout each area.

4. **What are the needs of the community?** The service area needs a variety of services including child care, health care, employment, transportation, mental health and substance abuse counseling, and educational support.

5. **What is happening in the community in which the agency is located?** Many mothers are losing their income maintenance benefits. The need for services will increase as more parents must find child care, especially non-traditional child care such as overnight care. The community appears to be experiencing an overall drop in income and an increased level of transience. Crime rates are also on the rise.

6. **How are the relationships between the agency and other individuals and organizations in the community? In what ways might the agency draw upon those relationships in order to deal with the anticipated opportunity or challenge?** Relationships within the community and with other agencies are very good. AFC is respected and supported by both members of the community and other service providers. It is also respected by local and state government officials and funders. Although financial support from the community is unlikely to be forthcoming due to the limited income of most residents, AFC might be able to draw more volunteer support from the community. It might also consider involving some community members in its public relations processes. Its strong relationships with other agencies and government officials suggest the possibility of forming additional collaborative relationships to improve or broaden service alternatives for its service area.

7. **Are there any external threats to funding or services that exist, such as new programs in the areas offering similar programs? What is the current political climate?** The current political climate is conservative; current state and federal administrations are not sympathetic to low-income and working-poor family issues. They have not made funding for day care, after-school programs, vocational programs, and other issues impacting families a priority. Also, two for-profit agencies providing similar services have moved into two of the three neighborhoods.

GENERATION AND PRIORITIZATION OF ALTERNATIVES

After the work group has completed external and internal scanning, the next step is to look at possible scenarios that might develop, and what the agency's responses might be. In addition, the group should determine what forces are likely to affect each contingency during its implementation and the manner in which the effectiveness of each alternative might be evaluated. All this information should be helpful when the alternatives are prioritized.

Before the final plan is conceived, it may be important to revise the problem or opportunity statement a final time. Although a clear statement will have been prepared at the beginning of the process, practitioners often find that factors discovered during their research may cause the statement to need revision. Imagine, for example, that an agency serving people who are HIV positive discovered the only other agency in its community that provides such services was about to close its doors. This might make their early estimates for level of need obsolete, requiring them to seek more funding than was earlier anticipated.

Once the group has finalized the problem statement, it should develop alternative plans to address the problem or opportunity. Every possible scenario should be considered and alternatives created that would consider as many of those scenarios as possible. Once alternative approaches have been designed, they can be evaluated in terms of the degree to which they are likely to be successful given the anticipated conditions. The plan deemed most likely to succeed would become known as Plan A, the next most likely as Plan B, and the next as Plan C, and so on until all the plans had received names.

For example, if Alternatives for Children were to lose United Way funding one year, the work group might propose undertaking a capital campaign and raising parent fees as Plan A. Recognizing that this alternative might fail, it might recommend that Plan B apply for funds from a foundation. Should both of these alternatives fail, Plan C might be closing one or more programs and reducing the number of clients served.

When devising backup plans, it is crucial to take the following into consideration:

1. The impact each alternative will have on agency culture
2. The impact each alternative will have on staff
3. The impact each alternative will have on clients
4. The impact each alternative will have on agency functioning
5. The impact each alternative will have on the community
6. The potential legal and political ramifications of each alternative

COMMITTING THE PLAN TO WRITING

In nearly every instance the plan should be committed to writing. Putting the words on paper will help to clarify intentions and ensure that all work group members are in agreement regarding the proposal. It will also help the group communicate its intentions clearly to those who will implement the plan as well as other stakeholders. Although there is no single correct format for writing up a contingency planning report, the following suggestions should be helpful.

The report should begin with a title page followed by a second page containing a brief introduction and a statement of the problem or opportunity the plan is intended to address. The introduction should explain the circumstances that lead to the planning being undertaken. It should be followed by a transition into the problem or opportunity statement. See Box 3.3 for an example of a sample introduction and problem statement.

The second section of the report should contain the results of the committee's work in identifying conditions and processes. It should be headed by a title that reflects its contents, like "Relevant Conditions and Processes." It

---

  SAMPLE INTRODUCTION
AND PROBLEM STATEMENT

This report has been compiled in response to a request from the board of directors of Alternatives for Children. During its February 2004 meeting, the board recognized an impending problem that would likely affect its ability to offer a full range of services in future years. It appointed a work group composed of various stakeholders associated with the agency to study the problem. The group met six times over a three-month period in order produce a contingency plan for dealing with the problem. This report contains the results of its work.

Problem statement: Due to decreased funding from the United Way, Alternatives for Children may find it hard to offer the same level of programs and services to families and children. Given the current political and social situation of the county, replacement funding may be difficult to acquire because government grants and contracts may be difficult to secure.

should include a discussion of the tools used to obtain the information, any experts who were consulted, and the results of its efforts. The anticipated effects of any conditions described in the report on the targeted problem or opportunity should be clearly explained.

The third section of the report might be entitled, "Results of Internal and External Scanning." It should explain the process of internal and external scanning for readers who may not be familiar with the techniques. It should then describe the aspects of the agency and its environment that were examined and explain the findings. The effect that the findings may have on the future of the agency and the alternatives proposed should also be clearly explained.

The next part of the report should contain the alternative plans proposed by the work group. Each plan should be clearly described and its advantages and disadvantages explained. It might also be helpful to offer suggestions as to how the plan's implementers might recognize when the time has come to abandon one alternative and move to another.

The final section of the report should be a summary and should simply recap the contents of the report. The report should be thorough but concise. It is important that its recommendations are clear and that no misunderstanding is likely to arise regarding its proposals.

OBTAINING FEEDBACK AND MAKING FINAL REVISIONS

After a plan has been committed to writing, the committee should review it and seek input from outside sources. Other stakeholders who were unable to participate with the group may be able to provide valuable insight at this point. Members of the work group might also want to do a short overview of the plan at a retreat or staff meeting to inform agency employees and to obtain their input. Finally, the recommendations should be considered and the useful ones incorporated into the report.

USING THE MACRO PRACTITIONER'S WORKBOOK

The case study for unit 1 is designed to be used to complete the worksheets from the Macro Practitioner's Workbook included in Worksheets 3.1 through 3.6. The case study may not supply all the details you need, so feel free to use your imagination to create realistic answers wherever it is necessary to do so. The answers to the questions on the worksheets will provide the raw material for writing a report. Use the format described in the "Committing the Plan to Writing" section and summarized in Box 3.4 when you write it.

 OUTLINE FOR A CONTINGENCY PLANNING REPORT

1. Title Page
2. Introduction and Statement of Problem (or Opportunity)
3. Relevant Conditions and Processes
4. Results of Internal and External Scanning
5. Alternative Plans
6. Summary of Findings and Recommendations

SUMMARY

In this chapter we have learned the basic techniques of contingency planning, a vital strategy for today's agencies. By following the processes described, practitioners can help to ensure that their agencies both survive and prosper. Those who fail to plan in today's environment are unlikely to survive.

Activities for Learning

1. Working in a small group, list some times at which contingency planning might be necessary for an agency. How might the agency anticipate these situations in time to do thorough planning? What types of resources should practitioners be sure to have available to deal with these kinds of situations?

2. Compose a list of the stakeholder groups that exist at your practicum or workplace. Which of them have the characteristics most conducive to effective strategic planning? What might each bring to the table? Are there other factors that might make you reluctant to ask them to be a part of the work group?

3. Working in a small group, practice the brainstorming process. First, imagine a problem that an agency might face. Next, compose a list of questions. Finally, with one person acting as facilitator, practice the brainstorming process as though you were participating as a member of a strategic planning work group.

Questions for Discussion

1. Imagine an agency with which you are familiar. Imagine and list the internal and external conditions that the agency might need to consider in order to conduct effective strategic planning. If you want to take it a step further, contact a member of the executive staff and ask for their input.

2. What trends do you think are occurring that affect social service agencies today? What trends exist for substance abuse agencies, for mental health agencies, and for child welfare agencies?

3. What kind of feedback do you think a work group might receive from those who review it before the final report is published? How might you distinguish between valuable input and input that is not valuable? How would you keep from objecting to suggestions out of pride of ownership alone?

Key Terms

Brainstorming—a type of group activity in which members of a group contribute ideas freely and without any form of censure until every idea has been expressed or a set time period has expired. Group members may then review and edit the suggestions.

Forecasting—a tool used in various sorts of planning in which individuals or groups use discussion, data review, or computer modeling to try to predict the performance of social trends.

Internal and external scanning—the process of reviewing conditions both inside and outside the agency to determine what conditions exist that may affect the agency's future.

Work group—a group of stakeholders assembled for the purpose of conducting strategic planning.

References

Edwards, R. L., Yankley, J. A., & Altpeter, M. A. (1998). *Skills for effective management of nonprofit organizations*. Washington, D.C.: NASW Press.

Ellis, R. A. (2003). *Impacting social policy: A practitioner's guide to analysis and action*. Pacific Grove, CA: Brooks/Cole.

Ginsberg, L., & Keys, P. R. (1995). *New management in human services 2nd edition*. Washington, D.C.: NASW Press.

Krueger, R. A. (1994). *Focus groups: A practical guide for applied research*. Thousand Oaks, CA: Sage.

Netting, F. E., Kettner, P. M., & McMurtry, S. L. (1998). *Social work macro practice 2 edition*. Washington, D.C.: NASW Press.

Osborn, A. F. (1963). *Applied imagination: Principles and procedures of creative problem solving* (3rd ed.). New York: Scribners.

Patton, C. V., & Sawicki, D. S. (1993). *Basic methods of policy analysis and planning* (2nd ed.). Englewood Cliffs, NJ: Prentice Hall.

WORKSHEET 3.1 | CONSTITUTING A WORK GROUP

1. Who are the stakeholders for your agency or community? List them by category, for instance: members of the board, administration, direct service workers, support staff, volunteers, clients, and so on.

   STAFF members
   Other agencys
   board members
   Community volunteers

2. Which people from each group will you ask to be a part of the work group? Why will you choose that person? (Remember to limit the group to eight to ten people.)

   Board members
   STAFF

3. Whom will you choose to facilitate the group?

   Board members

WORKSHEET 3.2 | DEVELOPING A PROBLEM OR OPPORTUNITY STATEMENT

1. What problems or opportunities will you address in your contingency plan?
    Problems: *when a staff person leaves the project is indifiently delayed untill that position is Finds a replacement.*

    * Income for agency begins to drop as a result of its inability to produce an up-to date resourse guide,

    * agency looses credibility as a result of its inability to provide the service to its members agencies need

    Opportunities:

    to work with other non-profit agencys

2. Write a concise statement that thoroughly and accurately describes the problems or opportunities the work group will address.

    Because there is no direct services to the community at large, there is difficulity in secRing funding. How do we secure funding. How do we keep our credibility in tact throughout the community and other non-profit agencies that we work with.

WORKSHEET 3.3 | IDENTIFYING BARRIERS, POSSIBILITIES, AND PROCESSES

1. Identify the processes you will use to anticipate the factors that may impact the agency, problem, or opportunity in the future.

   Let staff do research on how other organizations that do similar things, have approuched thier proBlems, and you could do it by computer, mailer w/ questionaer.

2. If you will use groups, identify potential members for each group and describe what you hope each member will bring to the group.

   STAFF member - info from other organizations

   Board members - contact other boards and how thier boards have dealt w/ similer barriers.

3. If you will use a technical process, such as forecasting, identify the source from which you will obtain an expert to assist you, and the means of compensation of that expert, if necessary.

4. If you will use a literature review, identify the people or group that will conduct it.

   STAFF - they know more about what they need to research, the organizations that they need to look into

WORKSHEET 3.4 | RESULTS OF INTERNAL AND EXTERNAL SCANNING

1. List the internal conditions that could hinder the work group's plan and describe the effect each might have.

- loss of funding
- loss of staff
- poor or no support from supervisory staff
- having regular staff meetings, o

2. List the internal conditions that could benefit the work group's plan and describe the effect each might have.

- management does an excellent job of managing monies
- keeping a good reputation about the agency in the community
- having regular staff meetings w/ a strong supervisor.

3. List the external conditions that could hinder the work group's plan and describe the effect each might have.

- funding
- competition from other agencies working in the same area
- more people loosing their jobs, and so it makes a change in attitude, and brings change to the neighborhood.

4. List the external conditions that could benefit the work group's plan and describe the effect each might have.

- having a good reputation in the community
- programs they provde
- the people they serve

WORKSHEET 3.5 | GENERATION OF POSSIBLE SCENARIOS AND RESPONSES

1. Refine your problem or possibility statement in light of what you have discovered during your research into trends and the internal and external conditions.

2. Develop three or more alternatives for addressing the problem or opportunity.

— providing services outside the area they are already serving
— different types of funding
— working w/ local law enforcement, and job training agencies

3. Considering what you know about trends and the internal and external conditions, rate your alternatives as Plan A, Plan B, Plan C, and so on.

WORKSHEET 3.6 | COMMITTING YOUR PLAN TO WRITING

1. Write a title page including the type of activity that has been performed (contingency plan), the name of the agency for which it has been performed, and the names of the work group members.

2. Write an introduction to the report that includes the problem or opportunity statement, the circumstances under which the planning was initiated, and a transition into the next section.

    This report has been compiled in response to a request from the Board of directors.

3. Write a summary of the work group's activities and findings during their identification of trends and processes. Begin it with a centered subheading: "Relevant Conditions and Processes."

    During it meeting the board recongnized an impending problem that would likely affect it's ability to offer a full range of services in future years.

4. Write a summary of the group's activities during the internal and external scan. Begin it with a centered subheading: "Results of the Internal and External Scan."

    The bard appointed a work group, composed of various stake holders acciocated w/ the agency to study the problem. The group meet 6 times overa 3 month period in order to produce a plan to deal w/ the problem.

5. Write a summary of each of the group's proposed alternatives (Plan A, Plan B, and Plan C) and a rationale rating them in that order. Begin it with a centered subheading: "Proposed Alternatives."

6. Write a "Summary of Findings and Recommendations" report including a one-sentence summary of each alternative.

    due to decreased funding from United way, they may find it hard to offer the same level of programs + services to families and children.

4 CHAPTER

RECRUITING COLLABORATIVE PARTNERS

CHAPTER OUTLINE

Why Collaborate?

The Challenges of Collaboration

Factors to Consider Before Engaging in Collaborative Efforts

Selecting Collaborative Partners

Recruitment

Establishing Roles, Responsibilities, and Boundaries

Using the Macro Practitioner's Handbook

Summary

As we've noted, social service agencies experience continuous change in their task environments that impacts both the availability and their need for resources. To complicate matters even further, there is a growing demand for a multitude of services that enable agencies to provide more comprehensive alternatives to clients and communities. One way agencies are able to meet increasing demands despite diminishing resources is by developing collaborative partnerships with other organizations. Ellis (2003, p. 70) defines collaboration as "working together through planning and action to accomplish a specific goals or series of goals." Brody and Nair (2000, p. 327) state that "collaboration occurs when one or more organizations perceive that their own goals can be achieved most effectively and efficiently with the assistance and the resources of others." Collaborative partnerships, therefore, are joint ventures between two or more organizations to achieve specific goals by planning and implementing the plan together.

This chapter provides basic information on collaboration. It begins with a discussion of the benefits of collaboration, then describes the general principles involved in developing partnerships. It then provides specific guidelines to follow in developing collaborative ventures. Finally, the chapter includes worksheets designed to walk practitioners step-by-step through the process of developing collaborative relationships with other agencies.

WHY COLLABORATE?

Collaborative partnerships exist in many forms. Some, such as multiagency task forces and **multidisciplinary committees**, are quite common. Others types, such as joint ventures, are formed when two or more agencies partner to access resources are becoming increasingly common. In fact, one agency may have several partners. For example, an agency serving senior citizens may join with state agencies to ensure that their clients are receiving adequate nutritional and medical services. That same agency might partner with local schools to establish a volunteer program where seniors help in classrooms and enter into a joint venture with advocacy groups to support a hotline for reporting elder abuse.

Collaborative ventures benefit organizations in a number of ways. One example is the broad range of services a group of partners may provide. A single agency may find the task of serving clients with complex needs daunting. When some of those needs are totally outside the agency's expertise, the task may be impossible. By partnering with other agencies, a pool of resources and expertise can be created, permitting the collaborative group to efficiently and effectively meet clients' needs (Brody & Nair, 2000). For instance, an agency providing job training might discover significant substance abuse and mental health issues among some of its clients. If the agency had collaborative partners with organizations with expertise in these areas, the effectiveness of the training could be enhanced by referral to one of the partners.

Another benefit of collaboration is that it may increase the probability that an agency will receive external funding. **Requests for proposals** often specify that applicants must provide letters of support and memoranda of understanding from others with whom they will work. Government agencies who contract with private organizations often want to see evidence that those organizations will utilize other resources already present in the community. These partnerships are often particularly appealing if they incorporate several disciplines or professions.

A third benefit of collaboration is that agencies can often access resources, such as staff, technology, community contacts, political alliances, and funding sources from other partners. For instance, an agency might be able to get help in developing a computer database to track clients in a project from a partner with more technologically skilled employees.

Partnerships can provide publicity for all the member agencies. Cohen (1998) notes that a collaborative partnership may be a way to attract the attention of the media. Certainly, a major effort by a group of agencies to address a significant social problem is likely to draw media attention, particularly if it is accompanied by a substantial grant or contract.

Partnerships may help agencies reach goals described in their strategic plans, such as broadening services to a new community or new target population. Because, as we saw in chapter 1, strategic plans are a road map for fulfilling the agency mission, it is important that the goals contained therein be accomplished. The additional support and resources brought by the partnership can make those goals more attainable.

Program development and expansion may be necessary, but it can also be fraught with risk. There are often costs involved, such as those required for hiring and training staff, purchasing equipment, and funding increased operating expenses. It may be prohibitive for a single agency to assume the liability for all these costs. The potential liability of each cost is decreased by spreading the risk across several partners.

1. A group of partners can provide a broad range of services.
2. Collaboration may increase the probability that an agency will receive funding.
3. Agencies with partners can access additional resources such as staff, technology, community contacts, political alliances, and funding sources.
4. Partnerships provide good publicity.
5. Partnerships may help agencies reach goals described in their strategic plans.
6. Partnerships may also reduce the risk for establishing new programs or expanding existing programs.
7. Smaller, less established agencies may be sheltered from the demands created by program development.

THE CHALLENGES OF COLLABORATION

As we've seen, collaboration has many benefits. However, developing and maintaining partnerships also presents many challenges. Most of these challenges can be anticipated and prepared for, thereby enhancing the probability that the effort will succeed.

One risk faced by the partner agencies is that one or more agencies may lose its autonomy as a result of the partnership. This is particularly true for smaller agencies that provide services the same or similar to those provided by larger, more established partners. The probability of loss of autonomy can be minimized by clearly defining the role of each partner in the collaborative agreement. The process of role definition is discussed in greater detail in a later section of this chapter.

Another potential problem in collaborative efforts is that an agency may be forced to compromise when that is not desirable. The compromise may involve anything from agreeing to give up clients the organization has expected to receive to making decisions that might compromise the agency's ethical standards. Obviously, while the former might be negotiable, the latter would be unacceptable. The potential for such disagreements should be discussed and strategies for dealing with them identified before partnerships are formed.

The potential for ethical issues warrants further attention. It is important that social workers carefully consider the potential consequences of partnerships with other agencies and professions. Collaboration among those whose values conflict may lead to ethical dilemmas or may create a situation where one partner violates the ethical code of another. Issues that may arise due to ethical conflict should be thoroughly discussed prior to entering into a collaborative agreement, and a solution that is acceptable to all parties should be identified. It is possible to partner with those whose ethics conflict with one's own, but it must be done with clarity and understanding on the part of all those involved. One example would be when an agency that operated in accordance with the Social Work Code of Ethics chose to partner with an agency composed of attorneys who provide legal services. Attorneys may have an ethical obligation to protect clients who admit to engaging in such acts as child abuse or elder abuse, while social workers are bound to report such incidents. Although it may not be possible to anticipate every conflict, issues must be discussed, solutions agreed upon, and resolutions committed in writing before collaborative agreements are consummated.

Yet another potential challenge might arise if a member agency did not fulfill its part of the agreement. In such a situation, other partners would be obliged to confront the offending partner, perhaps resulting in strained

| BOX 4.2 | A PARTIAL LIST OF THE CHALLENGES OF COLLABORATION |

1. Agencies may find it difficult to maintain their autonomy.
2. Partners may be forced to make undesirable compromises.
3. Confrontations with underperforming partners may lead to strained relationships or severed ties between the agencies.
4. Failing to establish roles and appropriate boundaries may lead to conflict.
5. Partners may find it difficult to share credit for successes.
6. If one partner receives negative publicity, other partners may experience consequences.
7. Conflict may arise between individuals assigned to work in the partnership.

relationships or severed ties between the agencies. The possibility of this sort of misunderstanding underscores the importance of a clear and thorough agreement in which roles and responsibilities are described. It also illustrates the importance of accurate documentation in which the activities of each partner are clearly recorded.

Partnerships may also encounter problems if some member agencies find it difficult to share the credit for the group's accomplishments. Positive media attention is important to everyone, and group members should freely share any favorable attention they receive. Once again, procedures for such situations should be outlined in partnership agreements, and channels for communication between agencies should be clearly identified when media opportunities arise.

Just as agencies benefit from positive publicity, they suffer when media attention goes badly. If one agency involved in a partnership receives negative publicity, other partners may also experience negative consequences even if they are not directly involved in the incident. For example, if a juvenile dies while in the care of a residential facility, the actions of partners who provide wraparound services might be questioned. Written agreements may provide little defense to a competant provider because public perception is so dependent on the position the media takes regarding the role of all partners. Perhaps it is best if each member agency develops a plan for dealing with this eventuality as a part of its public relations plan. Further, the partners might discuss how they could handle publicity problems should they arise.

Just as conflict may arise between partner agencies, it may also occur between individuals assigned to work within the partnership. This can have a number of negative effects, including diminished program effectiveness, a negative organizational culture within the partnership, and strained relationships between agencies. Although a well-crafted agreement can help to minimize the probability that such situations might arise, it cannot totally eliminate them. The potential for conflict between program participants requires that agencies closely monitor the activities of employees assigned to work within the partnership and intervene effectively when problems arise.

FACTORS TO CONSIDER BEFORE ENGAGING IN COLLABORATIVE EFFORTS

Collaborative efforts can solve many of the problems created by today's agency task environments. There are times, however, that collaboration may be contraindicated. To proceed with developing a partnership under the wrong circumstances can be devastating to one or more agencies. Several

BOX 4.3 | CRITERIA FOR DETERMINING THE
DESIRABILITY OF COLLABORATION

1. The potential partners' goals must have commonality.
2. The potential partners must have similar beliefs, values, and political views or must have a reasonable way of accommodating their differences.
3. The potential partners must be able and willing to communicate effectively.
4. The potential partners must have minimal problems with personality differences or must have effective ways of compensating for them.
5. Potential partners must have sufficient financial stability.
6. Potential partners should be willing and able to compromise and negotiate differences.

criteria can be used to identify those occasions on which it may wise or unwise to proceed.

One very important factor is that the partners' goals have commonality. This is not to say that their goals must be identical or that they may not be different in some areas indirectly related to the partnership. It does mean that inasmuch as the proposed venture is concerned, the interests and goals of the agencies must be similar, and the actions they plan to jointly undertake should be beneficial to all. Generally, even when the interests of agencies are very similar on goals related to the proposed venture, they should not be oppositional in other areas.

Just as goals must have commonality, agencies who partner must share similar beliefs, values, and political views in order to optimize the probability of success. This is not to say that agencies with perspectives that vary in several ways cannot be successful in collaborative efforts. In many areas, for example, social service agencies and law enforcement agencies have formed excellent partnerships. Social service agencies typically have a primary concern with maintaining the rights of individuals and families. Law enforcement agencies have a primary concern with ensuring the safety of the community. These values conflict when law enforcement personnel insist on incarcerating and punishing criminals, while social service agencies advocate for treatment and rehabilitation. Some agencies, however, have found commonality in the desire to protect the community by rehabilitating those who can be helped. The result have been powerful partnerships that have been leaders in effective intervention.

When agencies with different perspectives collaborate, communication is very important. Agency leaders must clearly communicate their own positions, yet must constantly seek commonality. Compromise becomes a desirable alternative, and mutual planning becomes essential.

Personalities are also an issue in collaboration. Even when goals, values, beliefs, and political positions are the same between agencies, the partnership can become off track by a conflict between high-level administrators or between designees who work together within the partnership. Several strategies are available to partnerships threatened by personality difficulties. When top-level leadership conflicts, each leader may choose to assign a designee selected by an outside party or some other member of the collaborative. When someone other than top executives are representing the interests of their agencies and conflicts occur, upper administration may consider replacing one or both of the representatives. (Replacing both may create a considerable problem, such as a lack of institutional memory.)

Those entering partnerships should also be as certain as possible of the financial stability of the agencies with which they make agreements. Those who enter into collaborative arrangements with agencies that fail may find they are suddenly responsible for twice the work they had intended. Long-term friendships and good intentions do not provide financial stability. The result of partnerships that include an unstable partner may be the loss of not only the financially weak agency, but also of the other partners.

Agencies should not enter into collaborative partnerships if they are unwilling to compromise, if roles are not clearly defined, or if the agencies involved and populations served will not benefit in some meaningful way. If the cons outweigh the pros, then it is not in the best interest of the agency to enter into partnerships with others. If the agency finds that a partnership forces it to engage in practices that are either unethical or in direct opposition to its own mission and values, it should forgo the partnership and seek others with which to form collaborative ventures. However, if an agency finds that collaborative partnerships provide additional needed resources and are able to ethically and effectively compromise, it may wish to enter into a partnership. These decisions can be successful but they must be made carefully, with deep thought and careful communication.

Partnership must not be entered into lightly, as many agencies may either benefit or be harmed through collaboration. Practitioners must be able to discern how their agencies will be affected by the agreement. Additionally, those who work for state or federal agencies must decide whether potential partners are responsible and capable of achieving the stated goals.

SELECTING COLLABORATIVE PARTNERS

Selection of collaborative partners happens in a variety of ways. Often the selection process is informal, with one agency approaching another simply because they are known to one another or because they have worked together in the past. In some communities the list of potential partners may be short because the number of agencies is small. In other cases there may be a variety of potential partners from which to choose.

Whenever possible, partners should be selected in a careful, rational manner. A list of potential partners should be developed and the strengths and weaknesses of each discussed. Those included on the list might be other agencies serving the same population, agencies with similar values and goals, and agencies that can bring special or unique resources to the partnership. When compiling the list it is important to be creative. There may be agencies that are not obvious choices as partners, yet might bring important resources to the table. Once the list has been prepared, the agencies listed should be evaluated in the light of a series of questions. These questions might include:

1. Is the potential partner already involved in other collaborative efforts? If so, do they have sufficient resources to become involved with the proposed initiative?
2. What kind of reputation does each potential partner have? Do they work well with others? Can they be trusted to fulfill their responsibilities to the initiative?
3. Is each partner financially stable?
4. Are there internal problems at any of the agencies that could interfere with the success of the initiative?
5. What would each agency bring to the table? What would they be expected to bring?

By answering these questions the list of potential partners can be narrowed and the role of each potential participant defined.

RECRUITMENT

After identifying a pool of potential partners, the next step is to approach them to discuss the collaboration. The approach you take will largely depend on what you are comfortable with and what is in-line with your agency's culture and practices. Recently, one of the authors of this text had the opportunity to speak with a former employee of a prominent philanthropic organization who is currently working as an independent consultant. When asked about methods for recruiting partners, he simply stated that "you pick up the phone and make a call." Although this seems simple enough, proper preparation can help to improve the chance of success.

Determine Whom You Will Approach

The first step in proper preparation is to determine whom you should approach. Practitioners may feel inclined to call the executive director of a potential partner and appeal to her regarding the initiative. This may not always be the best approach, however. There may be others within the agency who have substantial influence who can be approached, convinced of the viability of the proposed initiative, and recruited to help approach the executive director. For example, it may be that the clinical director of an agency is creative, innovative, and has substantial influence with the executive director. In such a case, it might be best to approach the clinical director, convince her of the viability of the partnership, then approach the executive director together.

Decide How You Will Approach Them

The actual approach can occur in many forms. If you know the person you intend to approach, a simple phone call or lunch invitation may be adequate. In other situations potential partners may be contacted at a task force meeting or social event. When the recruiter does not know persons within the agency, he might ask a third party, known to both, to make an introductory call. The manner of the approach should be dictated by the likelihood of its success.

Determine What You Want to Accomplish in the Conversation

It is important that the recruiter have a clear goal for the approach. Under most circumstances, the goal will not be to convince the potential partner to commit to the initiative immediately. A more reasonable goal is to schedule a meeting in which all the potential decision makers from both agencies can talk through relevant issues. Alternatively, the goal might be to convince the prospective partner to read some literature about the proposed initiative. The recruiter should know exactly what she wants and make that request specifically.

Determine What You Will Say in the Approach

It may also be helpful for the recruiter to write a script of what she intends to say and to rehearse it several times. Although it is unlikely that she will be able to follow the script verbatim, she should be sufficiently familiar with it to ensure that she is able to communicate her ideas clearly, quickly, and accurately. If the goal is to schedule a meeting, the script should contain a greeting, a transition into a brief summary of the initiative, an invitation to discuss the initiative, and a request for a meeting to do so. If the recruiter hopes to encourage the prospect to read literature, the script would still contain the greeting and a brief summary of the initiative, but would also include an offer

| BOX 4.4 | STEPS TO RECRUITING COLLABORATIVE PARTNERS |

1. Determine whom you will approach
2. Decide how you will approach them
3. Determine what you want to accomplish in the conversation

4. Determine what you will say in the approach
5. Plan and conduct your recruitment meeting
6. Prepare and sign your agreement

---

of the literature and a request that it be reviewed. The recruiter might also promise to make a follow-up call within a few days. A sample script might read, "Hello, Ms. Wilson, how are you? I'm calling you today because I'm working on an exciting new idea for delivering wraparound services to foster homes in rural communities. I think I know where we could get funds to support it. I'm approaching you because your agency has a wonderful reputation and offers some of the services that ours does not. I would like to get together with you and your executive committee to discuss the idea and determine whether it might be a project we could do together. Can we schedule a meeting next week?"

Plan and Conduct the Recruitment Meeting

The meeting in which a potential partner is recruited should also be planned carefully. The recruiter should do everything possible to ensure that all the key decision makers are present and should be certain that she has the authority to make decisions for her agency or has her own key decision makers present. She should have an agenda in mind, should have rehearsed her presentation, and should be prepared to answer any questions that might arise. The expectations for the prospective partner should be clearly stated, as should the contributions the recruiter's agency is willing to make. If the meeting results in an agreement, the next steps should be planned and a tentative time line developed. One or both agencies may designate employees to continue the process while establishing some feedback mechanism to upper-level administrators. In more complex situations, the initial meeting may become the first in a series of negotiating sessions in which the partners work out an agreement as to areas of responsibility and courses of action.

Prepare and Sign the Agreement

The final step in recruitment of partners is to formulate and sign the agreement. The agreement may be as simple as a letter of agreement or as formal as a contract prepared by attorneys. Its nature should be determined by the expected roles and responsibilities of the partners and the degree to which legal recourse may be required in the future. For example, when agencies agree to do no more than provide services to one another's clients, a letter or memorandum may be sufficient. When money changes hands as a result of the partnership, a contract may be more appropriate.

The agreement should include the name and nature of the initiative; the names of the partner agencies; a description of the roles, responsibilities, and boundaries of each of the partners; and a summary of the planning and communication mechanisms that will be used for the initiative. It should end with places for signatures by the decision makers.

BOX 4.5 | A STUDY IN ROLE DEFINITION — BOOSTING
ACADEMIC PERFORMANCE (BAP)

A small Chicago nonprofit agency, Boosting Academic Performance (BAP), has the opportunity to apply for funding for a pilot program. If selected, this grant would support programming to increase academic performance and college attendance for high school students from three zip codes on Chicago's west side. Historically, families from these three zip codes have had low incomes and have often been headed by single parents. They typically experience high crime rates, elevated levels of teen pregnancy, high unemployment, high rates of substance abuse and incarceration, and an increasing use of income maintenance programs. The residents also have poor access to supportive services, such as health, mental health, and substance abuse treatment programs. The high schools located within these three zip codes have been on probation for several years, graduating only a faction of the students who enter as freshmen. An even smaller group goes on to attend college.

BAP is located in one of these three zip codes, causing agency staff to have limited interactions with children and families living in the other two areas. Additionally, although the agency provides mental health services such as counseling, testing, and some case management, their services are somewhat limited.

Agency staff believe that students would benefit from a comprehensive approach to services in which they not only receive tutoring and increased educational opportunities, but in which a full range of services to meet other needs is also offered. They develop a proposal for a program that would incorporate mental health counseling, tutoring, advocacy, case management, medical services, and substance abuse treatment to the clients. Realizing their own limitations, agency staff decide to recruit collaborative partners to provide some of these services. After careful consideration, they identify two other agencies, each located in one of the two other zip codes to approach as partners. While BAP intends to provide tutoring, educational support, mental health assessment, and some mental health counseling, it hopes that its partners, a mental health/substance abuse treatment agency and a medical/dental clinic will provide the other necessary services.

ESTABLISHING ROLES, RESPONSIBILITIES, AND BOUNDARIES

The step of establishing roles, responsibilities, and boundaries for each partner is sufficiently critical to warrant further discussion. Unclear boundaries can lead to resentment and hostile interactions, while role confusion can result in the failure of critical components of the initiative. The results of the discussion should be committed to writing and preferably included in the partnership agreement.

One aspect of this stage of planning is to determine what components of the initiative each partner will be responsible for managing. Referring to the case study in Box 4.5, the agency recruiting other partners plans to provide mental health counseling and testing to clients. Additionally, they would be responsible for program evaluation as well as submitting the grant proposal, creating a budget and managing funds, and reapplying for the additional funding if needed. One of the other partners would be responsible for providing tutoring and mentoring, while the other would do the case management and referral services.

When agencies share the responsibility for the same portion of an initiative, clear boundaries must be established so that neither intrudes into the other's area of responsibility and so that no tasks are left incomplete. For instance, if two agencies are responsible for writing a grant application, it should be clearly understood who will write what portion, who will assemble and submit the final product, and who will be responsible for collecting the supporting documentation. Each participant must understand not only what it is to do, but must refrain from intruding on the other's area of responsibility unless specifically asked to do so.

Collaborative partners must also establish patterns of communication and feedback between the agencies. Clear chains of command should exist, and each partner must understand whom is to be contacted in order to deal with problems or call attention to opportunities. Some reporting system should be agreed upon so that all partners are constantly appraised of the progress the initiative has made. For example, one of the partners might be designated to collect information and prepare a monthly report for all the partners. The agencies would need to agree on the contents of the report and make that information available to the reporter. Regular meetings might also be scheduled in which partners could discuss problems and plan for the future.

Examples of these decisions can be drawn from the example in Box 4.5. In this case, all three partners might select a staff member to perform client intakes. The partners might share the responsibility for grant writing and advertising the program. While the names of all partners might be included on brochures, the mental health agency's mailing address might be used on program letterhead and brochures. One agency might agree to handle all press inquires and write press releases. The partners would also need to designate a staff person at one agency to coordinate interactions between the partners.

USING THE MACRO PRACTITIONER'S WORKBOOK

Worksheets 4.1 through 4.3 include step-by-step guidelines that will allow practitioners to develop strong collaborative relationships with other agencies. They can be practiced by using the case study provided at the beginning of unit 1. As with the other worksheets, it may be necessary to use a bit of creativity from time to time to complete the details.

SUMMARY

In this chapter, the development of collaborative partnerships have been discussed. The identification of prospective partners has been considered, along with various means of recruiting them and several principles for establishing partnership guidelines. In a time of increasing uncertainty and instability in the social service community, the ability to partner effectively with others is a key to both survival and success.

Activities for Learning

1. Identify a collaborative initiative currently operating in your community. Arrange a meeting with one of the partners. During your meeting ask the partner about how their partnership was originally formed, what kinds of agreements it has with the other partners, and what challenges and opportunities the partnership has experienced.
2. Think of an initiative that your agency or practicum site might form with other agencies. List the various areas of responsibility that would exist as a result. What areas seem to naturally belong to one agency? What areas might easily be taken by any one partner or shared between the partners? How might the partnership make these decisions?
3. Working in a small group, develop a script for approaching a potential collaborative partner for an imaginary initiative. When you've finished, take turns role-playing your approach with other group members.

Questions for Discussion

1. Why are collaborations so desirable? Why are they not used more frequently? What kinds of challenges to collaborative ventures are present?
2. What would you do if you could not find a partner among those on your original list? Where else might you look for a partner? Who else in your community might be able to help you identify other alternatives?
3. What characteristics would you hope to find in a good collaborative partner? What could you do to ensure that you exhibit those same characteristics?

Key Terms

Collaboration—a cooperative arrangement in which two or more agencies share the responsibility for the completion of some venture.

Multidisciplinary committees—small groups deliberately composed of individuals with various types of professional training to allow the group to benefit from the perspectives of each.

Recruitment—the process of attracting and forming agreements with potential collaborative partners.

Request for proposals—otherwise known as RFPs, these are announcements by a funding source that state grant dollars will be made available to those who submit successful applications.

References

Brody, R., & Nair, M. D. (2000). *Macro practice: A generalist approach* (5th ed.). Wheaton, IL: Gregory Publishing.

Cohen, T. (1998). Managing public policy advocacy and government relations. In R. L. Edwards, J. A. Yankey, M. A. Altpeter, *Skills for effective management of nonprofit organizations* (pp. 119–126). Washington, D.C.: NASW Press.

Ellis, R. A. (2003). *Impacting social policy: A practitioner's guide to analysis and action.* Pacific Grove, CA: Brooks and Cole/Wadsworth.

WORKSHEET 4.1 | IDENTIFYING POTENTIAL PARTNERS

1. Write a complete description of the initiative you hope to develop.

    By collaberating w/ surrounding areas, I hope that this organization and others will be able to operate a regional point effort in operating a child abuse and neglect division, and be able to bring the surrounding communities together in a community mobilization project

2. List the agencies in your community that provide the services planned for the initiative or related kinds of services.

    Dept of Human Endeurs -
    Child Welfare Advisory Council - Research
    Human Services Dept -
    School of Social Work - Students
    United Way - monies

3. List the agencies in your community that have a common interest in the benefits you expect clients or the community to derive from the initiative.

    Dept of Human Endeurs
    Human Services Dept
    United Way -

4. For the agencies listed above, note each of the following:
    a. What resources might each agency bring to the initiative?

    Dept of Human End. - STAFF, outside contracts
    United Way - funding, grant writing
    Human Services -

    b. What motivation might each agency have for participating in the initiative?

    Since all work with clients from the community that are in need of community resources, funding, getting there company name out..... Better community relationships

c. What barriers might exist to prevent each agency from participating?

The actually effort it will take to work together, since they each have thier own needs for monies and shaffeing in a small community

d. What problems might each agency bring to the initiative?

They might conflicts w/ maintaing autonomy
- they might have to comprimise
- Strained relationships between agenceys

5. Based on the answers to the first four questions, select one or two agencies to approach in regards to becoming collaborative partners.

WORKSHEET 4.2 | RECRUITING COLLABORATIVE PARTNERS

1. Consider the agencies you have decided to recruit for a collaborative venture. Who is the person who must be approached at each agency? What is the best way to approach that person? Will you need to involve a third party in the approach?

    Dept of Human Services- Upper manag. They where around for many of the earlier attempts of intervention and would have a good understanding- Call + set-up meeting

    United Way- someone who helps write thire grants -face to face meeting.

2. Decide what it is that you want to accomplish in your initial contact. Do you simply want to schedule a meeting to discuss the initiative more fully? Do you want to make a complete presentation and proposal at that time? What are the strengths and deficits to both approaches?

    I would lay most of it out on the table, but suggest that all angency that are interested in the idea, have a meeting so that everyone could hear what each agency thinks,

3. Write a script of what you would say in your approach to each agency. Be sure to include a greeting, a transition into a discussion of the initiative, an invitation to discuss the initiative, and a request for a meeting to do so.

4. Plan an agenda for the meetings you will have with prospective partners.

    A. Meeting called to order
    B. Thank-you FOR coming
    C. Basic Into to those @ meeting
    D. Presentation of initiative
    E. Disscussion
    F. END

WORKSHEET 4.3 | FORMING COLLABORATIVE RELATIONSHIPS

1. List the various tasks and areas of responsibility associated with the initiative. What portion should each partner be responsible for managing? Will any areas of responsibility be shared? How will decisions be made about who is responsible for what?

    all desions would be made by the group.
    Tasks would be agreed upon by those in the group. There
    is always a chance that there would be shared
    responsibilities.

2. What boundaries will need to be established within the collaboration? What measures will need to be put into place to ensure that these boundaries are honored?

    There needs to be a list of who is doing what. Each
    person who agrees to do a task with Be responsible
    For themself. There has to be a "trust" factor that comes
    into play.

3. Who will be the point of contact in each agency? Who will be responsible for coordinating the agencies' activities? What kind of reporting system will be put in place?

    There a two ways to go about this. One the committee
    can choose a point of contact, or the agency
    who intitiated the collaboration would be point of
    contact. This person would then be in charge of
    all coordination between partisapating agency. They
    would compile reports, send them out, and have
    minutes from each meeting.

GAINING SUPPORT AND MINIMIZING OPPOSITION

CHAPTER 5

CHAPTER OUTLINE

VIBES

Strategies for Identifying Stakeholders and Stakeholder Groups

Political Alliances and Interacting in the Political Arena

Additional Techniques for Gaining Support

Other Techniques for Minimizing Opposition

Using the Macro Practitioner's Workbook

Summary

Social workers and other human service professionals encounter both support for and opposition to the initiatives they try to develop. Support for their ideas may be ample or scarce. When it is ample, they must locate and enhance it. When it is scace, they must encourage and create it. Similarly, opposition may be minimal or abundant. In either case it must be won over, neutralized, or eliminated.

It is important to understand the sources of both support and opposition. In many cases, they originate from basic ideas and philosophies that individuals hold or that groups share. For example, opposition may be based on a strong assumption on the part of the broader community that the group to be helped is undeserving of aid. This is often the case with initiatives designed to help the homeless, those with addiction problems, or convicted felons. At other times, opposition may occur because of competition between agencies or other turf battles. Whatever the nature of the opposition, practitioners must be equipped with the knowledge and skills necessary to overcome it. Similarly, practitioners must understand the nature of support to ensure that it is properly mobilized.

Unfortunately, the processes of understanding support and opposition can be daunting. Practitioners must determine what position others may take regarding their plans, what those group's motives are, with whom the groups are aligned, and what strategies might be utilized to deal with each situation. This can best be accomplished through a structured, methodical process. In this chapter we'll talk about such a process. The first step in this method involves identifying and understanding the motives of both the support and the opposition.

VIBES

Much of the opposition social workers experience is due to conscious or unconscious bias on the part of society's dominant groups. Both institutional and individual **prejudice** and **discrimination** create barriers to success for specific populations of people. These barriers perpetuate the **oppressive conditions** the groups have historically experienced. Social workers are ethically obligated to seek to remove these barriers by addressing prejudice and discrimination. The Social Work Code of Ethics (National Association of Social Workers, 1996) states

> The primary mission of the social work profession is to enhance human well-being and help meet the basic human needs of all people, with particular attention to the needs and empowerment of people who are vulnerable, oppressed, and living in poverty. . . . Fundamental to social work is attention to the environmental forces that create, contribute to, and address problems in living. . . . Social workers promote social justice and social change with and on behalf of clients.

The efforts of social workers on behalf of oppressed and vulnerable populations often bring them into contact with groups who either support or oppose their work. For example, practitioners trying to ensure that recent immigrants to a community participate in Head Start programs may experience resistance from current members of those communities that oppose the immigration. Alternatively, practitioners might find support among groups of previous immigrants who have become a part of the community and wish to help welcome others. (Another example of support and opposition is offered in Box 5.2) The degree of support or opposition varies according to a complex set of perspectives each holds. Understanding these perspectives is an important key to anticipating how the groups will react to an initiative and deciding how the reaction of each group will be treated. Burch (1996) has developed a useful model for understanding the perspectives of various groups.

Burch (1996) suggests the factors that motivate individuals and groups can be grouped into five categories that he terms "VIBES." VIBES stands for Values, Interests, Beliefs, Ethics, and Slants.

Values

Burch (1996, p. 26) defines values as "a criterion for deciding desirability." Ellis (2003) expands on Burch's ideas by stating that values are "fundamental convictions about what is desirable or morally correct." Additionally, because values are constructs, their validity cannot be proven. Values are held both by individuals and groups. For political purposes, those who are members of the same group tend to hold similar values. When several individuals hold common values, the probability that they might unite behind a common cause supported by those values is enhanced. For example, the value shared by individual social workers that all people should receive equitable treatment in society might lead them to unite in a campaign to ensure the poor have greater economic opportunity and better health care. Similarly, a group of people with a conservative value system might band together to oppose

BOX 5.1 | A BRIEF DESCRIPTION OF VIBES

Values

"a criterion for deciding desirability" (Burch, 1996, p. 25)

"fundamental convictions about what is desirable or morally correct" (Ellis, 2003, p. 63)

Interests

"the benefits or consequences that people will experience as a result an event" (Burch, 1996, p. 25)

Beliefs

"the acceptance of something as true, real" (Burch, 1996, p. 33)

Ethics

Ethics are those values and beliefs that have been codified in some way (Burch, 1996; Ellis, 2003)

Slants

"a particular tendency or inclination, especially one which prevents unprejudiced consideration of a question" (Burch, 1996, p. 25)

"slants are not as strong as beliefs, but often affect the way people see things without even knowing it" (Ellis, 2003, p . 64)

Source: H. A. Burch. (1996). *Basic Social Policy and Planning.* Binghamton, NY: Haworth Press.

BOX 5.2 | SUPPORT AND OPPOSITION FOR A HALFWAY HOUSE

A halfway house for recently released felons has decided to expand to a new location in the same city. After soliciting funds and finding a building to house the organization, the city council women for that district inform the executive director that some of the residents of the neighborhood are not happy with their prospective neighbors. They oppose the initiative because they believe all criminals are morally inferior and do not deserve a chance at rehabilitation. Further, many fear that the presence of such people would represent a threat to their safety and well-being. Realizing their initiative may be defeated unless opposition is minimized and support is recruited, the executive director and program staff recruit church groups and the local civil liberties union to support their cause. Together they launch a campaign to target the city council members and local neighborhood associations. The efforts include an education campaign, a series of public service announcements, and door-to-door canvassing of homes in the community to persuade stakeholders that a halfway house is both just and safe.

these efforts, insisting on their common value that people are capable of raising themselves up by their own bootstraps.

Look again at the example in Box 5.2. Although agency administrators and staff may value the ability of clients to access services and to live in a positive environment, these values may not be shared by some in the neighborhood. Residents of the neighborhood may place a higher value on community safety, thinking that the presence of a residence for former criminals may jeopardize their security. This attitude may lead them to form a group that creates barriers to the development of a halfway house. Other groups, however, may place a high value on rehabilitation and support for the disadvantaged. These residents may become supporters of the halfway house.

Interests

Interests refers to the benefits or consequences that people will experience as a result of an event (Burch, 1996). Those who stand to gain or lose as a result of an initiative may be considered stakeholders. Allison and Kaye (1997) define **stakeholders** as those who have a stake in the success or failure of an agency or initiative. In the situation described in Box 5.2, stakeholders would include agency staff, current and future clients, residents in the neighborhood, city council men and women, and neighborhood business owners.

Interests may be of several different types. Stakeholders may have a vested interest, meaning that they already have an advantage the proposed program may negate. They may consider the public interest or what would most benefit a large group or population. Stakeholders might also have a private or special interest generated by the interests of a group to which they belong.

It is also important to remember that values and interests interact. In Box 5.2, the values of those opposing the halfway house that emphasize community safety (private interest) may interact and be amplified by a fear that property values will decrease (vested interest). On the other hand, those who value providing rehabilitation opportunities may also have an interest in recruiting the low-cost labor the halfway house may bring into their community.

Beliefs

Burch (1996, p. 33) defines beliefs as "the acceptance of something as true, real." Beliefs are different from values in that a value is a conviction we have about what is good and desirable, whereas beliefs concern our perceptions of the world and how it works. An example of a belief that might impact the halfway house proposal in Box 5.2 would be if those advocating for the house had a deep conviction that there was sufficient power in the community to block their efforts. Such a conviction might lead to halfhearted efforts to minimize the opposition. On the other hand, a strong belief in the basic goodness of others might cause them to vigorously pursue their efforts despite what they perceive as overwhelming odds.

Ethics

Ethics are those values and beliefs that have been codified in some way (Burch, 1996; Ellis, 2003). For example, social workers have the Social Work Code of Ethics (National Association of Social Workers, 1996), which guides members of the professional community in practice. Sometimes ethics may come in direct conflict with personal values and beliefs. In such cases, those who ascribe to a code of professional ethics must give greater priority to the principles of the code than to their private system of values.

Ethical standards can cause groups to support an effort. In the case of the halfway house, the local chapter of the National Association of Social Workers might be mobilized to provide support on the grounds of its ethical obligation to advocate for oppressed groups. In other cases, however, conflicting ethics might produce opposition to proposed programs. For example, a group of social workers supporting the halfway house based on its mandate to "help people in need and to address social problems" (National Association of Social Workers, 1996) might be opposed by attorneys hired by residents of the community. The attorneys' ethics would require them to support the position of their clients.

Slants

Burch (1996, p. 36) defines slants as "a particular tendency or inclination, especially one which prevents unprejudiced consideration of a question." Ellis (2003) elaborates on this concept, stating that "slants are not as strong as beliefs, but often affect the way people see things without their even knowing it."

| BOX 5.3 | CATEGORIZING GROUPS BY THEIR VIBES |

SAME—Groups whose views are sufficiently similar to those who are proposing the initiative so as to make it impossible to distinguish between the project-related goals of each group

SIMILAR—Groups of persons who share the principle tenets of one's own group, but may differ regarding the specific proposal at hand

DIFFERENT—Groups that share the views of those who support the initiative on some aspects of VIBES, yet differ with them strongly on others

OPPOSITIONAL—Groups that have virtually no aspect of their VIBES in common with those who are supporting the change

Source: R. A. Ellis. (2003). *Impacting Social Policy: A Practitioner's Guide to Analysis and Action*. Pacific Grove, CA: Brooks and Cole.

An example of the way in which a slant might affect the proposed halfway house would be if a stakeholder was somewhat neutral regarding the opening of the house, but found herself swayed toward opposition by an almost forgotten statement of her grandfather in which felons were depicted as morally depraved and unredeemable. Similarly, one who was mildly opposed to its presence might be appealed to through reminders of forgotten family values about the dignity of all people.

Using VIBES to Structure Strategy

Ellis (2003) suggests that stakeholders can be divided into four basic groups, those for whom the VIBES are the *same* as one's own, those in which the VIBES are *similar*, those where VIBES are *different*, and those whose VIBES are *oppositional*. He goes on to suggest that specific strategies should be employed when dealing with each of these groups.

Groups with the *same* VIBES are composed of people whose views are sufficiently similar to the group sponsoring the initiative so as to make it impossible to distinguish between the project-related goals of each group. With groups whose VIBES are the *same*, practitioners should use two basic strategies: partnering and planning. Partnering refers to the process of developing an alliance, reaching an agreement as to areas of responsibility, establishing processes of communication, and designating areas of expertise and authority.

Groups with *similar* VIBES are constituted by persons who share the principle tenets of one's own group, but may differ regarding the specific proposal at hand. In such cases, the primary strategies should be collaboration and compromise. Collaboration refers to opening and maintaining communication, sharing in the planning process, and sharing the responsibilities for completion of the necessary task. It is different from planning in that collaboration often involves some sort of compromise. Compromise occurs when one or more groups gives up some portion of their position in order to accomplish a greater goal.

The third type of group includes those with *different* vibes. These groups may share the views of those who support the initiative on some aspects of VIBES, yet differ with them strongly on others. For example, an influential family in the community described in Box 5.2 might have a member who has a criminal history, yet has successfully reformed. This family might share the conviction that those with criminal records should have the opportunity to rebuild their lives, yet also desire to protect its interest in property values. Practitioners supporting the initiative might be able to appeal to the family's conviction that those who have criminal records should have a chance to rebuild their lives to gain their support and perhaps the support of the *different* group. This illustrates one of the two primary strategies for dealing with those who have different VIBES: persuasion. Persuasion requires appealing to those VIBES which are shared by the *different* group so that the group agrees to support the initiative. The second strategy is compromise. Compromise involves giving up some portion of one's own position in order to gain compromises from the opposing group.

The final kind of group that practitioners may encounter are those whose VIBES are *oppositional* to their own. These groups have virtually no aspect of their VIBES in common with those who are supporting the change. Lacking some other influencing factor, like one of those described in the "Political Alliances and Interacting in the Political Arena" section following, oppositional groups are unlikely to be persuaded to support the initiative. Strategies for dealing with groups with oppositional VIBES include neutralization and negation. Neutralization means that some method is found to cause the oppositional group to refrain from opposing the initiative. Negation refers to the process of disabling or discrediting the opposition to the extent that they are unable to negatively affect the proposal.

STRATEGIES FOR IDENTIFYING STAKEHOLDERS AND STAKEHOLDER GROUPS

As the strategy for mobilizing support and minimizing opposition is developed, it is critical that all the possible stakeholders and stakeholder groups be identified. Several strategies should be implemented to accomplish this.

Asking the Experts

One strategy for identifying the various constituencies is to ask those who are experts in the area. Experts include those who have worked in the field for years, those who have received services from agencies in the field, funders, advocates, government officials, and legislators. They may also include members of the media such as newspaper, radio, or telephone reporter. Experts can often provide information not only on who the stakeholders are and what position they are likely to take, but may also suggest strategies that will enhance the probability of success with that group.

Obviously, it is important to know as much as possible about the VIBES of the experts before approaching them. Otherwise you may find that they have misled you or have provided information that is less than adequate. You can acquire information about the experts in the field from other people you know who work in or have been involved with the field or, in the case of public figures, from websites and media records.

Networking

A second strategy for identifying stakeholders and stakeholder groups involves networking. Gummer and Edwards (1995, p. 75) define a network as "a major informal communication channel for getting information that cannot be gotten through official means." Networks can also be formally constituted groups, such as task forces and committees. Networking can provide key players with information not easily obtained through other channels. When an agency attempts to build support or diminish opposition, it is a good idea for members of that agency or task force to use their networking skills. They can do this by asking for information and input from their associates who are friends or members of groups in which they participate.

Practitioners should begin to network with others before they actually experience political encounters. Students can initiate this process by attending National Association of Social Worker (NASW) meetings, school functions, job fairs, community organization events, and other activities at which they may come in contact with social workers already in the field. School provides a wonderful opportunity for students to become involved in task forces and coalitions during internships. Additionally, fellow students will prove to be useful resources once they are in the field. Professional social workers can network with others by attending coalition meetings, participating in task forces, staying active in the local social work alumni association, and keeping in contact with former professors.

By attending meetings, participating in task forces, participating in political campaigns, and making contact with other agency staff and policy makers in person or by telephone, agency staff can begin to form networks composed of like-minded individuals and agencies. These networks can be excellent sources of information for those who are seeking to enhance support for or minimize opposition to their initiatives.

Checking the Record

It is sometimes possible to check public records to determine where individuals and groups are likely to stand on a specific issue. Government workers or elected officials may be on record as having supported or opposed similar issues in government documents or on legislative roll calls. Newspaper or other media records can provide insight into the past choices of many individuals and groups, providing a basis for determining what their future behavior is likely to be. The Internet may also be a source of information. Websites from the executive or legislative branches of government may be useful, as may the sites of political action committees or other activist groups.

POLITICAL ALLIANCES AND INTERACTING IN THE POLITICAL ARENA

Social workers are sometimes hesitant to become part of the political process. However, in order to fulfill their obligation to advocate for vulnerable and oppressed clients, practitioners must be prepared to enter the political arena. Gummer and Edwards (1995, p. 47) write,

> The aversion of human services professionals (and professionals in general) to organizational politics is largely attributed to the central role that the acquisition and exercise of power plays in the political process. . . . Americans tend to focus on the negative aspects of power, seeing it primarily as an instrument for destruction. . . . Human service managers must acquire a positive attitude toward the use of power. They must learn to view managing organizational politics as a legitimate part of their professional role and to acquire the skills necessary to become effective participants in the political process.

According to Gummer and Edwards (1995), practitioners must learn to think and behave politically. Not only must macro practitioners embrace opportunities to participate in the political process, but they must maximize opportunities to form political alliances whenever possible. When an organization or coalition faces opposition, alliances cultivated in more peaceful times can help minimize that opposition.

The first step to successful political interaction is to understand the processes it involves and to become a part of those processes. Pelton and

| BOX 5.4 | TYPES OF POLITICAL ALLIANCES |

Alliances based on common VIBES

Alliances based on personal relationships

Alliances based on political debt

Alliances based on partisan obligation

Alliances based on political pressures

Alliances based on other factors

Baznick (1998) write that practitioners must be aware of the policies that influence their organizations as well as the processes that create that policy and must learn to affect both. They identify three dimensions of the political arena that practitioners must understand and become a part of to influence policy and politics. These three dimensions are:

1. The formal public dimension composed of the processes of information sharing and monitoring of agreements between governmental agencies and nongovernmental, not-for-profit agreements.
2. More informal interactions that affect and are composed by private interactions and agreements that exist as a result of networking and the development of interpersonal relationships.
3. Informal public interactions between a public organization or elected officials and the public (Pelton and Baznick, 1998).

Understanding these dimensions of political interaction will help practitioners concentrate their efforts when trying to gain support or minimize opposition. Attempts to gain information and allies can be channeled appropriately. Further, this understanding will help in the cultivation of strategies.

Additionally, Pelton and Baznick (1998) believe that for practitioners to successfully operate in the political arena, they must study the key players. Knowing who the key players are and how they are likely to respond can help agencies develop successful strategies. Practitioners can form political alliances and understand the other alliances that may affect their initiative by utilizing all the strategies discussed previously.

Ellis (2003) identified six types of political alliances, including those based on common VIBES, personal relationships, political debt, partisan obligation, political pressures, and other factors.

Alliances based on common VIBES are the first type of group. These groups are united by similarities in values, interests, beliefs, ethics, and slants. Formal alliances based on common VIBES include political action committees and special interest groups such as the National Organization of Women (NOW) or the National Association of Social Workers as well as other types of advocacy groups. Other groups are less formal and may be transient in nature, formed only until a specific initiative either comes into existence or is defeated. A discussion of the strategies for dealing with groups with various types of VIBES was included in the section of this chapter entitled "using vibes to structure strategy."

Alliances based on personal relationships include longstanding friendships, family relationships, sexual relationships, and other forms of personal intimacy. These relationships are often clandestine and therefore may be more difficult to detect than other types. Insight may often be gained through conversations with people who have been involved in politics or public service for a long period of time.

Some social workers may be reluctant to capitalize on alliances based on personal relationships. This is understandable given the scandals such as the ENRON debacle in which personal relationships played a role in creating and concealing gross misconduct. It is important, however, to understand the degree to which these alliances can be useful in advocacy for vulnerable and oppressed populations. Often the populations for which social workers advocate lack both political power and expertise. Cultivating alliances based on personal relationships may be the only way for the practitioner to help these populations access the power and expertise they need to overcome the barriers that sustain the oppressive conditions they experience.

Resistance from alliances based on personal relationships can be minimized in a number of ways. A strategy that is often successful is to find a person who is not a part of the alliance but who has a strong personal relationship with one or more of the alliance's members. That person can then be persuaded to use their influence to alter the perceptions or actions of the alliance. A much more extreme measure is to publically expose the alliance. Politicians and other power brokers are typically opposed to having these types of relationships exposed to public scrutiny. Making knowledge of them publicly can quickly neutralize the most powerful of foes.

Alliances based on political debt are formed when politicians and other power brokers support one another's initiatives in exchange for future support. Such alliances are common in the political arena. Once again, practitioners may be hesitant to become involved in this type of alliance. In fact, care should be exercised to ensure that the future cost of the alliance will not be too great and that it will not place them in an ethically compromising situation. However, alliances based on political debt can be useful when appropriately constructed.

These types of alliances are best assembled by those to whom the debt is owed. It is unlikely to be effective to approach someone saying, "Senator Smith says that you owe him so you need to support my plan." It will probably be better if Senator Smith does the approaching, or precedes your request with a phone call. If Senator Smith instructs you to make the approach, it would be wise to ask his advice as to how you might phrase your request.

Practitioners can employ a number of strategies when opposing alliances based on political debt. Among these are: (a) recruiting the cooperation of a third party to whom an even greater debt is owed by the alliance or a member of the alliance, (b) accessing similar alliances among those who support the proposed initiative, and (c) exposing the nature of the alliance to the voting public.

Alliances based on partisan obligation are a product of political party affiliation. Ellis (2003, p. 85) writes, "Some alliances are based on partisan obligation; that is, the issues being debated are central to a stakeholder's own political group that the stakeholder feels a strong obligation to support the group's position." It will benefit any initiative if its authors can find an alliance that is willing to support its cause. They are among the most powerful forms of alliance and often require extraordinary resources to overcome.

Just as alliances based on partisan obligation can be to the benefit of practitioners who are advocating for change, they can be powerful weapons in the hands of those who oppose it. Several strategies are available, however, for dealing with those in opposition.

These strategies include using political pressure from others to whom members of the alliance owe favors, convincing key players that the initiative is in the best interest of the public (while showing them how to sell this concept to the public), and convincing members of the alliance that the initiative closely mirrors their party's philosophy (Ellis, 2003).

Alliances based on political pressures arise from donor and voter support (Ellis, 2003). At times, the influence of major donors and of large blocks of voters can have a great influence on the decisions of political leaders. Individual practitioners may lack the power to influence politicians with political pressures. Herein lies another example of how building a coalition through networking can be beneficial. By developing networks with others, such as key political players, the media, and other power brokers, practitioners can put themselves in a better position to influence political processes. Practitioners and small coalitions should not underestimate their potential political power. Powerful people often sit on the agency boards, volunteer for agencies, or are affiliated in some other way with coalition members. Practitioners can use these relationships to exert political pressure on those who oppose their initiatives.

Strategies for minimizing the influence of alliances that are based on political pressures include: (a) developing other alliances that will oppose those who are creating barriers, (b) mobilizing public opinion through media campaigns and public meetings, and (c) persuading major funders to support the initiative.

The final category, *alliances based on other factors*, serves as a reminder that political decisions are very complex and can be a product of some combination of the influences described above or the result of some totally unforeseen or unexpected occurrence.

The existence of these sorts of alliances demonstrates the importance of creativity and flexibility on the part of practitioners who honor their obligation to enter the political arena. They must both look for unexpected opportunities to align with those who can help them and be prepared to deal with unexpected challenges from groups that have formed as a result of unusual influences.

ADDITIONAL TECHNIQUES FOR GAINING SUPPORT

There are many other techniques that can be used to gain or mobilize support. These are discussed in the previous chapter about building coalitions and the next chapter, which discusses developing a public relations campaign. Each of these should be considered when political strategies are developed.

OTHER TECHNIQUES FOR MINIMIZING OPPOSITION

Various other techniques can be employed to minimize opposition. As stated previously, the strategies that an agency or coalition decides to utilize are largely based on what they feel comfortable doing, the situation in which they find themselves, and the resources they have available. In this section, three additional techniques will be discussed that can often be used by practitioners and organizations who have varying levels of comfort with political processes.

Managing impressions are important aspects of minimizing opposition. Regardless of the other methods an advocacy group decides to employ, it is critical that it control the ways that the public, politicians, and others perceive the initiative. Gummer and Edwards (1995) emphasize the importance of leaders being able to influence and direct the perceptions of people both inside and outside their own organizations. Specific strategies are available to those who wish to control perceptions.

First, practitioners should work with staff and/or other collaborative partners to ensure that they present a unified front when dealing with opponents and those external to their group. Particularly for high-profile initiatives, it is crucial that internal conflicts be diminished, or at the very least minimized, so they do not surface in public places. All participants should discuss issues at length to ensure that everyone involved is educated about the initiative's history as well as the motivation for undertaking its development. In more high-profile situations, it is imperative that all staff in all the involved agencies be educated about the initiative. If some are not on board, practitioners should engage them in a discussion, simultaneously validating their concerns and conveying the importance of the initiative.

Additionally, the group sponsoring the initiative should designate a spokesperson who can educate the public, the press, and other interested parties about the motivation and benefits of the initiative. The designee should be able to speak articulately and convincingly about the initiative and field questions in a frank, nondefensive manner.

The sponsoring group should be able to describe any prior studies or evaluations demonstrating the effectiveness of the initiative in other places. Current statistics regarding the population who will benefit from the program or the initiative should be easily accessible. In particular, the spokesperson should be well versed in reports and outcome studies that demonstrate the need the initiative is intended to address.

Publicity campaigns are an effective means of controlling perception and building the support of the general public and specific constituencies. Practitioners should learn how to write press releases and to interact with reporters and media staff who write advertisements and news releases. Spokespersons for the group supporting the initiative should make themselves available to reporters for interviews. Yet another way to utilize media outlets is to have supporters of the initiative write letters to the editor or op-ed pieces for local newspapers.

Organizational demonstrations can be employed as well. Practitioners can prepare a demonstration, contacting local media to ensure that there is ample coverage. It is often a good idea to invite a large, supportive group of people to attend these demonstrations to convey the impression that the initiative is both exciting and has substantial community support. Media outlets often have designated reporters who cover local politics or social service events. Practitioners should know who those reporters are and cultivate relationships with them as well.

Human interest pieces featuring past or current clients may also help minimize opposition. While clients should never be exploited to benefit an initiative, many may be willing to tell their stories in a public setting as a means of helping others with similar problems. Using the example from Box 5.2, former felons who have been through a halfway house program and have built successful lives might be willing to talk about how the program helped change their lives. Staff members or other community members may also have stories, as long as the confidentiality rights of clients are closely guarded. These kinds of efforts both provide positive coverage for the initiative and help dispel myths by attaching a human face to a social issue.

Public education campaigns can help to minimize opposition that stems from ignorance. For example, many people feel that entitlement programs, such as TANIF, are a waste of public funds and benefit only the undeserving poor. Because of the way the media and politicians sometimes skew statistics, many Americans honestly believe that exorbitant amounts of tax dollars fund this program every year, when in reality this is not the case. Printing fliers with current statistics and facts to distribute at churches, community events, and fairs is a good way to get your message out there, while dispelling commonly held beliefs and myths. Additionally, practitioners should offer their services to community groups, civic organizations, and faith-based and religious organizations for speaking engagements. Community meetings scheduled specifically for the purpose of educating the public can also be helpful.

USING THE MACRO PRACTITIONER'S WORKBOOK

The worksheet on the following pages will help you apply the techniques described in this chapter. Use the case study included in the introduction to unit 1 for this exercise. In some cases you may lack access to the information needed to answer every question. In these cases you should simply imagine feasible scenarios and use those to provide answers.

SUMMARY

In this chapter the basics of gaining support for or minimizing opposition to programs and initiatives that you may be a part of when engaged in macro practice were included. VIBES were discussed and learning to group stakeholders in terms of their level of agreement with our own was brought up. Specific strategies for dealing with those groups as well as various types of political alliances were also shown. Finally, learning to manage the perceptions of others regarding programs and initiatives in order to maximize the probability that the effort will succeed was an important last point in this chapter.

Activities for Learning

1. Select a current story from the local news regarding a social service program or initiative that is experiencing opposition. Working with a group of classmates, use Worksheet 5.1 to identify several means of minimizing opposition. What strategies will you use? What do you think your likelihood of success will be and why?
2. Select an area of social work practice (for example, homelessness, substance abuse, domestic violence, or children and families). Identify stakeholders in your community relative to those groups. Are the VIBES of these groups the *same*, *similar*, *different*, or *oppositional* to your own? What strategies might you use to deal with those groups?
3. Select an area of social work practice. List the groups you might become involved with in order to network with those who have interests common to your own. Ask others in the field (direct practitioners, administrators, politicians, advocates) what groups you should add to your list. Then attend at least two of those groups and make an effort to meet people there. Report to your class on the results.

Questions for Discussion

1. Think about the area of social work practice in which you are most interested. What are your own values regarding that population? What values are included in the Social Work Code of Ethics? What conflicts are likely to arise between your own value system and those of the Code of Ethics?
2. How would you create and submit a public service announcement to a local radio station? (Hint: This information is not in this book. Trying calling a local station to find out.) Do they have a format in which they expect you to submit the announcement? What assistance will they provide you?
3. Imagine that you need to prepare a demonstration for a new program proposed for a domestic violence program in your community. What kinds of information will you want to provide in your presentation? What sources will you use to acquire outcome information and relevant local data? How will you organize your presentation?

Key Terms

Discrimination—treating a specific group in a biased, disadvantaging manner as a result of some characteristic or characteristics the group possesses that is different than that of the dominant group.

Oppressive conditions—conditions of social denial for a minority group that exist because members of the dominant group think and act in prejudicial and discriminatory ways.

Prejudice—opinions or perceptions about specific groups that are formed without specific proof or evidence but that are used to maintain a for the social disadvantages experienced by the group.

Stakeholders—those who have some sort of interest in a program or initiative.

References

Allison, M., and Kaye, J. (1997). *Strategic planning for nonprofit organizations: A practical guide and workbook*. New York: John Wiley and Sons.

Burch, H. A. (1996). *Basic social policy and planning*. Binghamton, NY: Haworth Press.

Ellis, R. A. (2003). *Impacting social policy: A practitioner's guide to analysis and action*. Pacific Grove, CA: Brooks and Cole.

Gummer, B., and Edwards, R. L. (1995). The politics of human service administration. In L. Ginsberg, and P. R. Keys, (Eds.), *New management in human services*, (2nd ed., pp. 57–71). Washington DC: NASW Press.

National Association of Social Workers (1996). *National association of social workers code of ethics,* Available online: www.naswdc.org/pubs/code/default.asp

Netting, F. L., Kettner, P. M., McMurtry, S. L. (1998). *Social work macro practice* (2nd ed.). New York: Longman.

Pelton, E. D., and Baznick, R. E. (1998). Managing public policy advocacy and government relations. In R. L. Edwards, J. A. Yankey, M. A. Altpeter, *Skills for effective management of nonprofit organizations* (pp. 119–126). Washington DC: NASW Press.

WORKSHEET 5.1 | GAINING SUPPORT AND MINIMIZING OPPOSITION

1. Describe the target population and the demonstrated need.

The surrounding community and other social service type organizations. Low income, elevated crime rate, transience

2. Using VIBES, identify the values, interest, beliefs, ethics, and slants of **each** stakeholder or stakeholder group. In the sections below, list the stakeholders or groups by name and describe the position each is likely to hold.

Values

DHE- that people need thier services
DHS- that the same people need thier services

Interests

DEE- Serving the people in the community
DHS- that they are serving to commonly

Beliefs

DHE- that there is a need for the services
DHS- that there is a need for the services

Ethics

DHE- they are to help people in need and to address thier social problems

DHS- that they are to help people in need and to provide help for thier problems

Slants

DHE – That many have already tried and that they get nowhere.

DHS – They will be competing for the same people

3. Group the various stakeholders in terms of whether their VIBES are the same, similar, different, or oppositional.

all the stakeholds have the same VIBES

4. What techniques can be used to develop strategies, minimize opposition, and enhance partnership or collaboration? What are the advantages and disadvantages of each?

5. What strategies can be used for operating in the political arena? With whom might you choose to use these strategies?

The Dept of Human Services, they are a government organization with political ties, they would have more "connections" w/in the political arena.

6. Identify political allies and opponents in the following categories.
Alliances based on common VIBES

Alliances based on personal relationships

Alliances based on political debt

Alliances based on partisan obligation

Alliances based on political pressures

Alliances based on other factors

7. Which alliances will your agency utilize in order to help minimize opposition? What strategies might you use to enhance partnership and collaboration?

Keeping in touch w/ the surrounding communities schools, churches, local government

8. What can your agency do to manage impressions?

Positive media, going out to the community, getting the local churches and school board involved

9. Will the agency utilize media resources? What are some ways that the agency could do this?

mailngs,
local posters about new project.
inserts @ grocery stories
Try to get news coverage

10. What are other techniques can be used to minimize opposition that were not mentioned in this chapter?

- Backing from poliacal parties
- other state agencies
- other counties that have done the same thing
- national new soverge
- lobbyist

6

DEVELOPING A PUBLIC RELATIONS PLAN

CHAPTER OUTLINE

What Is Public Relations and Why Is It Important?

Developing a Public Relations Plan

Working with the Media

Public Relations Crisis Planning

Ethics and Public Relations

Public Relations for Community Practitioners

Using the Macro Practitioner's Workbook

Summary

Public relations, that is, the processes by which an agency makes others aware of its existence and manages the ways other perceive it, is a critical part of every agency's work. There are at least two levels on which it occurs. One level has to do with the good will (or lack thereof) produced by the daily operations and interactions of the agency. The second level includes activities consciously and deliberately undertaken to increase the visibility of the agency and to ensure that it is perceived positively by others in the community. The first level is a product of the manner in which business is conducted and clients are served. It is not, therefore, a part of the discussion in the current chapter. The second involves specific activities carefully planned and strategically implemented. These activities might include a media campaign, a direct mail initiative, or a series of visits to other agencies. These kinds of public relations efforts can have a powerful effect on the way in which your agency is perceived. They must, however, be well-conceived and carefully executed. Public relations can be a challenge for many practitioners whose training is likely to have focused more on direct service to clients or management of organizations than on writing radio advertisements.

Successful public relations requires having a plan. It also involves analyzing your community, as well as identifying your customers or stakeholders. Specific goals, objectives, and strategies must be written in a clear and understandable form. Budgets must be developed and evaluation mechanisms put in place. Some agencies may be fortunate enough to have full- or part-time employees who are trained in public relations. Others may be unable to afford such staff and may be forced to do most or all of the work on their own. It is for the administrators in that sort of agency that this chapter is written. It offers step-by-step guidelines for planning and implementing a public relations campaign, as well as references to resources that can be easily accessed for additional information.

WHAT IS PUBLIC RELATIONS AND WHY IS IT IMPORTANT?

Public relations refers to the activities undertaken by an agency to manage the way in which it is perceived by the public. At one time this was not seen as a important function. However, as the task environment has changed, it has become increasingly clear that agencies must be concerned not only with making others aware of their existence but also by managing the ways in which they are viewed by others. A good public relations campaign can increase the probability that clients will know about and choose to avail themselves of the services offered by the agency. It may also increase the probability that the agency will receive funding by increasing its name recognition and credibility. In addition, a strong public relations campaign can cause an agency to reassess the degree to which it is being true to its mission and the degree to which it is meeting the needs of its clients. A good public relations plan can challenge an agency's creativity and help virtually every facet of its existence, including program development, fund development, staff satisfaction, and client satisfaction (Mattson, 2003; Wales, 2002).

Other reasons that public relations is important include:

1. It may raise awareness of specific issues important to an agency.
2. It can improve the agency's image in the community.
3. It may increase quality and quantity of the board of directors and volunteers.
4. It can improve staff satisfaction.
5. It can help the organization prepare for crisis situations.

Public relations campaigns may utilize a variety of activities. These may be in many forms, including: (a) planned word of mouth campaigns, (b) e-mail broadcasts, (c) use of an agency website, (d) brochures and fact sheets, (e) public speaking initiatives, (f) newsletters, (g) press releases, (h) media coverage or advertisement, (i) direct mail campaigns, (j) banquets, and (k) fundraising events. Although most campaigns should include some combination of these activities, it is important that these issues be considered carefully and a plan developed with specific goals. It is equally important there be a goal for each activity and that these goals be related to the campaign's overall goal. The activities might be viewed as pieces of a puzzle, in which they are linked together to produce a single, overall result (Mattson, 2003; Wales, 2002).

DEVELOPING A PUBLIC RELATIONS PLAN

A public relations plan should include both annual and monthly components. The annual plan should be directed toward the overall goals and should be supported by the activities for each month. The overall plan can be created by following the steps below (Mediatrust, 2004).

Steps to Creating a Successful Public Relations Plan

1. The agency should first assess its current perception by the community. This step, often termed, "situation analysis," includes questions across several dimensions. For example, the planners will need to know how well known the agency is both in the community at large and in the social services community. In many cases, they may also want to assess the degree to which the agency is known to local, state, or federal funders. In addition, they will want to know whether others understand what their agency does, how well others believe the agency fulfills its task, any special strengths that may exist due to the perceptions of others, and any challenges that may exist because of what others believe.

2. The second step involves the development of a goal statement. The statement should be brief, clear, measurable, and feasible, and should be directed toward building on the strengths or addressing the challenges identified during the assessment.

3. The third step is the development of objectives. Guidelines for the development of goals and objectives were supplied in the first two chapters of this book. The objectives should be measurable, time limited, and directed toward achieving the goals.

4. As with strategic and contingency planning, the development of objectives should be followed by the designation of tasks, the assignment of responsibilities, and the construction of communication mechanisms. The tasks should include each major activity that must be completed in order to ensure that the objectives are met.

5. Goal and objective development must include a discussion of the audiences the campaign will be intended to address. The need to appeal to specific audiences should have become clear during assessment. If, for example, the planners discover that there is an overall lack of awareness of the agency and its services in the general population, the general population will become a **target audience**. If it is determined that state funders are not sufficiently aware of the agency and its services, that group would become a target audience.

6. Once the target audiences have been identified, planners must develop the message or messages they wish to transmit. They must determine what it is they wish the target audience to do as a result of exposure to the message, then tailor the message in such a way that it is effective. The planners are likely to need more than one message if there is more than one target audience.

7. After the message(s) have been developed, the planners must determine what method can best be used to get it to the target audience. Several issues must be considered and balanced. One issue has to do with effectiveness versus feasibility. The planners might decide, for example, that television advertising would be the most effective means of reaching their audience. Television spots, however, can be very expensive. They might elect for some other, less costly alternative in the presence of a limited budget.

8. The next step is to finalize goal statements, objectives, tasks, assignments, and then record them in the form of an action plan. Everything should also be recorded on a time line, with the monthly steps and activities clearly specified.

9. The plan should also include an evaluation component. During evaluation, those who implement the plan should ask specific questions about its effectiveness. Feedback mechanisms should be put in place to allow

ongoing review of the implementation and effectiveness of the public relations efforts. When a plan is not working, the problem should be examined and the deficiencies corrected.

A Sample Public Relations Plan: The Family Center

The section below contains a sample public relations plan that might have been developed by following the steps outlined in the previous section. The plan would be committed to writing and might include a title page (including a title for the document), the name of the organization for which it was developed, and the names of the planners who submitted it. It is included below beginning with a **situation analysis**.

Situation Analysis:

The Family Center has greatly increased the number of clients in the past year, thanks to donor support and increases in funding for programs. It is well known in the community and offers unique services for children at risk of abuse and neglect. While other agencies offer counseling and in-home services, the Family Center is the only agency in this community that focuses on child abuse prevention and that does not charge for its services. It has relied heavily on a core group of volunteers but the volunteer base has not grown with the agency. In order to best serve the clients, more volunteers should be recruited to assist in a variety of tasks.

Goal Statement:

To double the number of active volunteers the Family Center uses to deliver child abuse prevention services during the next 12 months.

Objectives:

1. To increase the number of volunteers recruited in each month from five to eight.
2. To increase our retention of volunteers by 25%
3. To recruit three former volunteers per month to return to service.

Target Audience:

Primary audience: Retired social workers, psychologists, psychiatrists, teachers, attorneys, and mental health counselors.

Secondary audience: Women who do not work outside of the home, part-time workers, and church groups.

Volunteers are needed to serve in the following capacities:

1. Special events planning
2. Direct mail campaign
3. Child care
4. Teaching parenting classes
5. Parent mentoring

Message:

The Family Center wants volunteers to know that they can protect children by working with our agency. Stories of those who have been successful while volunteering with us need to be told. The theme will be, "Volunteers make a world of difference." The accompanying logo will feature the earth with children standing on it holding hands. At the center of the earth will be the words, "The Family Center, professionals and volunteers working together to save the lives of children."

Getting the Word Out:

A series of **public service announcements** will be run on local radio along with a series of advertisements in the local paper. Both will be written by Mr. Jacks, a board member who has an advertising agency. Speaking engagements will be scheduled with professional groups, civic clubs, and churches. Mr. Pickett will call former volunteers about returning to the agency.

Plan of Action (This Example Includes January Through May Only):

January:

Mr. Jacks will write an advertisement for the local paper and public service announcements for local radio and submit these to the appropriate people.

Ms. Wilson will compose a list of all local churches, civic groups, and professional organizations.

Ms. Alcorn will recruit and organize a speaker's bureau from board members, agency employees, and current volunteers.

Ms. Culligan will prepare and print brochures to be distributed by speakers.

Mr. Pickett will write a phone script to use in recruiting former volunteers and outline a speech to be used by the speaker's bureau.

Ms. Radigan will develop the theme and logo for the agency.

The results of these efforts will be reported in a meeting to be held at the agency office at 10:00 A.M. on the last Friday of the month.

February:

Ms. Wilson and Mr. Jackson will speak at four churches, the morning Rotary, and the morning Civitan.

Mr. Jacks will continue the media campaign by submitting public service announcements to local television stations.

The number of volunteers recruited during this month will be compared to the average monthly number recruited last year.

The results of these efforts will be reported in a meeting to be held at the agency office at 10:00 A.M. on the last Friday of the month.

March:

Ms. Wilson and Mr. Johns will speak at four churches, the lunch Rotary, and the lunch Civitan.

Mr. Jacks will work with local television and newspaper reporters to develop a human interest story about the successes of a current volunteer.

The number of volunteers recruited during this month will be compared to the average monthly number recruited last year.

The results of these efforts will be reported in a meeting to be held at the agency office at 10:00 A.M. on the last Friday of the month.

April:

Dr. Kravitz will hold a volunteer appreciation banquet to be covered by the media.

Ms. Davis and Mr. Johns will speak at four churches, the Masonic Lodge, and the Eastern Star.

The number of volunteers recruited during this month will be compared to the average monthly number recruited last year.

The results of these efforts will be reported in a meeting to be held at the agency office at 10:00 A.M. on the last Friday of the month.

May:

Ms. Honeycutt and Mr. Neily will speak at four churches, the quarterly meeting of the National Association of Social Workers, and the quarterly meeting of the National Education Association.

Mr. Jacks will submit public service announcements to local media and will run the newspaper advertisement again.

The number of volunteers recruited during this month will be compared to the average monthly number recruited last year.

The results of these efforts will be reported in a meeting to be held at the agency office at 10:00 A.M. on the last Friday of the month.

Evaluation Plan:

The success of the initiative will be determined by comparing the average monthly number of volunteers recruited for this year to the average number recruited last year.

WORKING WITH THE MEDIA

Media coverage is a valuable way of increasing an agency's visibility and reputation in the community. It rarely just happens, however. Relationships with media sources are built with people at those sources and often require planning and relationship building over a period of time.

There are several different ways to develop relationships with people from the media. Often a specific reporter is assigned to cover social service agencies. A simple phone call and invitation to an agency event may be adequate in these cases. A little research may be required in other situations. Potential contacts at newspapers, for example, can be identified by noticing the bylines of those who write the kinds of articles an agency might need to have in print. Similarly, it is often possible to identify radio or television reporters who would be receptive to the agency's story by their on-air demeanor and the kinds of things for which they express support. It may also be effective to simply call the switchboard at a media organization and ask for the social services reporter.

Reporters often respond better to human interest stories than to pieces that are nothing but news. This is where a success story from a client or a volunteer may be particularly helpful. Facts and statistics may convince people, but stories motivate and excite them. The media often finds the opportunity to report success stories to be compelling because of these qualities.

It is essential to prepare a **press kit** before approaching the media. The kit should be professional, easy to understand, and clearly communicate the message the agency wants to send. Remember that your goal is to catch the reader's attention, make a lasting impression, and motivate them to action. Ultimately, you want members of the media to cover not only this story, but other stories in the future.

According to Lautenslager (2002) your press kit should include:

1. *An introductory letter:* This letter should explain what your organization does and why the media should be involved. It should also detail the other contents of the kit.

2. *A document containing basic agency information:* This document should provide some background on your agency. Information on agency history, mission, and staff are important. Information about the board of directors is also important.

3. *A brochure containing program information:* For smaller agencies this might be a simple fact sheet attractively outlining the services offered by the agency. Some summary data might also be included, such as the number of clients served or the amount of change observed among those served.

4. *A summary of past media coverage:* An information sheet about past radio spots or the clippings from previous newspaper articles may help to convince the press that your agency is newsworthy.

5. *The proposed press release, public service announcement, or sample news stories:* If the rest of the kit has done its job, the reporter should be ready to see the news piece you are asking to be considered. The version you give them will probably be edited for publication. The sample you offer should also include a date of release.

Public Service Announcements   Newspapers, radio stations, and network television stations often provide free public service announcements for nonprofit organizations. The Federal Communications Commission requires that stations donate a certain amount of air time to serve the community. In addition, many have a community calendar where they will announce events. Newspaper pieces should be brief, concise, and sensitive to the editor's concern about preserving column width. Television and radio spots often range from 10 to 60 seconds, so the message for those media must be equally clear and concise. Each should be clearly labeled "Public Service Announcement" and should include a date of release.

Press Releases   These brief summaries serve to notify the press about an event or accomplishment, anticipating that they may lead to coverage through some media source. The manner in which the release is written is critical; harried reporters and news writers prefer to have a release that requires as little revision as possible. They need the basics: who, what, where, when, and why. If possible, pictures should be included, as should quotes and other features that will make the story interesting. The release should also contain the name and phone number of a contact person from whom additional information can be derived. After the release has been sent and aired it may be useful to contact the editor and discuss why it was or was not chosen. This can provide useful insight as to how releases should be written in the future (Prebyl, 1997).

Newspaper Articles   At times, agencies may be given the opportunity to contribute their own articles to local papers. In such cases it is important to remember that newspaper reporters write succinctly, including mostly fact with little embellishment. Practitioners should keep the following rules in mind when given the opportunity to write articles for the paper.

1. Lead with the most important information
2. Keep your work brief, simple, and to the point
3. Answer who, what, where, when, and why
4. Use the active voice and strong, active verbs

5. Check and recheck your grammar, spelling, and facts
6. Provide accurate contact information

Editorials and Letters to the Editor   Staff, volunteers, and board members should take advantage of writing letters to the editor in order to increase awareness. Board members and other stakeholders may also participate, bringing the strength of an outside perspective to the effort. When potential writers lack knowledge of how to write for newspapers, assistance can sometimes be found through journalism departments at local colleges and universities.

PUBLIC RELATIONS CRISIS PLANNING

Although many agencies operate for years without experiencing any sort of public relations crisis, problems that threaten the way in which the agency is perceived by the community can arise at any time. Some have experienced an injury to a client; others have had employees who became involved in ethical or moral difficulties that have subsequently become public. Scandals of any sort can have dire consequences for an agency. Therefore it is vital that practitioners develop a plan for dealing with public relations crises that may arise, and that each participant in the plan understand his part. The next section details the steps that should be followed to ensure that a successful plan is developed. It is adapted from a model developed by Sandra Clawson (2004).

Steps in a Public Relations Crisis Plan

Be Prepared   Agencies should have a spokesperson designated to speak with the press during public relations crises. Whenever possible, this should be someone with experience interacting with the media. In the absence of experienced personnel, the spokesperson should be someone who is well-spoken, politically savvy, and is able to think quickly on her feet. A protocol should also be developed to ensure that the spokesperson receives accurate information and assistance in order to prepare her statement in a manner that is consistent with the desires of agency administration. The press should be referred directly to a designated person, perhaps the spokesperson. A script should be developed as to what is to be said in that initial call. If the call is unexpected, a statement should be prepared in which the spokesperson promises information within a prespecified period of time. Those who need to participate in preparing the statement should also be identified in advance. For example, members of that group might include the executive director, the board chair, and an attorney who is a member of the board.

Get All the Facts   The second step in public relations crisis management is determining what led to the crisis. Questions should be asked such as, "Was it a human or mechanical error?" "Did the crisis occur as a result of poor quality control or poor judgment?" The statement should articulate the consequences of the crisis and the steps that will be taken to avoid such problems in the future. Calls from the press should be either taken immediately or returned promptly. Agency employees and board members should be notified of the crisis and told to whom they should refer any press inquiries.

Tell the Truth   The agency response should never try to hide or deny what has happened. It is accountable to the community and has an obligation to report accurately. Those preparing the statement should, however, ensure that the truth be told in as favorable light as possible, and that implications of impropriety

TYPES OF PUBLIC RELATIONS ACTIVITIES

1. Planned word-of-mouth campaigns
2. E-mail broadcasts
3. Use of an agency website
4. Brochures and fact sheets
5. Public speaking initiatives
6. Newsletters
7. Press releases
8. Media coverage or advertisements
9. Direct mail campaigns
10. Banquets
11. Fundraising events

that are incorrect are effectively refuted. The response should anticipate what the public's concerns will be and address those concerns directly.

Respond Quickly All inquiries need a response, and a rapid response ensures that the agency's version of the story is available to the early news reports. A call log might be developed in which the name of the caller, the date and time of the call, and the nature of the inquiry are recorded. This could help to ensure that calls are returned quickly and that none are lost during the process.

Of course the ideal way to respond to a crisis is by avoiding it altogether. Careful planning, training, and quality control can help avert many problems. When crises do occur, however, it is vital that practitioners be prepared to respond effectively.

ETHICS AND PUBLIC RELATIONS

It is important to emphasize that public relations is about presenting an agency in the best possible light. It is not about dishonesty or exaggeration. The Social Work Code of Ethics requires a high level of professional conduct that would be violated by a misrepresentation of the facts. Practitioners must be careful not to cross the line between positive public relations and unethical conduct.

PUBLIC RELATIONS FOR COMMUNITY PRACTITIONERS

This chapter was written with organizational practice in mind. This was done because public relations is more often the concern of agency administrators than of community practitioners. There are, however, times when those who practice in the community may need to publicize some facet of their work or interact with the media. The guidelines in this chapter can be easily adapted to accommodate those situations. For example, each of the communications methods described in Box 6.1 could be used by a community organizer. Those who need to develop an ongoing plan can easily use the step-by-step guidelines included earlier in this chapter. Worksheets 6.1 and 6.2 can be used with equal ease for either organizations or communities.

USING THE MACRO PRACTITIONER'S WORKBOOK

The worksheets from the Macro Practitioner's Workbook contain two separate activities related to public relations. The first worksheet is designed to lead you through the step-by-step creation of a public relations plan. The second will help you create a public relations crisis plan. Use the case study for unit 1 to complete both worksheets.

BOX 6.2	STEPS TO CREATING A SUCCESSFUL PUBLIC RELATIONS PLAN

1. Assess the agency's perception by the community
2. Develop a goal statement
3. Develop objectives
4. Designate tasks
5. Identify the audience

6. Develop the message
7. Determine the method of transmitting the message
8. Develop an action plan
9. Create an evaluation plan

SUMMARY

This chapter has described the importance of and the procedures to establish a good public relations plan. Agencies must do effective public relations work in order to survive in today's task environment. They must be able to develop strong and effective plans, deal effectively with the media, and be prepared for public relations crises. Public relations programs should not, however, be used for deception or exaggeration. Rather, they should be used in a manner consistent with the high ethical standards of the Social Work Code of Ethics.

Activities for Learning

1. Call a local agency and ask its executive director for an appointment to discuss its public relations plan. Use this chapter to construct a questionnaire to use during your interview. (Be careful that your questions do not insinuate that the agency's plan is ill-conceived.) Report the results to your class after your interview.
2. Spend a two-week period reading the newspaper, listening to radio news, and watching television news. Which reporters seem likely to be supportive of a story regarding a social service agency? Call the offices of each organization and inquire as to their procedures for accepting public service announcements. Report your results to the class.
3. Working in a small group, talk about the kinds of situations that might arise in an agency with a public relations crisis. Discuss the ways in which you would present those to the press and the public. What would you do to ensure that you present the agency's position in the best possible manner, yet remain true to the Social Work Code of Ethics?

Questions for Discussion

1. What kinds of people would you try to recruit to your board for help with the public relations portion of your agency's work? What might each bring to the agency? What approaches might you use to recruit them?
2. Identify the media outlets in your area (newspaper, radio, television). How might you approach each of them regarding an agency event? What would you include in your media kit?
3. What kinds of public relations crises have agencies in your area experienced recently? How did they handle those crises? What mistakes did they make? How might they have handled the situations better?

Key Terms

Press kit—a collection of documents and other items that present an agency and its proposed public relations idea's to members of the press.

Public relations—the processes by which an agency makes others aware of its existence and manages the ways others perceive it.

Public service announcements—announcements provided free of charge for nonprofit organizations as a community service.

Situation analysis—the process an agency uses to assess the way in which it is currently perceived by the community.

Target audience—the group or groups to which an agency directs its public relations efforts.

References

Clawson, S. (2004). *Crisis communication plan: A PR blue print*. Available: www3.niu.edu/newsplace/crisis.html.

Lautenslager, A. (2002). *The ingredients of a press kit*. Available: www.entrepreneur.com/article/0,4621,304700,00.html.

Mattson, K. (2003). Public relations is a powerful tool for establishing and maintaining credibility. *Expert PR*, 4 (11). Available: http://www.baccis.com

Mediatrust. (2004). *Writing a PR or communications plan*. Available: www.mediatrust.org/online_guides/prplan.html.

Prebyl, J. (1997). The anatomy of a press release. *Library Media and PR*. Available: www.ssdesign.com/librarypr/content/f4pr.shtml.

Wales, M. (2002). *Profiting with PR power, part II: Building your strategic PR plan*. Available: www.tmcnet.com/tmcnet/columns/cc090902.htm.

WORKSHEET 6.1 | DEVELOPING A PUBLIC RELATIONS PLAN

Situation Analysis

1. How well known is the agency in the community, among funders, and among the other agencies?

It's is pretty well known. There are 3 or 4 major agencies that play a role with this agency. The agency through does have a reputation in the community

United Way
School of Social Work
Dept of Public Administration

St. Dept of Juvile Justice
Human Services Dept
Child Welfare Adv. Council
Local Law enforcement

2. How is the agency positively perceived?

Contractors provide high quality Services
local schools want to work closely w/ for foster care children

3. How is the agency negatively perceived?

they are drasticlly underfunded
Lack of innovative parterning w/ other organizations
history of hiring people w/ little or no job skills that are required
over-all poor perception of agency

4. Who holds these positive and negative views of the agency?

other agencys
the community at large

5. Who understands what the agency does?

Other silmilar agencies.
it's board members.

6. Who does not understand what the agency does?

the communty @ large

Goal Statement

1. What perceptions identified during the situation analysis would you like to promote?

What and who the agency does, who they serve

2. What perceptions identified during the situation analysis would you like to change?

—STAFFING ISSUES
- the relationship w/ other similar agencies
- public opinion of agency.

3. What else would you like to accomplish?

Funding

4. Use the guidelines in chapter 1 for the development of a goal statement in order to develop a goal statement(s) for this public relations plan.

To operate a regional agencies for the support of child abuse & neglect that

Objectives

1. What steps will your agency need to take in order to accomplish each of the identified goals?

   1. Better staffing
   2. Better relationshp w/other agencies
   3. More positive media coverage
   4. More funding
   5. Better support in the community as a whole

2. Use the guidelines in chapter 1 for developing objectives in order to develop objectives for each of the goals identified above.

   1. To train and hire better qualified staff with 4 months
   2. To increase funding each year
   3. To develop a public relations dept
   4. To develop better relationship w/other organization by inviting other organizations to "buy" into the project.
   5. adding more volunteers from the community to partispate on the board.

Tasks

1. What tasks will your agency need to perform in order to accomplish each of the identified objectives?

   1. Bring in trainers, better hiring practices.
   2. Better and more communication w/ other agencies
   3. Better working relationship w/ media, and a connection to 1 or 2 writers who might be invited to sit on board
   4. Apply for more grants, or hiring an outside accounting firm to monitar $.
   5. Seeking out members of the community that want to positive influence-

2. Use the guidelines in chapter 1 for defining tasks in order to develop tasks for each of the goals identified above.

3. Organize the goals, objectives, and tasks into a single document.

Audiences

1. Although you have probably identified the audiences you wish to address during the steps above, it is time to further define those audiences. Have your goals, objectives, and tasks clearly specified the people and groups you hope to reach?

2. Are there other audiences you need to reach that have not been identified in the processes above?

- other forms of funding.
- NASW
- Lobbyist

3. Are there audiences that require special care when they are approached?

No

Message

1. List the audiences you intend to reach.

- Local community at large
- Local agencies / organizations
-

2. Match the audiences to the goals identified above.

all of the audiences would benefit from all the goals stated above.

3. Write a statement of the message you want to send to each audience.

The Dept of Endover would like the community to know they they can protect child by working with other agancies and within thier own agency.

Method

1. For each of the groups and messages above, identify three alternative methods that might be used.

2. Rate each alternative with regard to its feasibility and its effectiveness.

3. List the method that will be used to get the chosen message to each group.

Develop an Action Plan

1. Examine all the goal statements, objectives, tasks, messages, audiences, and methods identified previously. If they require revision, do so.

2. Incorporate the goal statements, objectives, tasks, messages, audiences, and methods into a written action plan using the "Sample Public Relations Plan" model in this chapter.

3. Identify and describe the methods that will be used to evaluate the effectiveness of the public relations plan as a part of your action plan.

WORKSHEET 6.2 | DEVELOPING A PUBLIC RELATIONS CRISIS PLAN

Be Prepared

1. List the possible alternatives for a spokesperson during a public relations crisis. List the strengths and weaknesses of each. Which person will you choose as spokesperson?

I would choose the represtive or staff person from the main body Dept of Human Endeoveors

2. Develop a protocol for dealing with public relations crises. When someone approaches the agency, to whom should they be directed? What should the person receiving the inquiry say? How will the spokesperson, after receiving the initial press contact, answer the immediate questions? What steps will that person take to convene a group to plan a response, should that the appropriate and necessary? Who should comprise that planning group?

If thier is a media dept they should be able to answer all questions, without having to really give out information. They could also put out a media release before the crisis hits a head.

3. Write a script that receptionists or other staff might use in response to an approach from the press.

Thank-you for inquiring about our organization, we have a public relations dept that help you with any if not all of your questions. we also have a brochure that we can mail to you.

Get All the Facts

1. What are the facts in the case? What caused the incident to happen? What other factors contributed to the incident? What might have prevented the incident from occurring?

2. Write a statement using the information above and circulate it to the public relations crisis group. Ask for their input.

3. Revise the statement according to the recommendations of the group.

Tell the Truth

1. Review the statement prepared in the step above. Does it report the truth? If not, ensure that it does.

2. Review the statement once again. Does it report the facts in a manner that is consistent with the Social Work Code of Ethics? If not, ensure that it does.

3. Review the statement once again. In the light of the truth and of ethical considerations, does it present the situation in a manner that places that agency in as positive a light as possible. If not, ensure that it does.

Respond Quickly

1. Develop a call log to track requests from and record responses to inquiries from the press and others.

Date | Time | Caller name/ organizaton | Inquirey | Intials of call taker.

2. Identify a central location in which the log will be kept.

The log should be kept in two places. The main phone area, and the public relation dept.

3. Develop a protocol that will ensure that anyone receiving inquiries will record those inquiries on the call log.

Using a 2 or 3play call log-in book. Should have date, time, person calling, area for inquiries and intial area for who took the call.

EFFECTIVE COMMUNICATION

FOR AGENCIES, GROUPS,

AND COMMUNITIES

INTRODUCTION

A critical aspect of any form of macro practice is communication. Some communication occurs within agencies, work groups, and communities. Other interaction is between groups, while still other contact occurs between individuals who are members of groups. Although it would be impossible to provide an example of every possible situation in which macro practitioners are required to communicate, it is possible to use examples that provide basic guidelines that can be used in any setting. That is the goal of this unit. Three chapters are provided. Chapter 7, "Effective Communication in Agencies, Groups, and Communities," includes both basic information about the communication process and insight as to how communication can be enhanced in any group setting. Although the narrative is written with a focus on agency-type settings, shaded boxes are included that apply the principles the narrative describes to community practice. Chapter 8, "Forming a Task Force or Committee," may be useful to any macro practitioner (as well as direct service workers who are asked to participate in episodes of macro practice). Practitioners at any level may be asked to be a part of some group that has a specific, time-limited purpose. Such groups, often called "task forces" or "ad hoc committees," require a specific composition in order to be successful. This chapter can be used by any practitioner who is asked to compose or participate in a group that is charged with a specific, time-limited task. Chapter 9, "Working with a Board of Directors," is written as though it were intended for agency personnel but is intended to address the needs of community practitioners as well. Because social workers at every level are likely to have some involvement with either boards of directors or those who interact with boards of directors, it is important that they understand how interactions with boards work. By working through the chapter worksheets, assuming the role of an agency practitioner other social workers can develop a greater understanding of those interactions.

It is worthwhile to note that some of the chapters in this unit (chapter 8 in particular) might have just as easily been placed in another unit. In the case of chapter 8, the contents are closely related to some of the chapters in unit 1. It has been included here because it provides a good example of activities and communication that occur between an organization and either outside individuals or other organizations. Similarly, the chapter on public relations planning in unit 1 might have been included here using the logic that it represents a form of communication between agencies or community groups and the media. In fact, many aspects of any form of social work practice tend to overlap, making their classification difficult. Social workers are able to construct a successful practice by putting the pieces together. The intent of this book is consistent with that goal.

As with unit 1, use the case study provided in this unit to complete the worksheets for each chapter. You will notice that the unit 2 case study simply continues from the first, adding information that will allow you to build on what you did in unit 1. Feel free to refer back to the first case study for anything that might be useful in this unit.

EFFECTIVE COMMUNICATION CASE STUDY

The setting is the same as it was in the case study for unit 1. You continue to hold your position as District Administrator for the Department of Human Endeavors (DHE). In that capacity you are also assigned to head the Disadvantaged Communities Subcommittee (DCS) of the Council of Communities (CC). Several weeks have passed and you have learned a great deal about your responsibilities in both roles. Although you recognize that multiple needs exist in both areas, you recognize that none of them can be accomplished without enhancing communication patterns within your organization and among your partners in the community. You pull out *The Macro Practitioner's Workbook* and use the worksheets from each chapter of unit 2 to help you with the process.

Organizational Practice Information

You recognize the need for a meeting with your direct service workers. Some of them are doing excellent and dedicated work, making every effort to meet the needs of clients and managing impossibly large caseloads. Others are less consistent, doing excellent work with a few children and families while neglecting others. Still other workers appear to be doing little. The result is that many of the children in the care of the organization for which you are responsible receive few or no services. Allegations of abuse and neglect go uninvestigated. Children in foster care receive few or no visits. Children who are eligible for adoption are ignored. Foster and adoptive parent recruitment lags. Worker inactivity seems to be the most difficult and most prevalent out of the many problems your organization experiences.

You realize that you need to take disciplinary steps with your employees, but you also realize that they have worked in a culture that has accepted underperformance. You know that you must ensure that they understand your expectations before you take action. You also understand that your expectations must be written so that there is documentation of both what you expect and what consequences your staff will experience if they do not do as you expect. You also realize that some potentially valuable employees may need retraining, volunteer assistance, or some other form of support to straighten out the problems created by months and years of neglect.

You also realize that the problems are different between direct service workers and administrators. Direct service personnel have failed to provide the daily investigation, support, and supervision needed by families. Administrators and supervisors have failed to hold their employees accountable and to provide the support necessary to make them successful. You realize that the communication you need to make must occur in at least two meetings, one for the direct service staff and one for administrators and supervisors.

The improvements you intend to make will have a number of benefits. First, the clients will benefit from improved service. Children will be safer, happier, healthier, and will stand a better chance of either reunification with their parents or a good adoption. After resistance, employees have improved their performance, resigned, or been terminated. Employee morale and organizational culture will improve. Direct service personnel, supervisors, and administrators will take pride in their work and realize the importance of what they do. The community will benefit because families will be strengthened, and the dollars spent for child welfare will be more wisely spent.

Potential barriers to effective communication include employee skepticism, difficulty in scheduling a single meeting that many different employees can attend, and potential differences in understanding among the seven different cultural backgrounds of your direct service staff (three among your administrative staff).

Community Practice Information

In the weeks since you have assumed the role of lead community practitioner for the Addiesburg community you have assembled a work group consisting of Leila and Delores, both Caucasian, (you will remember them from the case study for unit 1), Samuel (an African American male who lives in the community and was key in the development of the Block Watch program), Ricardo (a Hispanic male who is the sergeant in charge of the local law enforcement's community policing effort for the area), Elena (a Hispanic woman who heads the middle school Parent-Teacher Organization), Marlene (an African American woman who heads the local Community Development Corporation), Antoine (a male of mixed ethnicity who is a middle-level administrator for the Department of Juvenile Justice), David (a Caucasian, the executive director for the Addiesburg Region Community Mental Health Center), Ellen (a Caucasian, a physician, and the medical director for the Addiesburg Medical/Dental Clinic), and Brother Mark (an African American minister who heads the Addiesburg Association of Churches). Your group has reached an agreement with a local university to have one of its faculty members (Marcos, a Hispanic male with a Ph.D. in Social Work) conduct a community assessment. Although the agreement is in place, your work group has not reached a decision about how the assessment will be funded. You schedule a meeting to deal with this issue.

EFFECTIVE COMMUNICATION IN AGENCIES, GROUPS, AND COMMUNITIES

CHAPTER 7

CHAPTER OUTLINE

Overview of Communication

Communication Structures in the Organization

Barriers to Effective Communication

Methods of Communication

Managing Meetings

Techniques to Improve Communication

Using the Macro Practitioner's Workbook

Summary

Effective communication is critical to the success of any agency. Good communication can avoid problems, create opportunities, and support the development of a positive organizational culture. Despite its crucial nature, the principles of effective communication are often misunderstood by agency administrators. McNamara (1999) states that some leaders erroneously equate communication with increased paperwork and bureaucracy and therefore fail to nurture existing communication channels. Communication affects not only how business is conducted within an agency but also the staff's perception of the value of communication to leaders and managers. Given that 60 to 90% of a leader's time is spent interacting with people, it is important to ensure that this communication is efficacious and accurate (Ludden & Capozzoli, 2000). In this chapter, ways to ensure that intra-agency communication occurs and its effectiveness will be discussed. Where the comments are also relevant to community work, a discussion of the application of those comments to community practice is included in a box entitled "Communication in Community Work." For example, relevant comments from this introduction are included in Box 7.1.

BOX 7.1 | COMMUNICATION IN COMMUNITY WORK

Effective communication is just as important in community work as it is in organizations. As is true for agencies, good communication can avoid problems, create opportunities, and support the development of strong relationships between participants in an initiative. Communication determines the manner in which an initiative is perceived by the community, by the partners in the initiative, and by citizens and power brokers in the surrounding city or municipality. As with organizations, a high proportion of a community practitioner's time is spent interacting with people. This makes it critical that social workers understand and consistently utilize the principles of effective communication.

OVERVIEW OF COMMUNICATION

Communication involves the exchange of information from one person or group to another. This is true in both informal, personal settings as well as in more formal agency or community settings. Communication is intended to inform, influence, and express feelings (Ludden & Capozzoli, 2000). People share knowledge about situations and needs by transferring information. They use communication to make plans, to change plans, and to decide to make no plan at all. Communication is so central that no organization or initiative can function without it. In fact, it is arguable that communication is a constant. In many cases, the decision to remain silent carries a distinct message. Because communication is ever present, practitioners must be vigilant to ensure that it is accurate, clear, and effective.

Montana and Charnov (1999, p. 27) describe organization communication as the "bridge between goals and the creation of performance standards and worker accomplishment." Strong communication can build trust and loyalty among staff, helping them work together to fulfill the mission of the organization. Staff may lack a clear understanding of how they fit into the overall work of the agency without effective communication. Further, if communication is not effective, misunderstandings may arise, creating disputes that inhibit the agency's work.

Principles of Effective Communication

McNamara (1999) notes four conditions necessary for optimal intra-agency communication. First, organizations must develop a culture that values and promotes communication. The importance and benefits of good communication must be expressed to staff and appropriate interactional skills should constantly be modeled by leaders. Second, strong communication skills must be emphasized in the agency's hiring procedures and taught to the staff who lack them. Third, effective use of group meetings can enhance communication within an agency. Meetings provide an excellent opportunity for leaders to model skills and demonstrate their support for positive interactions. Fourth, members of the organization must be willing to seek clarification and admit when they do not understand instructions. This requires the promotion of a safe, nurturing environment in which workers are encouraged to ask questions and seek needed clarification (McNamara, 1999). Box 7.2 applies these principles to community practice.

Process of Communication

Scientific literature contains extensive information about the patterns and processes of effective communication. This chapter will focus on two of the most fundamental components: developing and receiving a message. In keeping

BOX 7.2 | **COMMUNICATION IN COMMUNITY WORK**

The four prerequisites for effective communication identified for organizations are equally critical for community practice. First, just as organizations must develop a culture that supports good communication, the various committees and coalitions that compose a community initiative must value openness, honesty, and clarity. They must ensure that the perspectives of every member are respected and listen carefully to each idea and suggestion.

The second prerequisite involves the emphasis of strong communication skills during the recruiting process and a willingness to teach those skills to members those who lack them. These processes can be particularly challenging in the community, where volunteer participation is often critical. Practitioners must take the steps to ensure that all members of

the initiative contribute optimally to communication, yet are not alienated by the processes of selection and skill development.

The third critical factor has to do with the effective use of group meetings to model communication skills and demonstrate the support of leaders for effective interactions. Many of the processes of community practice occur in meetings. The opportunity to use those meetings for modeling and teaching is equally great for the community practitioner.

Finally, as with organizations, all the participants in a community initiative must be comfortable to ask for assistance, clarification, and further instructions. The culture of the initiative must make it possible for them to do so.

---

with this focus, the participants in an interaction are identified as **senders** and **receivers**. Senders are those from whom information is sent. Recipients are those to whom information is directed. Participants in an interaction continuously change places, sometimes sending, sometimes receiving.

Developing the Message

Before sharing information with the receiver, the sender must first create the message he wishes to send. Through an internal thought process, the sender organizes thoughts and selects the information that is important for the recipient to hear. The sender then encodes the process, putting the message into a form that will be understandable to the listener. Language is critical in this step. It is vital to use language that a recipient can understand. For example, using acronyms such as ADD or CHF with listeners who do not understand those abbreviations will lead to confusion and misinterpretation. The message is then transmitted in the most appropriate form to include verbal transmission, written, or electronic (Brody & Nair, 2000; Ludden & Capozzoli, 2000).

Receiving the Message

Once the sender has developed the message and shared it with the recipient in a clear and understandable manner, it is up to the recipient to receive it effectively. The more familiar the recipient is with the topic, the easier reception is likely to be. After the information has been assimilated, the recipient may accept the message, send back a message intended to correct the other participant, or choose not to respond. Received information may be either used immediately or stored for future use. A vital part of this process is the feedback a recipient returns to a sender. A decision not to respond may indicate a variety of situations along a continuum between the failure to understand the message or having been offended by the message that was sent. If appropriate communication has occurred, the recipient should affirm that the message is clear or should seek additional clarification. This step is often missed when recipients do not take the time to ask for additional information. Without this request, the sender may assume that the message is clear and move on to other business (Brody & Nair, 2000; Ludden & Capozzoli, 2000).

Examples of problems in the sender/receiver relationship can be seen in the following scenarios. If, for instance, an agency's new clinical director responded to a case manager's request for a consultation with a expression typical of some regions of the country, "I wouldn't care to," the case manager might interpret this to mean, "I wouldn't be interested in a meeting with you." In fact, in the traditions of his home region, the clinical director would have meant, "I would be very willing to meet with you." A simple follows-up statement from the sender such as, "What day would be most convenient for you?" or a question from the case manager like, "Do you mean that you don't want to meet with me?" might have clarified the situation. Similarly, a community worker approaching residents of a predominantly American Indian inner-city community might inadvertently communicate disrespect to the residents nonverbally by engaging in excessive eye contact or frequently interrupting their comments. In this case the sender (the community worker) might have avoided the problem by studying the Native American culture. Had she done so, she might have learned that both excessive eye contact and interrupting a speaker may be interpreted as signs of disrespect.

COMMUNICATION STRUCTURES IN THE ORGANIZATION

Although every organization has individualized methods of sharing information, some patterns are consistent between organizations. These patterns not only define the information flow, but can be helpful in identifying and diagnosing problematic conditions. Ineffective patterns that recur excessively or with inordinate intensity can be characteristic of the overall effectiveness of intraorganizational communication. For observational purposes it is helpful to consider these patterns within three contexts: top-down, bottom-up, and horizontal communication (Brody & Nair, 2000).

Top-Down Communication

Top-down (sometimes called downward) communication refers to information directed from upper levels of an organization to its lower levels. Downward communication is generally used to provide direction for the agency's work and is often conveyed in the form of policies, procedures, or rules (Ludden & Capozzoli, 2000). The degree to which this channel of information is effective plays significantly into the overall effectiveness of the entire organization. Brody and Nair (2000) emphasize the importance of keeping this path open and constantly monitoring its effects on staff morale. Managers can avoid many problems by sharing information about anticipated changes with lower-level staff and involving them in the planning phases. This approach helps staff feel as though change has not been dictated. Further, it emphasizes their importance to the organization and increases the likelihood that they will buy in to the proposed change. Asking for the input of lower-level staff tells them that they are important and that their expertise is valued (Brody & Nair, 2000; Montana & Charnov, 1999).

Communication patterns within any organization, group, or initiative that are predominately downward may create an authoritarian environment that generates fear, stifles creativity, and fosters resentment. Employees, volunteers, and partners are likely to resist and even undermine the efforts of those who use top-down methods extensively. Damage to the organizational culture can be substantial, the quality of work is likely to suffer, and employee turnover or the loss of partners can be expected to be high.

Bottom-Up Communication

Bottom-up (or upward) communication refers to the transmission of information from staff lower on the organizational hierarchy to those in higher positions. This information tends to be specific and grows broader as it passes through the higher levels. Information in these messages commonly focuses on attitude and morale of staff and, if used appropriately, can decrease the number of unrealistic decisions made by leaders (Ludden & Capozzoli, 2000). Examples of upward communication would include: (a) a description to an agency's executive committee of the problems experienced by direct service workers in accessing transportation for their clients, (b) a conversation between a project's bookkeeper and its operations director about anticipated revenue shortfalls, and (c) a report to the board of directors from a group of middle-level managers on the outcome of a recently completed project.

Conversations with direct service personnel can paint a vivid picture of the true condition of the agency. Although upper-level management creates the policies that determine how these individuals interact with clients, they rarely have a strong understanding of the daily interactions of direct service staff and the people they serve. Building formal and informal communication mechanisms into agencies tells staff members that their opinions are valued. It also provides upper management with critical information they need to ensure that the agency provides effective services. It is important that if the opinions of lower-level employees are not incorporated into new policies, the reason for that decision be clearly communicated back to them (Brody & Nair, 2000; Montana & Charnov, 1999).

Horizontal Communication

Horizontal communication refers to the sharing of information between staff on similar levels within the organization's hierarchy or between equal participants in groups and community coalitions. This information tends to focus on the details needed to do the daily work of the group. Examples include arrangements to accommodate schedule changes by clients, references to the availability of files, communications about shared projects, and discussions about covering responsibilities for others during breaks or vacations. Coworkers may also share information about difficult situations in the past or about resources they have been able to access. Good horizontal communication has many benefits. It encourages a positive organizational or group culture by promoting openness and helpfulness. It improves morale and increases the level of bonding. It also contributes to the quality of service and promotes continuity of care. Groups in which good horizontal communication occurs typically have teamwork and a sense of camaraderie and shared purpose. It serves the purpose of enhancing workers' ability to collaborate and to make the best use of resources. It creates the sense that individuals care about one another and their work (Brody & Nair, 2000; Montana & Charnov, 1999). A lack of communication can lead to feelings of isolation among group members, creating an unpleasant environment (Ludden & Capozzoli, 2000).

Ludden and Capozzoli (2000) also identify some of the problems involved in excessive or inappropriate horizontal communication. Principal among these is the fact that workers may lack the ability to see the organization or partnership as a system and may not understand the way their action or inaction affects the overall group. When this is the case, communication may foster discontent and increase the level of misunderstanding. Horizontal communication also becomes negative when inaccurate information is transmitted, personal conversations become excessive, and unwarranted fears about the future are circulated.

| BOX 7.3 | COMMUNICATION IN COMMUNITY WORK |

Good communication is just as important in community work as it is in organizations, but it tends to take on a different appearance. Agencies have more top-down communication (that is, authoritative communication from those with greater power to those with lesser power) than do groups working in the community. This is because so much work is done by committees, task forces, and volunteer groups where no bureaucratic structure is present. Horizontal communication (information exchanged by those with roughly the same level of power) receives greater emphasis because participants tend to be of equal or nearly equal rank and authority. Bottom-up communication is less frequent, once again because of the absence of a hierarchical structure. Community practitioners are likely to spend as much or more time communicating than are agency leaders, emphasizing the importance of mastering basic techniques of communication.

Community practitioners must often work to ensure that their communications are perceived as lateral, rather than top-down. They often bring greater levels of expertise and experience to an initiative, yet they must function as facilitators rather than managers. Similarly, they must learn to recognize the expertise of others, and refrain from interpreting vital contributions of skilled people as efforts at top-down communication.

The examples used in this section have focused on patterns of communication within organizations. These principles are also useful for community work. Box 7.3 offers insight as to how they might apply in that setting.

BARRIERS TO EFFECTIVE COMMUNICATION

Communication failures are often disastrous. Misunderstandings may lead to critical mistakes and frustration at many levels of the agency. Often such problems are the result of failure to overcome specific barriers to successful interaction. These barriers include internal and external noise, filtering and distortions, and emotional interference.

Internal and External Noise

Noise refers to conditions that may occur both internally and externally to the receiver that may prevent her from completely understanding the message. Internal noise occurs when the receiver experiences thoughts unrelated to the message being sent, or when she attempts to receive multiple messages simultaneously. External noise can come from a variety of sources, including other people's conversation, construction sounds, and television or radio broadcasts.

Administrators can take steps to minimize or eliminate internal and external noise. Conferences should occur in quiet rooms behind closed doors whenever possible. These rooms should be attractive but should not contain furnishings that are likely to distract participants. The chairs should be comfortable but not so much as to encourage drowsiness. Meetings should follow clear agendas in which topics are clearly distinguished and an obvious transition is made when topics are changed.

At times, communication must occur in settings that are less than optimal, such as a hallway or a lobby. When these situations occur, it is important to minimize the effects of both external and internal noise. External noise can be reduced by inviting the receiver to a more private corner and speaking very distinctly. Internal noise can be minimized by maintaining eye contact, clearly outlining the message, and asking for feedback to ensure that the message has been understood.

Filtering and Distortions

Some barriers are directly related to a recipient's incorrect encoding of the message. Messages are filtered by the recipient when only pieces of the message are received and encoded. Essentially, the recipient hears what he wants to hear and blocks undesirable content. For example, a manager might share with a staff member plans to increase salaries if the agency receives a pending contract. In his excitement about the raise, the worker might not process the factor the raise is dependent upon. Messages can be distorted as the receiver interprets the information incorrectly. Distortions commonly occur when the receiver is under stress. For example, consider a leader who approaches a worker voicing concern regarding his availability to dedicate 100% due to personal factors. Rather than hearing the concern, the already stressed worker hear's that his supervisor doubts his capacity to perform. The distortion might, therefore, raise the worker's level of anxiety. Distortions also occur due to physical factors that affect the recipient's ability to receive the message. For example, the receiver may miss part of a message if her attention is distracted, resulting in a misunderstanding of the message (Ludden & Capozzoli, 2000; Montana & Charnov, 2000).

Several techniques can be employed to minimize the probability of distortion. The sender should take steps to ensure that communication is clear, particularly when the receiver is known to have experienced frequent distortions in the past. These steps might include careful planning about what is to be said (perhaps even writing out or rehearsing it), repeating the message two or three times in different words, and asking the receiver to repeat the message back.

Emotional Interference

Barriers also exist as a result of emotional factors. Credibility issues or a speaker's past inconsistencies will also affect the way in which a message is received and encoded. The lack of trust created as a result of credibility issues has major effects on the morale of the organization (Ludden & Capozzoli, 2000; Montana & Charnov, 2000). For example, imagine that the staff presents several major obstacles affecting their abilities to perform to organizational leaders. The leaders make a commitment to address these barriers. However, the administration has taken no action after several months. As time goes by, workers are likely to become increasingly frustrated and resentful of their managers. Both their level of trust in management and their morale is likely to drop dramatically.

When emotional factors such as diminished trust and resentment interfere with communication, these factors must be addressed before effective interactions can consistently occur. In the previous example, administrators may need to explain the reason no action has been taken and may need to perform some good-faith steps toward resolving the problem to reestablish trust. Often these situations can be resolved with a combination of frank, honest discussions and sincere, meaningful actions directed toward resolving the emotional blockages.

An understanding of the barriers to communication is also important for community workers. Specific examples are discussed in Box 7.4.

METHODS OF COMMUNICATION

Organizational and community practitioners typically use a variety of methods of communication. Choosing the best option, or combination of options, must be based on a number of factors including: (a) the person or people who must send the message, (b) the person or people who will receive the

| BOX 7.4 | COMMUNICATION IN COMMUNITY WORK |

Unique conditions within any community may present unusual combinations of barriers to communication for community workers. Cultural differences, for example, may result in any of the barriers discussed in this chapter. For example filtering might occur if a community practitioner accepted the response from an Southeast Asian immigrant that things were fine with him and his family despite strong visible evidence to the contrary. In this case, the professional would be filtering out the visible evidence in favor of the client's statements, while ignoring the Southeast Asian custom of publicly minimizing problems in order preserve the dignity of the family.

Noise is a common problem in community work. Typically, many conversations are conducted on street corners or in busy centers of activity. Community meetings may be emotional and be the occasion for multiple individual conversations occurring simultaneously with a public speech or presentation. It is important that community practitioners use the techniques recommended in this chapter to overcome such barriers. Street corner conversations can be enhanced by taking a few steps away from traffic. Communication in meetings can be improved by providing frequent summaries of the information provided during a presentation and asking for feedback from the audience about comments that have been made.

message, (c) the nature of the message, and (d) the culture and climate of the agency within which the message will be delivered. Most practitioners use a combination of face-to-face, written, and electronic communication to meet objectives.

Face-to-Face Communication

Although old fashioned in comparison to today's technologically driven methods of communication, face-to-face interactions are still preferable in many circumstances. No other medium allows participants to share on an interpersonal level as effectively as does a direct conversation between two people. It allows for multiple levels of interaction (including direct sending and receiving) the opportunity to personally observe body language, and the occasion for instant questioning and clarification. Confidential information is often more protected than in other mediums. Information can be exchanged and questions answered on the spot rather than waiting for a written response. Possibly the greatest benefit of face-to-face interactions involves the opportunity to observe nonverbal communication, a major advantage considering most information is transmitted through nonverbal messages (Ludden & Capozzoli, 2000).

Written Communication

Written communications, such as memoranda and letters, have other benefits. In some environments, information is perceived as important only when it is written down. Written communication also provides the opportunity for accountability. An organization's mission statement, for example, is powerful in part because it defines the purpose of the agency in such a way as to allow its effectiveness and integrity to be evaluated. Policy and procedure manuals carry authority because they are consistent and readily available for reference. Written communication can also be replicated, while verbal communication can never be precisely reproduced. It offers the chance to convey a great deal of information that will not be lost because the recipient can refer back to it. Written communication does have its deficiencies, including a lack of opportunity for the observation of nonverbal messages and the inability to provide immediate feedback to ensure that the message was understood (Ludden & Capozzoli, 2000).

Electronic Communication

Electronic technology allows practitioners to maintain constant contact through devices such as telephone, e-mail, and fax. Staff from an unlimited number of locations can correspond through electronic exchanges allowing for the quick and efficient exchange of information. These media allow for the ready transmission of large quantities of information and the efficient storage of that information. They can help members of organizations and initiatives feel connected and supported by one another. Electronic communication can also have its limitations, however. It can be easily misunderstood and, if used in excess, can actually cause isolation rather than bonding within an organization or initiative (Ludden & Capozzoli, 2000).

MANAGING MEETINGS

Meetings are a beneficial means of getting important information to a large number of workers simultaneously. Communicating a policy change to individual employees, for example, can be time consuming and may delay the implementation process. These problems can be overcome through a meeting in which the policy change is clearly and comprehensively explained to all employees. Meetings have disadvantages, however. Assembling large numbers of employees consumes substantial agency resources, particularly if some must travel from remote locations. Workers also must take time from their regular duties in order to be present. Some may feel overwhelmed when the requirement of attendance is added to an already unmanageable day. For this reason, meetings should be used cautiously and should be managed judiciously. Brody and Nair (2000) recommend not holding meetings in some specific situations:

1. When communication by phone or memorandum is sufficient. Practitioners should not devote time to meetings when a phone call would be sufficient.
2. When the issues to be addressed are confidential. Private information should not be discussed in a group.
3. Poor preparation. Even when a meeting is scheduled, it should not be held if the facilitator is not prepared or if inadequate information is available. Employees and collaborative partners may experience frustration if meetings are disorganized or seem meaningless. Poorly planned and executed meetings will encourage disinterest or decreased participation in the future (Brody & Nair, 2000).

Because the success of meetings can be critical to agency operations, administrators should ensure that they have the greatest possible likelihood of being successful. Some basic guidelines for holding meetings are:

1. Because meetings are costly, practitioners must plan for optimal effectiveness and efficiency. The purpose and objectives of the meeting should be communicated to participants in advance and opportunities for feedback regarding its content should be provided (Brody & Nair, 2000; McNamara, 1999).
2. An agenda should be developed and circulated. The input of participants should be solicited whenever possible. The agenda should define the desired outcome for the meeting, list the topics that will be considered,

BOX 7.5 | A SAMPLE AGENDA

Agenda for Staff Meeting October 24, 2005 10:00 a.m. in the Tiara Conference Room

Call to Order—Mr. Admin

Approval of Minutes from the September Meeting—
Ms. Archivist

Discussion of the Problem of Decreasing Funding—
Mr. Poorly

Discussion of Available Options—Ms. Optimist

Discussion—Ms. Optimist

Vote on an Option—Mr. Admin

Formation of Subcommittee to Implement
Option—Mr. Admin

---

and include any actions that should occur, such as a vote or formation of a committee. The agenda should be honored in that the discussion should follow the written plan. Straying from the agenda may mean that important topics are not addressed and will likely result in a meeting that is too long. Important topics that arise that are not a part of the agenda should be tabled until the end of the meeting or scheduled for a later meeting. A sample agenda can be found in Box 7.5.

3. A meeting's opening moments are critical to its success. They should model the norms that are desired for the balance of the meeting. Starting on time communicates that participant time is valued. Initially, the agenda should be presented to ensure that everyone understands the meeting's purpose and plan. The facilitator's role should also be explained and any minutes of previous meetings reviewed and approved by the participants.

4. All participants must understand the rules under which the meeting will be conducted. Each meeting does not require establishing new rules but may involve reviewing those previously established. When a discussion of rules is needed, it should take place as a part of the meeting to ensure that all members are committed to the rules. Examples of rules include items such as confidentiality and the desired level of participation from attendees.

5. Time management is a major factor in the success of a meeting. Becoming overly consumed by one topic will mean that others on the agenda will go unaddressed. Ultimately, this may mean that a topic may go undiscussed for days, weeks, or months until the next meeting. The facilitator should ensure that participants move briskly but effectively through the agenda. Meeting participants can support this effort by holding other members accountable for irrelevant and lengthy discussion.

6. The evaluation of meetings is also very important. This is perhaps most easily done by simply asking for comments from participants. If they are unlikely to answer openly or if anonymity is an issue, a questionnaire may be circulated at the end of the meeting. The discussion or questionnaire should include such questions as: "How did you feel about the manner in which this meeting was conducted?" "Did the meeting meet your expectations?" "Do you think the objectives for the meeting were achieved?" and "What might have been done to make this meeting more effective?"

7. The meeting should end on time. The facilitator should briefly review the steps and assignments made during the meeting as well as the time and place of the next meeting. Because a positive, lasting impression, as well as the likelihood of participants returning for the next meeting, may be

| BOX 7.6 | COMMUNICATION IN COMMUNITY WORK |

Meetings assembled by community practitioners may require that special considerations be made. These considerations include:

1. *The time of the meeting.* The plan should accommodate as many potential participants as possible. For example, many people from participating agencies and organizations may prefer that meetings occur at a time that allows them to leave their offices to attend without being required to return at the end of the day.

2. *The place of the meeting.* Because community practitioners may be assembling meetings that include participants from a variety of locations, it may be important to find as central a location as possible.

3. *The representation of all stakeholder groups.* Although the inclusion of all stakeholder groups is important within agencies, it is often even more critical in communities. Those who feel excluded may be difficult to recruit in the future.

4. *The need for publicity.* The presence of media representatives may be particularly important for community meetings. Reports by the press can mobilize the support of government officials and power brokers as well as attract the attention and participation of additional community members.

5. *The need for the presence of outside decision makers.* At times it may help the cause of a community group to have those with the power to support or oppose their initiative present so that the sentiment of the community or the purposes of a work group are clearly understood.

---

dependent on the closing moments, the meeting should end on a positive note (Brody & Nair, 2000; McNamara, 1999).

Certain considerations regarding meetings are particularly important for community practitioners. Some of these are discussed in Box 7.6.

TECHNIQUES TO IMPROVE COMMUNICATION

Several techniques are available to enhance communication within an agency or community group. McNamara (1999) suggests the following methods.

Top-Down Communication Methods

1. Every member should receive a copy of the strategic plan. A constant awareness of the agency or initiative's mission, vision, and values will increase participants' understanding of the reasoning behind changes and new policies.

2. Organizational employees should receive a copy of the organizational chart and their job descriptions. These tools can enhance a worker's understanding of how her position contributes to the organization as a whole.

3. Protocols should be developed describing routine tasks and collected into an operating manual. These protocols assist employees in knowing what to expect in common situations.

4. Practitioners should hold regular meetings to celebrate accomplishments and to discuss needs and issues. This encourages open communication and, in organizations, communicates to staff that the managers are interested in their well-being.

5. Leaders should hold regular meetings with managers to proactively identify any obstacles the agency or initiative faces. A failure to intervene early on sets a pattern of reacting to crisis situations that could have been prevented.

Bottom-Up Communication Methods

1. Employees should communicate with supervisors on a weekly basis to discuss past and future activities. This facilitates the supervisor's job of building rapport and helps to anticipate problems and opportunities.

2. Staff and community partners should have the opportunity to meet in forum or round table environments with leaders to discuss concerns. This can enhance morale and help leaders gain an understanding of the perspectives of others.

3. Practitioners should never underestimate the importance of information received through informal channels, sometimes known as "the grapevine." Although it is a breeding ground for gossip, the grapevine often paints an accurate portrait of the working environment (McNamara, 1999).

Horizontal Communication

1. Administrators should create time to engage in casual, horizontal communication with staff. Although it is beneficial to do this during work hours, at times it is also beneficial to do it outside the office through outings, events, and so on.

2. Administrators should create opportunities to engage in both work-related and non-work-related communication with their peers.

3. Break areas should be provided near work areas to provide opportunities for employees to gather and talk.

4. Agency activities that either allow opportunities for communication or that require communication should be arranged regularly. Examples include staff lunches, group visits to other agencies, and supervisor's meetings. Community practitioners should ensure that collaborative partners and other participants also have casual or formal times to get together.

USING THE MACRO PRACTITIONER'S WORKBOOK

Worksheets 7.1 and 7.2 are included for the Macro Practitioner's Workbook. The first worksheet will take you through the steps necessary to plan effective communication. The second will help develop an agenda for a meeting. Use the case study for unit 2 to complete the worksheets.

SUMMARY

In this chapter, effective intra-agency communication was discussed. In doing so, some basic principles of communication were learned as well as some of the barriers that may interfere with effective interaction. Finally, ways of using this knowledge to improve communication within social service organizations were discussed.

Activities for Learning

1. Working in a small group, discuss a current event from the national media. Watch as the other members of the group interact. What are the senders doing to ensure that their messages are being received? What are the receivers doing to ensure that they understand? What barriers to communication are present? What might be done to enhance communication?

2. At a agency or community meeting, observe the interactions between participants. What kinds of noise are present? How do they affect the meeting? Are any efforts made to overcome them? Do you see evidence of any distortions? If so, what kind? What is done to overcome those distortions? What else might have been done? Do you see evidence of any emotional interference? How might those situations be handled?

3. Participate in a group discussion about the strengths and weaknesses of e-mail as a communication tool. What advantages do you see to e-mail? What are its disadvantages? What can be done within an agency to maximize its strengths and minimize its weaknesses?

Questions for Discussion

1. How can you use your newfound knowledge of the barriers to effective communication to enhance your relationship with your classmates, with faculty, with clients, and with others in your agency or community partnership?

2. What do you feel is the most damaging problem that may affect downward communication? What can administrators do to avoid this problem? What can practitioners do to avoid it?

3. Under what circumstances should administrators use a memorandum rather than a meeting to communicate with staff? When might a meeting be preferable? If a memorandum is chosen and administrators fear that the limited opportunity for interaction it provides is likely to generate problems, what measures might they take to alleviate those problems?

Key Terms

Bottom-up communication— the transmission of information from staff lower on the organizational hierarchy to those in higher positions.

Developing the message— the process of preparing a message to send. It involves organizing thoughts, selecting information, and encoding the message.

Horizontal communication— the sharing of information between staff on similar levels within the organization's hierarchy.

Receivers—those to whom information is directed.

Senders—those from whom information is sent.

Top-down communication— information directed from upper levels of the organization to lower levels.

References

Brody, R., & Nair, M. (2000). *Macro practice: A generalist approach*, (5th ed., pp. 107–115, 146–152). Wheaton, IL: Gregory Publishing.

Ludden, L. & Capozzoli, T. (2000). *Supervisor savvy: How to retain & develop entry-level workers*. Indianapolis: Jist Works., pp. 79–104.

McNamara, C. (1999). *Free basic guide to leadership and supervision*. Available: www.mapnp.org/library/mgmnt/prsnlmnt.htm.

Montana, P. & Charnov, B. (2000). *Management,* (3rd ed., pp. 216–220). New York: Barron's Educational Series.

WORKSHEET 7.1 | PLANNING A COMMUNICATION

1. Decide what you want to say
    a. Write a description of the issue you want to address.

    The work ethic of direct service personal
    How to change the buy-in process, so that everyone is
    working from the same thoughts and understandings

    b. Write an explanation of what it is that you wish to say about the issue.

    Would talk about what happened before and review the
    mission of agency, and talk about where to go in the future.
    The expectations of the agency and each individuals
    role they play.

    c. Review both to ensure that you have identified everything that needs to be said.

2. Decide how you want to say it
    a. Make a list of the things others will need to know before they will be able to understand your
        message.
        1. Mission of agency
        2. Job discriptions
        3. Where the agency is now and where you want it to
           go.
        4. How you are viewed by other agencies
        5. Clear message for the reason you are sending this
           message
    b. Write an explanation of how your message will benefit its recipients.
        1. Employees will know what direction agency is going in
        2. Opportunity to buy-in
        3. Understanding of roles different employees have
        4. Better communication
        5.

c.   Write an explanation of how your message will benefit clients or community members.

Clients will no that the agency is trying to better it's self w/ the clients as it' main reason. Better organization will give better understanding and faith to those who use it's services. It will also show that the agency wants to succeed.

d.   Write an explanation of how your message will benefit the agency or the community partners.

Same as above. But to other community partners it will show a "take charge" - time for change attitude, that is important to those who also share thier visions.

e.   Write a paragraph or two combining the above information and presenting it in the most effective way possible.

3.   Identify those who need to hear your message
   a.   List those people and groups who need to hear your message.

   1 Employees
   2. Clients
   3 Community partners
   4 Porspective clients
   5. Board members

   b.   Prioritize the list. Should one individual or group hear the message before the others?

   1. Board member
   2 Employees
   3 Community partners
   4 Clients

4. Tailor your message according to your audience
    a. Using the list of intended recipients composed in the step above, make a note of the things that will be needed as a part of effective communication with each recipient.

    1. Mission and direction in which it will take, agenda.for meeting copy of mission statement

    2. mission, Job discriptions, orgainzational flow chart, - Future notes

    3. Meeting w/ joint organizations
    4. News letter to explain changes

    b. Rewrite your message for each, taking these differences into consideration.

5. Overcome barriers to the transmission of your message
    a. List the barriers you anticipate encountering with each group.

    1. Board - people not coming to meeting
    2. Employees - resistence to change - accoutability
    3.
    4. Nobody really caring, because of past

    b. List at least two strategies for overcoming each barrier.

    1. Personal phone calls - more than one notice - eary copy of agenda
    2. Open forum to speak. Buy-in
    3. Wanting thier imput
    4. Community meeting

    c. Select the strategies you will use when you send the message.

    1. phone calls, mail,
    2. Notices
    3. phone calls, email, mail
    4. Newspaper, direct mailing. word of month

6.   Select a medium for transmitting your message
   a.   List the strengths and weaknesses of each of the following approaches:
      ___ memorandum

      - go for inhouse use only.
      -

      ___ letter

      - ok - people will read and throw-out, if it
      is well written they will save

      ___ individual contact

      Best to use · hard to get a hold of
      people, and asking for return calls

      ___ small group meetings

      - productive
      -

      ___ an agencywide meeting

      - time comsuming
      - cause anxiety
      - over-all communitation good

___e-mail
- *not very effective, people delete messages if they don't know where it came from; addresses change or fail.*

But could get quick responses back when working

___other
~Newsletter
~ media

b.   Identify in writing the way in which you will transmit your message to each individual or group.

personal contact - phone call
letter or flyer
email

7.   Evaluate the success of your efforts
a.   Write a statement of your desired outcome for each time the message is sent.

people will want to come to meeting

b.   Write a statement explaining how you will determine whether your outcome has been reached.

- determined by the number of people contacted and to the number that respond back.

WORSHEET 7.2 | DEVELOPING AN AGENDA

1. Set a date for a meeting that will allow the maximum possible attendance by the intended recipients of your message.

Board - Early evening meeting around 7:00pm
Employees- a little before lunch thru lunch

Community - during the day
    agencies

2. Send a memorandum to all the intended recipients:
   a. Informing them of the date and time of the planned meeting

We have scheduled a "board nothing" to be held
on TUE Sept 16 2005 to begin at 7:00pm.

   b. Informing them of the purpose of the meeting

The purpose of this meeting is review the agency
mission, and to share with the board the goals
of the agency for the next year.

   c. Asking for their ideas for additional agenda items

If you would like to add an item you feel
is important for a discussion, please forward it
to me by Sept 13, so that it may be added to the
final agenda for that evening

3. Prepare an agenda following the example in Box 7.5.

Meeting called to order
Approved for past minuets
Reading + discussion of Agency Mission Statement
Report of agency goals for next year
Discussion of goals
added agenda items
meeting closed

8

FORMING A TASK
FORCE OR COMMITTEE

CHAPTER OUTLINE

Determining Whether a Task Force Is Needed

Defining the Problem

Identifying Potential Task Force Members

Developing a Key Description of Each Prospective Member

Prepare a Script for Approaching Prospective Members

Prepare an Action Plan Approach for Each Prospective Member

Follow the Action Plan

Using the Macro Practitioner's Workbook

Summary

Task forces are collaborative efforts in which individuals, often from a variety of sources, come together to accomplish a specific, time-limited task. For example, the model developed by the Office of Juvenile Justice and Delinquency Prevention for addressing disproportionate minority confinement in the states utilizes multiple task forces within each state. At the highest level, a statewide task force is assembled consisting of representatives from the courts, Departments of Juvenile Justice, state representatives, and representatives from social service agencies, universities, and other sources. This task force coordinates the efforts of several local task forces who interact with the community to arrange research projects, initiate interventions, and collect outcome data regarding efforts to reduce the percentage of minority juveniles who are confined in state-operated facilities. The task forces are charged with a specific task: overseeing the processes related to disproportionate minority confinement. They are time-limited in that once their task is accomplished, they will cease to exist.

| BOX 8.1 | CASE STUDY |

A small nonprofit drop-in center with a staff of seven specializes in serving the homeless. Recently the city had started to conduct nightly "sweeps," rounding up homeless men and women and forcing them to move out of certain areas of the city. In addition to this, the mayor has put pressure on several single residency occupants hotels (SROs) to close in areas that he has marked for "urban revitalization projects." Realizing that the nonprofit has very few resources, limited staff, and no political ties, the staff decide to initiate a citywide task force, combining resources with larger organizations serving the homeless, other drop-in centers, local churches, and social work professors at the local universities. Through the task force, they are able to organize a large advocacy campaign, pooling monies and staff resources from different organizations to stage demonstrations, print up fliers, and lobby city council men and women.

Task forces are different from many other types of groups. They are distinguished here from collaborative efforts (discussed in unit 1) by their brief, task-oriented nature. They are included in this unit as an example of communication with other individuals and agencies. It is also practical for community practitioners, because they are frequently involved in task force activities.

Because they have a specific mission, task forces require a specific composition to be successful. This chapter describes the characteristics required by task forces, methods of recognizing them in potential members, techniques for recruiting those members, and the steps necessary to prepare for the task force's initial meeting.

It is important to note that some committees, particularly **ad hoc committees,** are similar to task forces in that they have a specific task to accomplish, and they will exist only until that task has been accomplished. When this is the case, the similarities between a committee and a task force are so great that virtually everything in this chapter applies to both. Therefore, the majority of the following discussion can be applied to both committees and task forces. In places where there are differences, those differences are identified and discussed.

The contents of this chapter are equally applicable to both community and agency practitioners. Either is likely to be asked to participate in or help put together a task force. Either needs to have the skills and knowledge provided in this chapter.

DETERMINING WHETHER A TASK FORCE IS NEEDED

Before forming a task force, it is important to determine whether it is needed, or whether it is the best alternative for addressing the situation at hand. Several factors may affect this decision, such as the need for a speedy resolution, the existence of other organizations with the same purpose as the intended task force, and the feasibility of addressing the issue at the current time.

One factor that must be considered before a task force is developed is the degree to which speed is needed in the completion of the desired task. Under unique circumstances a task force is able to work quickly. More often, however, they are composed of individuals from various sources with varying levels of available time and heavy commitments to other projects. A task force is useful when the need for substantial and diverse resources exceeds the need for a speedy resolution. If circumstances are such that an individual can access the necessary resources with relative ease, it is likely to be more desirable that the individual be assigned the task. One person is likely to be able to accomplish the goal more quickly than a task force could.

Another question to be asked before assembling a task force is whether some other organization already exists that is charged with completing the task. If so, it may be more beneficial to contribute resources to that organization than to form an additional one. If such an organization exists, issues of compatibility should be discussed with its members. Participants on both sides would need to consider comparability of goals, potential ethical conflicts, and consistency of acceptable methods. If these areas are sufficiently compatible, the two groups should consider joining forces.

A third factor that should be considered before forming a task force is the feasibility of addressing the issue at the current time. Although an issue may be critical and worthy of pursuit, internal or external forces may make it impossible to address at the current time. Problems that might make it undesirable to form a task force include a hostile political climate, a dearth of the resources needed to accomplish the task, and the recent failure of a similar task force formed to address the same issue.

DEFINING THE PROBLEM

It is critical that the issue is clearly identified and defined when a task force is formed to deal with it. The importance of problem definition has been discussed in several previous chapters. In the case of a task force, particularly one that has been assembled from groups outside the agency, problem definition is crucial. The group must be in agreement as to the nature of the problem and its desire to solve the problem.

Although the problem was probably identified when the decision was made to form a task force, it is important that the members of the group thoroughly discuss its perceptions of the problem before taking steps to address it. This discussion will ensure that the task force members are in agreement as to the nature of the problem. It will also help to identify any philosophical or ethical differences between the task force members early so that they can be dealt with without interfering with the process.

The task force should be given a draft problem statement with which it can work. Guidelines for the development of a problem statement are provided in chapter 1.

IDENTIFYING POTENTIAL TASK FORCE MEMBERS

Task forces and all committees with similar functions require four key components in order to function effectively. These components include: (a) key people or positions, (b) influence, (c) competence, and (d) motivation. In order for any task group to function effectively, people who bring these components to the table must be included.

The first critical component of task forces is **key people** or **positions**. This component refers to people who are needed by the task force because of the position they hold in the community. These people hold key positions that can bring the other resources, power, competence, and motivation to the group. Typically, they are people who are involved in the process in some way by virtue of their position. Examples for a local disproportionate minority confinement task force such as the one discussed in the beginning of this chapter include a judge or referee from a juvenile court, the top administrator for the local district of the Department of Children's Services, and the head of the local law enforcement agency. These would be important participants because decisions regarding the children who are taken into custody are made by these agencies.

The second category of people that should be members of a task force includes those with **influence**. Influence refers to the ability to influence decisions about the issue directly, the ability to affect funding, or the ability to influence other people who play roles in the process. Another word for influence would be power; the power to make things happen. People with influence include those whose positions and personal circumstances create interest for them and provide them with influence in the area. Examples include the mayor's office, a county commissioner, and a state legislator. Other examples, often forgotten in the development of task forces, include local power brokers who are not a part of either the social services or political communities. These include people who contribute substantially to local social service efforts and those who have relationships with people who are in formal positions of power.

People who lack an official position or the power to influence decisions but understand political realities and how those in power can be influenced have **competence**, a necessary ingredient for a task force. Members of task forces must find ways to affect the decisions that people in power make. In the example of the disproportionate minority confinement task force, members may encounter a juvenile judge who is resistant to its work or a police chief who does not wish to cooperate. Several options exist that may win the cooperation of these people. The options include several possibilities, from a personal request through media action. The task force should include people who have the competence to make things happen and will support the task.

Often the easiest people to recruit for a task force are those with **motivation**, that is, those who strongly desire to see a change in the chosen area. People with strong motivation are crucial to the success of the task force, but must not be mistaken for people who possess the characteristics in the other categories. People who bring motivation to a task force are often those who have no official connection with the task but who are directly affected by the issue involved.

It is important to remember that some task force members may bring more than one of these characteristics to the table. The task force needs to include each of these ingredients, but need not include individuals who possess one ingredient only. Although there are advantages to having the required characteristics spread across several members (for example, the loss is not as difficult to recoup if one member leaves the task force), there are also advantages to having a single member with multiple characteristics. The process is often quicker when one member of the task force is able to perform several of the tasks needed by the group. A person of influence, motivation, and competence can bring a great deal to any task force initiative.

When a task force is formed, a list should be developed including people from each of the categories described previously. The list will provide a structure that will ensure that all the necessary characteristics will be included. Those recruiting a task force can then use that list to develop a plan for approaching each potential member.

DEVELOPING A KEY DESCRIPTION OF EACH PROSPECTIVE MEMBER

After identifying potential members for the task force, the next step is to develop a key description of each prospective member. The key description is intended to provide a summary of the information that is needed to recruit the prospective member to join the task force. There are several components to a strategic description. These include the person's name, their agency, their phone number, their probable motivations for joining the task force, the way in which they will be contacted, and the role they will be expected to play.

It is important to consider the prospective member's probable motivations for joining the task force. In some cases, those who are assembling the group may need to convince a prospective member to join the group. In these situations it will be important to have thought through the ways in which the person or her organization might benefit from participation. This information can then be used as a selling point to convince the prospective member to participate.

It is also important to determine the manner in which the prospective member will be contacted. In some cases, the best approach may be a simple and direct phone call. In others, it may be important to involve a third party who has influence with the potential member. These kinds of decisions should be made in the planning stage whenever possible. The projected manner of approach should be included in the strategic description.

The strategic description of potential members should also include a summary of the role the prospective member will be expected to play. This is important for several reasons. First, the person recruiting the prospective member will need to have a clear understanding of what she is going to ask. Putting the request into writing will ensure that the recruiter knows what the group needs, and will help her communicate that need clearly. This will help to ensure that the potential member understands what her role will be should she choose to join the group.

PREPARE A SCRIPT FOR APPROACHING PROSPECTIVE MEMBERS

Before prospective members are approached, it is often useful to write a script of what will be said to them. Although it is unlikely that the recruiter will repeat the script verbatim, having thought through and written the request can help to make the process easier and can help ensure that all the important information is communicated. The following questions should be answered in the script.

1. *What is the prospective member being asked to do?* It will be important to let the prospective member know exactly what he will be expected to do, the amount of time commitment required, the number of resources that will be needed, and the amount of political capital that must be expended.

2. *Who is encouraging the prospective member to participate?* Many, perhaps most, of the people who are recruited to task forces are busy people with extensive responsibilities and heavy time commitments. They may be reluctant to take on another role. Often, by listing the influential people who consider them essential to the task force, the recruiter may be able to persuade them.

3. *Why is the prospective member important to the task force?* Each prospective member should be aware of which of the components (key people or positions, influence, competence, or motivation) he brings and why that is important to the task force.

4. *How will the prospective member's participation help him?* Hopefully, the prospective member will be able to realize some form of benefit from participating. Including this information in the key description can help to ensure that he is aware of that benefit.

PREPARE AN ACTION PLAN APPROACH FOR EACH PROSPECTIVE MEMBER

The key description forms the basis for the action plan. Each potential member is likely to require a different approach. Some will be accessible and will respond to a phone call or some other form of personal communication. Others may require an approach from a third party, someone who is known to both the recruiter and the prospective member. Regardless of the manner of approach, it should be carefully planned to ensure the highest probability of success.

The action plan should be developed in much the same manner as the strategic plan described in chapter 1. Goals and objectives should be clearly stated and grouped. Tasks should also be specified along with the name of the person responsible for each in the same way in which the results will be reported back to the planners. For example, if the goal were to recruit the commissioner of the state department of health, one objective might be to secure the support of two influential legislators and the second might be to arrange an appointment with the commissioner after the legislators have expressed their support. Tasks might include phone calls to the offices of those involved, the preparation of a letter or memorandum explaining the task force, and visits with the legislators and the commissioner.

FOLLOW THE ACTION PLAN

Once the plan has been developed, it should be followed closely, unless it becomes evident that it is not working. In the case mentioned previously, for example, if one legislator refused to support the plan, it might be necessary to contact some other influential person to enlist her aid. The need for this kind of flexibility suggests the need for an effective feedback mechanism that allows the planners to determine when changes should be made. In its simplest form, this might be no more than an oral report provided at a future meeting of the planners. The steps then, in following the action plan, would include:

1. Develop a system that provides feedback regarding the effectiveness of the plan and accountability for each person who is responsible for tasks
2. Identify the resources that are needed for additional support
3. Revise the plan as it becomes necessary to do so

USING THE MACRO PRACTITIONER'S WORKBOOK

Worksheets 8.1 through 8.5 are included for the Macro Practitioner's Workbook. Use the case study for unit 2 for the information to complete them.

SUMMARY

This chapter has focused on the development of task forces and task-oriented committees. A successful group requires four components: key people or positions, influence, competence, and motivation. Members should be recruited in such a way that all four components are included. An action plan should be developed and followed to enhance the recruitment process.

Activities for Learning

1. Ask someone in the social services community about task forces that have been assembled for various purposes in your community. Ask them about whether the groups were successful. If they were successful, what made them that way? If they were not successful, why did they fail? Did their plans require any adjustment in order to be successful?
2. Pick a problem in your local service delivery system. List people who could bring all four necessary components to a task force that might be convened to address the problem. What might be some ways you would approach those people?
3. Working in a small group, answer the following questions. What kinds of benefits might task force members experience as a result of their participation? Is it an ethical issue that they might benefit in some way? Is it an ethical issue that you might use that potential gain as an inducement for them to join the group?

Questions for Discussion

1. What advantages might a task force have over a single individual working alone? What disadvantages might it have? How might the disadvantages of a task force be minimized?
2. Consider that a committee is being formed to deal with some issues within your agency. Which of the principles in this chapter would you be able to use to form the committee? Which could you not use?
3. How might you determine when a plan to build a task force would need revising? How could you be certain you were not acting too quickly?

Key Terms

Ad hoc committees— committees formed on a temporary basis to accomplish a time-limited task.

Competence— one of the four vital components of a successful task force, competence refers to the capacity to deal with people and political issues in an effective manner.

Influence— one of the four vital components of a

successful task force, influence refers to the power to make things happen within an organization or community.

Key people or positions— one of the four vital components of a successful task force, key people or positions refers to those who can be identified as crucial because of the official positions they hold.

Motivation— one of the four vital components of a successful task force, motivation refers to a strong desire to see that the task force accomplishes its goals and the willingness to do whatever is necessary to make it effective.

References

Brody, R., and Nair, M. D. (2000). *Macro practice: A generalist approach* (5th ed.). Wheaton, IL: Gregory Publishing.

Ellis, R. A. (2003). *Impacting social policy: A practitioners guide to analysis and action*: Brooks and Cole.

Gummer, B. and Edwards, R. L. (1995). The politics of human ser-

vice administration. In L. Ginsberg, and P. R. Keys, (Eds.), *New management in human services*, (2nd ed., pp. 57–71). Washington, DC: NASW Press.

Pelton, E. D., and Baznick, R. E. (1998). Managing public policy advocacy and government relations. In R. L. Edwards, J. A. Yankey, and M. A. Altpeter,

Skills for effective management of nonprofit organizations (pp. 119–126). Washington, DC: NASW Press.

WORKSHEET 8.1 | IDENTIFICATION OF POTENTIAL MEMBERS

1. List the key people and positions you will need to recruit for the task force.

Marlene— communty development
Daud — ex dir. Com. Mefital Heath center
Child welfare Advisory Counal
St. Dept Juval Justice
Church leade

2. List the people who can bring influence to the task force.

Marlene
Child welfare

3. List the people who can bring competence to the task force.

Daud,
Marlene
St. Dept
Human Serves

4. List the people who can bring motivation to the task force.

Church leader

WORKSHEET 8.2 | DEVELOPING A STRATEGIC DESCRIPTION OF EACH PROSPECTIVE MEMBER

Person	Agency	Phone	Motivation for Joining	Point of Contact	Expected Role
Marlene –	Community development		Continued growth in community	work.	organizational influence w/ other agencies
David –	Community mental Health		works in same settings, uses same clients	work	Similar spreading can work w/ other agency's contacts
local com Leader	Churchs		Community @ large	?	contact w/ local com. Leaders & parents
R. Child welfare agency	Child Welfare agency		welfare to clients and children	agency.	policies/ procedures

WORKSHEET 8.3 | PREPARING A SCRIPT FOR APPROACHING EACH PROSPECTIVE MEMBER

1. What is the prospective member being asked to do?

By into a task Forse that will review pocy + produres at other orgainzahuns

2. Who is encouraging the prospective member to participate?

The Head of Committee

3. Why is the prospective member important to the task force?

They bring information to the task force that will help set-up new quidlines to the changes in communication

4. How will the prospective member's participation help him?

Over all connections w/ other orgainzatuns the success of the outcome to what they bring

WORKSHEET 8.4 | PREPARE AN ACTION PLAN FOR RECRUITING MEMBERS

Goal: _____

Objective 1: _____

Task 1 _____

Person Responsible _____

Accountability Method and Date _____

Task 2 _____

Person Responsible _____

Accountability Method and Date _____

Task 3 _____

Person Responsible _____

Accountability Method and Date _____

WORKSHEET 8.5 | **FOLLOW THE ACTION PLAN**

1. Develop a system that provides feedback regarding the effectiveness of the plan and accountability for each person who is responsible for tasks.

2. Identify the resources that are needed for additional support.

3. Revise the plan as it becomes necessary to do so.

9

WORKING WITH A
BOARD OF DIRECTORS

CHAPTER OUTLINE

Overview of Board Membership

Roles and Responsibilities

Board Structures

Selecting Board Members

Training Board Members

Fundraising

Using the Macro Practitioner's Workbook

Summary

Historically, the successes and failures of an organization have been viewed as indicators of an executive director's capacity to lead and accomplish objectives. In recent years, a number of factors have operated simultaneously to cause a shifting of the emphasis on the executive director alone to include the board of directors as well. Although boards of directors have virtually always been responsible for the management of the agency through their management of executive directors, the recent reemphasis of their role makes the ability of agency administration and **board members** to work together increasingly important. Consider the following factors.

The uncertain, turbulent task environment in which today's agencies operate has been cited in several chapters of this book. The conditions described in those chapters emphasize the need for a team approach to agency management in which the resources brought by an active, effective board of directors can make the difference between the survival and the death of the agency. Board members may participate in service delivery, contribute to the hiring process, raise financial support, or engage in many other supportive activities.

Today's agencies also have a need for diversity in their knowledge and skill bases. Although competent clinical staff may be relatively easy to find, other skills are often beyond the budgetary reach of the agency. Smaller agencies may find accounting assistance, legal advice, and business acumen for which they lack financial resources among the members of their board.

Yet another factor that has elevated the importance of an effective board is the recurrent emergence of scandals in the corporate world. These scandals have emphasized the need for multiple levels of accountability within an organization. The burden of accountability is not solely on the executive director but extends to members of the board as well. In most jurisdictions, a member of the board of directors can be held accountable for illegal acts or mismanagement of funds on the part of the organization. In fact board members typically have a **fiduciary responsibility** with regard to the agency's conduct. This emphasizes the importance of careful selection of and effective interaction with the members of the board of directors.

Although this chapter is written specifically to teach organizational practitioners to work with members of their boards, it is also important for community practitioners. Community practitioners will work with executive directors, agency employees, and people who are members of boards of directors. It is important that they understand the roles of each as they interact with them. The narrative in this chapter, as well as the exercises in its worksheets, will help them gain that understanding.

OVERVIEW OF BOARD MEMBERSHIP

For the purposes of this text, a board of directors can be defined as a group of volunteers who oversee and guide an organization. Holland (1998, p. 7) defines board members as "people in whom power is entrusted by the community to act as fiduciaries and to guide their organization with caring, skills, and integrity." Carver (1997, p. 3) notes that this group has an exceptional level of authority, so that its power "is exceeded only by owners and the state."

Board members are sometimes considered the "trustees" of the organizations they manage. This text, therefore, will use the terms "trustee" and "board member" interchangeably. The regulations and **bylaws** that guide organizations were written to ensure that boards of directors serve as checks and balances to the actions and authority of the agency's paid administrators. The relationship between the organization itself and the board of directors is so intertwined that formation of a board is one of the first steps in creating a new organization. Organizations cannot even apply for 501c3 status until a board of directors has been named. The precedent for board involvement is set when an organization submits its articles of incorporation, which identifies those private individuals who are committed to ensure that agencies operate using ethical methods.

Trustees are often referred to as organizational watchdogs or guardians of the public good and for good reason. When considering the number of 501c3 agencies that currently exist in the United States, the need for protection from fraud is enormous. Reiss (1990) estimated that in 1990, there were approximately 900,000 nonprofit organizations in the United States alone. Nonprofit organizations are charged with the task of meeting the needs of society that governmental agencies do not and could not fulfill. In return, agencies are rewarded with exemptions from paying taxes and other special treatment from the federal and state governments. In order to encourage contributions to these entities, private citizens can deduct donations to charitable organizations from taxes. Reliance on private citizens for financial support increases the need for board members to serve as responsible fiduciaries. The owners of nonprofit organizations are the communities in which they were created to serve. With that in mind, it is safe to say that board members work to protect the community that dedicates its resources to the organization

(Carver, 1997). When accepting resources, board members are giving their promise that money will be used for exactly what it was donated for. One instance of impropriety can mean the death of an organization and the demise of many reputations.

ROLES AND RESPONSIBILITIES

The board of directors for any organization, regardless of its tax status, is ethically and legally responsible for carrying out several key functions. When recruiting new members, many candidates are told that they will not be required to do anything other than carry the title of board member. This type of board involvement jeopardizes the existence of the organization and has potential legal implications for the board members. In order to lead the organization effectively, board members should attend regular meetings to remain informed of what is happening within the organization. However, attending meetings regularly is just the beginning. Research identifies four primary responsibilities that board members have: (a) reviewing activities of the organization, (b) securing funding for the organization, (c) reviewing the mission of the organization, and (d) collaborating with the executive director.

Reviewing the Activities of the Organization

One of the major areas of responsibility of the board of directors is to ensure that the activities of the agency will equip the organization in order to achieve its mission on both on a short- and long-term basis. With that function in mind, a board must have at least some involvement in the organization's daily activities. Without such involvement, it is unlikely that members will ever gain a good understanding of what the organization is doing. Those who do no more than attend meetings are likely to grasp big-picture issues such as budget and strategic planning but are unlikely to understand issues involved in client satisfaction and employee retention. For example, a board member who does no more than attend meetings may appreciate the contingencies of a budgetary crisis but be unable to perceive that micromanagement by an inexperienced executive director is alienating employees and preventing the agency from retaining valuable personnel. The executive director is, in fact, the key to successful management by the board. The board selects the executive director and entrusts him with daily operations. An effective and dedicated executive director will be able to manage those operations well, requiring minimal daily oversight and periodic intensive activity by members of the board.

Securing Funding

A second major function of members of the board of directors is securing the funding needed to sustain its operations while acting as monitors to ensure that funds are being spent appropriately. All members of the board are responsible for raising funds in some way. They may choose to write and sign letters for direct mail campaigns, approach foundations or local businesses for support, organize and participate in fund raising events, or make personal contributions. As noted earlier, they are also charged with making sure funds are used appropriately. Although the executive director creates an annual budget and is largely responsible for spending that funding, the board possesses the fiduciary responsibility to make sure that state and federal regulations are followed and that the funds are spent in a manner that is consistent with their purpose. The board must review the budget on a quarterly and annual basis (many choose to do so monthly) and can be held legally responsible for any improprieties.

Reviewing the Mission

A third primary area of responsibility for the board of directors is to review the organization's mission to make sure it is clear and appropriate within the current task environment. In doing so, they ensure that they can recognize where agencies are successful and where they have shortcomings. Ultimate responsibility for maximizing areas of effectiveness and addressing deficiencies lies with the board. By reviewing the mission and adapting either the mission statement or the agency's activities to changes in the agency's environment, board members can ensure that the agency is faithful to its purpose and delivers needed services to the population it is intended to serve.

Collaborating with the Executive Director

It is through collaborative oversight of the executive director that virtually every other task for which a board of directors is responsible is accomplished. The roles of an executive director and of the board are so enmeshed that an organization cannot be successful without the two working together. In nonprofit and for-profit settings, the board is responsible for the recruiting, hiring, and firing of the executive director. She conducts the business of the agency, then reports the activities, successes, and failures to the board on a regular basis. The board should, therefore, be continually engaged in the process of identifying major organizational issues and prioritizing the organizations' goals and activities in collaboration with the executive director (Holland, 1998). This process can occur through informal discussions or forums that focus on testing ideas and problem solving. Often the primary forum for such discussions is a monthly board meeting.

BOARD STRUCTURES

Boards are frequently composed of 15 to 20 members who serve for a period that is defined in the organization's bylaws. In creating an organization and recruiting a board, it is important to recruit members and to maintain a list of prospective members. It is also important to remember that a board of directors is composed of a group of volunteers. Because of its volunteer nature, it may be difficult to arrange for the entire board to be present at many meetings. Also, the probability of having some members resign from the group is high. Board resignation should not be perceived as a bad omen or a predictor of organizational failure, it is simply a reality of work in the social service world. Addressing this reality with an active, aggressive recruiting program can ensure that the agency is able to conduct business, and that loyal board members are not overwhelmed with responsibilities.

Many boards build term limits that define the number of consecutive years members can serve into their bylaws. This schedule has positive and negative consequences. On the positive side, the board has an opportunity to replace weak members at the point of their rotation. Although boards typically have the authority to dismiss inactive or problematic members, requesting the resignation of one member may be politically harmful to the organization. In essence, rotating schedules presents a socially acceptable method of firing undesirable members. However, these schedules also create the risk of losing an effective board member who may be recruited by another community organization. Dedicated and influential board members are highly sought after. One method of ensuring that active members remain involved is to recruit a member rotating off the board to a standing committee (Wolf, 1999).

A board may choose to create committees that focus their attention on specific objectives in order to maximize its effectiveness. Often, committees are composed of members that have specific areas of expertise. For example, an accountant might chair a committee that deals with agency finances. A group of people with media experience might head a public relations committee. Similarly, the board might create advisory groups to educate themselves and the agency administrators on areas of specialization. By drawing on the strengths of the community to compose its board of directors, agencies can access needed knowledge and skills while building a rapport with community stakeholders and possible future board members (Carver, 1997; Edwards, Yankey, & Altpeter, 1998).

SELECTING BOARD MEMBERS

Organizational leaders have discovered that building a board is a difficult task. It requires persistence, creativity, and dedication to create a good board. It requires the same qualities to keep a strong board functioning once it has been composed. Administrators must think strategically to identify all the needs of an organization and then compare them to the resources that are currently available. As board members' terms end, the strengths and skills of those remaining must be assessed. That assessment should then become the basis for the recruitment of new members, that is, new members are recruited to replace those who have "rolled off" the board (McNamara, 1999). Ideally, the collective board should possess skills related to:

1. Fundraising, including grant writing and event planning
2. Public relations
3. Contract and tax preparation
4. Organizational management
5. Working with target populations

The board should also have a strong knowledge of the community and connections to local leaders and stakeholders. A strong board can serve as a springboard to recruiting future members. When joining the board, members commit to linking the organization with others they know. Their acquaintances may provide the members needed to replace them.

In selecting members, it is important to remember that the board is a group of volunteers; meetings that involve continuous, unresolved conflict may not encourage members to attend meetings regularly when there are other obligations vying for their attention. Interpersonal dynamics can either facilitate board accomplishment or distract attention away from addressing important responsibilities (Carver, 1997). Hadzima warns against recruiting family members and friends for board membership (2002). Although members of these groups are likely to be dedicated to furthering the vision of the organization, family or friends may be unable to provide sufficient objectivity or may become bogged down with interpersonal baggage not related to the organization.

TRAINING BOARD MEMBERS

In order to maximize the benefit of having access to a board, the organization must dedicate itself to equipping members to do their job. Part of equipping members involves providing relevant training and information on an ongoing basis. One trait of a highly effective board is a desire to learn and understand the organization's purpose and objectives. This knowledge must encompass every detail of the organization, including the target population, economic environment, and public policy affecting the organization. Board members cannot be experts on every subject and should leave the clinical work to the professionals; however, an understanding of the challenges faced by workers each day will influence decision making and strategic planning.

One method of educating the board involves dedicating a portion of the regular meeting to training on a topic affecting the organization. Organizations use a variety of methods to deliver training. For some, the most effective presentation involves gathering a group of individuals who have specialized knowledge with regard to the operation of the organization. This group, perhaps several clients or direct practitioners, would then discuss its perspective on the agency with the board.

Board members may also require training that teaches them how to participate as board members. Some organizations assign mentors to new board members. These mentors may be responsible for educating new members about the history of the agency along with its mission and activities. Many organizations host a board retreat providing members the opportunity to bond with one another while conducting the business of the agency. Holland concludes that the purpose of any training is to establish a common vision and shared enthusiasm as to where the organization should be going (1998).

FUNDRAISING

Fundraising constitutes a major portion of any nonprofit organization's activities. Whether it involves the creation of grant applications or organizing a special event to raise money, nonprofit organizations are dedicating increasing amounts of time and energy to securing additional funding. Rather than spending time on fundraising, frontline staff should be focused on direct service delivery. The board of directors should take a major role in raising funds. This allows others within the organization to perform the specialized tasks for which they are trained.

Funders look to the level of board support as an indication of the organizations' ability to achieve the objectives it has proposed. One indicator of support is the level of financial contribution members make to the organization. For this reason, board members are frequently mandated to provide some level of personal financial support. This mandate varies between organizations. Some organizational bylaws state that trustees must make a financial contribution not below a certain level, while others may state that trustees must raise a minimal amount or donate a definite amount of hours to serving the organization. This practice has become more widely accepted as nonprofits struggle to build a diverse board that also includes representation of a population served by the agency. For example, a nonprofit agency that serves single mothers in a low-income neighborhood may wish to include a single mother from the neighborhood on the board of directors. An obligation to make a financial contribution to the nonprofit may be impossible for this woman, who will likely bring an invaluable amount of expertise to the table.

She might be able to contribute her time and expertise rather than make a monetary donation.

Not every board member will be willing to approach friends and acquaintances to ask for financial support for the organization. Others may have confidence in their networking skills and be at ease with using their connections to access funds. The role of each board member should vary based on her talents and strengths. Fundraising activities may include researching a topic for a grant proposal, assisting with planning the logistics of an event, or writing fundraising letters to community resources.

Effective fundraising requires some training. Imagine, for example, sending a board member to a prospective donor with an inadequate understanding of the agency's program. Money might be contributed based on misconceptions about the services an agency provides, which could result in the possibility of having to refund the donations. Members should have a strong understanding of the purpose and mission of the organization before attempting to represent it to the community.

USING THE MACRO PRACTITIONER'S WORKBOOK

Worksheets 9.1 and 9.2 constitute the Macro Practitioner's Workbook for this chapter. By working through the questions in the worksheet, it should be possible to identify the necessary components for a board, select people to approach who have those qualifications, and identify training issues that can be used to strengthen the board once it has been created. Please use the case study provided at the beginning of unit 2 to complete the worksheets.

SUMMARY

In this chapter, the basics of composing and interacting with a board of directors have been discussed. There are certain characteristics a board must possess in order to operate effectively. Those characteristics can be identified in potential members to ensure that they exist within the group. Further training can enhance the ability of the board to perform its responsibilities, ensuring that the agency can operate responsibly and effectively.

Activities for Learning

1. Working in a small group, list characteristics of a good board of directors, then list the people known by the group members who could contribute those characteristics to a board. Look at the list with your fellow group members. What standards will you use to decide whom you should ask first when there are several possibilities? What sources will you use to identify other options when no one is known to the group members?
2. With other members of your class, discuss possible ways of training board members. What resources would you use? Would it be a group format, individual, or some combination of group and individual? Would you use a mentor system, why or why not?
3. Working in a small group, imagine the following scenario. You are the executive director of an agency with a 15-member board. According to the bylaws of the organization your board cannot do business without ten of the members being present. Because the board has the ultimate authority to approve or disapprove decisions and has not been able to vote in two months, your agency is immobilized. What do you do?

Questions for Discussion

1. What are the advantages of having a board of directors? What are the disadvantages? How could you ensure that the disadvantages do not outweigh the advantages on your board?

2. A powerful and prestigious member of your community is a member of your board. Unfortunately, a provision in the bylaws states that members who miss more than three consecutive meetings will be removed from the board. This person has missed five consecutive meetings. Additionally, only six months remain before she will roll off the board. What do you do and why?

3. The chair of your board resigns more than a year before he is scheduled to roll off. No other members of the board are willing to assume his responsibilities. What do you do?

Key Terms

Board members—a group of volunteers who have been entrusted with the financial and operational responsibility for running an organization in a responsible and effective manner.

Bylaws—the written rules by which an organization operates.

Fiduciary responsibility—the responsibility of board members to ensure that the agency operates in an appropriate and responsible manner financially.

References

Carver, J. (1997). *Boards that make a difference*. San Francisco: Jossey-Bass Publishers.

Edwards, R., Yankey, J., & Altpeter, M. (1998). *Skills for effective management of nonprofit organizations*. Washington, DC: NASW Press.

Hadzima, J. (Dec. 23, 2002). *Outside directors—Do you need them and where to find them*. Available: http://enterpriesforum .mit.edu/mindshare/hadzima/ outside-directors.html

Holland, T. (1998). Strengthening board performance. In R. Edwards, J. Yankey, & M. Altpeter (Eds.), *Skills for effective management of nonprofit Organizations*. Washington, D.C.: NASW Press.

McNamara, C. (1999). *Guidelines for recruiting new board membership*. Available: www.mapnp.org/library/boards/ recruit.htm.

Reiss, A. (1990). Bottom line: A working board of directors. *Management review, 79,* 37–39.

Wolf, T. (1999). *Managing a nonprofit organization in the twenty-first century*. New York: Simon & Schuster.

WORSHEET 9.1 | COMPOSING A BOARD OF DIRECTORS

1. Whom do you know who can provide the following characteristics to a board?
    Fundraising

— United Way Represtatue
- wealth Local leadee
— Some motivated to be successful in the project

Public relations

— media relatwons person
- local person w/ influcerce +trust in commun ty
- Church leaders
— parent/teacher organnation

Contract and tax preparation

CPA
accountant
busness manaqer @ one of the orgaizatuns
Lawyers

Organizational management

DirectoR feom a successful agency

Working with target populations

other agency invdvedw/ target populatins
gorert agencyies

2. What supporters do you have that might help you identify people with the necessary characteristics?

other orgainzations
employees who are great workers
people who have been on board

3. Who are the people your supporters have identified who can provide the following characteristics to a board?
    Fundraising

    Public relations

    Contract and tax preparation

    Organizational management

Working with target populations

4.   List the potential board members and the way in which you intend to approach them.

WORKSHEET 9.2 | SUSTAINING A BOARD OF DIRECTORS

1. List the members who are rolling off your board and the critical characteristics each brings.

2. List the critical characteristics that have been lacking, even before the members rolled off.

    fundraising
    goodmedia

3. List the missing characteristics and identify people you know who can provide those characteristics.

4. Whom do others recommend that provide the names of people who could contribute the missing characteristics?

5. How will you approach the people on your list?

    By personal phone calls, followed up by a letter to restate the conversATIoN.

EFFECTIVE RECRUITING

AND HIRING

INTRODUCTION

Unit 3 contains three chapters that combine to offer a basic description and the necessary worksheets to help you simulate the hiring process for an employee. The chapters and exercises are equally applicable to those who are already in practice. Although it may seem that these are advanced procedures more applicable to actual courses in administration, they are included in this book because they are among the basic activities that so many recent graduates are called upon to utilize, regardless of whether they have studied to work in micro practice or macro practice. There is some evidence that crossover between the two areas may be as high as 40% within three years of graduation. It is therefore vital that every practitioner have the basic knowledge and skills to manage the recruiting and hiring processes.

On the surface, the recruiting and hiring processes might seem important only for organizational practitioners. Many circumstances arise, however, that make knowing and being able to navigate those processes equally important for community professionals. One example occurs when an initiative receives funding for a part- or full-time employee. This would require the community practitioner to either conduct or participate in a recruiting and hiring process. Another case would be when a partner agency hires an employee who will be partially assigned to the initiative and asks the community practitioner to participate in the hiring process. In this case, the practitioner could make a more effective contribution by knowing and understanding the process.

The chapters are written as though they were for organizational work. The reason for this is simple. The day a community worker hires an employee, she functions as an organization, making the process virtually identical for either setting. No distinction is, therefore, necessary in the chapters of this unit.

The first chapter in unit 3, "Creating Job Descriptions and Classified Ads," explains the theory behind and the processes of developing written advertisements designed to attract potential employees. Advertising can be expensive (in some cities even a brief ad may cost over one thousand dollars if run for multiple days). The delays created by publishing a poor advertisement can be even more expensive. It is for this reason that an entire chapter of this book is dedicated to the process.

Chapter 11, "The Hiring Process," provides an overview of the steps needed to successfully recruit and hire employees. In order to make good hires, employers must understand how processes such as job analysis, job description development, advertising, interviewing, and the actual offer itself fit together. "The Hiring Process" and its related worksheets provide that understanding.

"Conducting Interviews," chapter 12, offers detailed guidance for the face-to-face portion of recruiting and hiring. Preparing an interview guide, readying the interview site, managing the in-person contact time, and procedures to follow are all included. The worksheets will allow you to practice preparation using the case study provided on the following pages.

As with each unit in this book, the case study for unit 3 is a continuation of the study from the previous units. Hopefully, there is enough information provided in the study for unit 3 to complete the exercises here. If you need additional information, however, feel free to review the information from units 1 and 2.

EFFECTIVE RECRUITING AND HIRING CASE STUDY

It is now your third month as regional director for the Department of Human Endeavors. During the first two months you have accomplished all the tasks outlined in units 1 and 2 of this text. Those things completed, you are ready to move to the next challenge.

Organizational Practice Information

One of the most important tasks of your third month is to identify someone to serve in one of the two administrative positions that answers to you directly (associate administrators, AAs). You were able to fill one of those positions in your second week on the job by promoting a Program Operations Specialist (POS), Ms. Woodard, into the position. You talked with Mr. Brown about the possibility that he might take the other position, but reached the mutual conclusion that the time was not right. You spent several additional weeks considering other members of the organization, ultimately deciding that no one was a good match for the position at this time. As a result, you decide to recruit candidates from outside the organization. The job for which you will be recruiting requires the direct supervision of five POS's, each of whom manages a field office that conducts every aspect of child welfare service. Each office also has a support staff of seven supervised by an Administrative Manager (AM). AAs are also responsible for participating in three organizational committees and serving as a liaison between their field office and other individuals and organizations in the community. The AA also does a substantial amount of writing and public speaking.

State regulations require that the AA hold at least a Master of Science in Social Work (MSSW) and three years of management experience. Child welfare experience is preferred but not required. The AA will work primarily in the field office, but will sometimes be required to visit other agencies and the homes or schools of children in care. The salary range is $55,000 to $69,999.

You receive over 100 applications for the position, discovering that only 10 meet the basic requirements. Of those ten, three appear to be very strong candidates. Your secretary calls those three and schedules appointments with them. Although you are conducting interviews with all of them, space restrictions allow the discussion of only one of them here. Use the information provided to complete the worksheets for chapters 10, 11 and 12. Where no information is provided (such as for the questions asking you to formulate interview questions) use your imagination to compensate.

Joseph Wynn is a 38-year-old male who has served in various administrative capacities with the Department of Juvenile Justice in another state for the last 10 years. Prior to that, he worked for four years as a case manager for a nonprofit child welfare agency. Before entering the field he received his MSSW from a prominent university. He has also received specialized training in several aspects of child welfare and juvenile justice from the Child Welfare League of America. Mr. Wynn has managed large numbers of employees who were responsible for the care of children. He offered three personal references, all of whom speak highly of his character and personal habits.

Community Practice Information

The community initiative has rapidly obtained funding and secured enthusiastic participation from the community. The level of activity has risen beyond the ability of your administrative assistant to handle the workload. The funding your work group obtained was sufficient to allow you to hire a full-time administrative assistant who will be dedicated to the initiative. You and your work group initiate the process of recruiting and hiring.

The administrative assistant will be responsible for handling incoming telephone calls, e-mail, and regular mail correspondence sent to the initiative. Housed at the Attiesburg Community Mental Health Center, she will have two incoming lines and three e-mail accounts to manage. She will need to be able to deal with electronic correspondence in both Microsoft Word and Corel WordPerfect and will be responsible for entering data and preparing reports using Quattro Pro. In addition, she may, at times, be asked to help prepare a presentation in PowerPoint. She may also occasionally be required to deal directly with partners or community members who come to the office with questions. She will report directly to you, but will also perform initiative-related secretarial services for other members of the partnership.

The administrative assistant will be expected to have a bachelor's degree from an accredited university. She will need to be able to operate a computer, a copier, and a postage machine. The salary will be $25,000 per year. Because the administrative assistant will be considered a state employee, the salary will include all state benefits.

IO

CREATING JOB DESCRIPTIONS AND CLASSIFIED ADS

CHAPTER OUTLINE

Overview of Job Descriptions

Contents of Job Descriptions

Cost-Benefit Analysis of Job Descriptions

Writing Classified Advertisements

Tips for Writing

Using the Macro Practitioner's Workbook

Summary

Organizations face constant change and challenge. One of the challenges they face with great frequency is hiring. Employees leave their employers for a variety of reasons. Some find jobs that provide a higher income or greater satisfaction. Others may move to another geographical area or seek a position in which they will have more time for their families. Still others are terminated by their employers. Whatever the reason an employee leaves, her departure creates a challenge for the employer. Decisions must be made. Are the knowledge and skills the departed worker brought to the agency still necessary for its success? If not, are others needed? If the new employee will be asked to bring new and different contributions to the agency, what will those contributions be? In light of the answers to these questions, how will this affect the job description and classified advertisement?

Even when departed employees are not being replaced, successful agencies often go through the process of role clarification and task assignment with each member of the organizational structure. This process is a component of strategic planning and occurs both with positions existing within the agency and with those being added. This chapter will focus on the process of defining roles and creating job descriptions. Further, it will discuss using those documents to achieve other organizational functions, such as creating advertisements for hiring.

OVERVIEW OF JOB DESCRIPTIONS

Job descriptions "are a list of responsibilities and functions that are required in a particular position" (Winning, 2000, p. 12). As roles and responsibilities change, job descriptions should be altered to reflect those changes. Organizations often create descriptions for every position, from board member and CEO to the frontline staff. These documents are like a legend for the agency's road map to success, defining who will do what on the road to fulfilling the agency's mission. Creating a job description involves a process of collecting and analyzing information about the position itself (Career Search Consultants, 2003), providing a picture of how positions fit together to accomplish the agency's work.

Wolf writes that when creating job descriptions, the purpose is to answer several fundamental questions (1999, p. 22):

1. What is the job? An integral step in the process involves identifying what the needs of the position are. This includes looking at the functions that are essential to the position (Rice University Human Resources, 2000). In other words, the position exists to perform a specific function that requires specialized expertise that is currently unavailable or insufficiently available within the organization.

2. Why is the position necessary and how does it contribute to the overall needs of the organization? This question requires an organizational evaluation as a system. Intradepartmental needs must be considered, such as the degree to which each fulfills its part of the mission. Other interdepartmental needs must also be considered, such as the way in which the various units within the agency interact.

3. How is the work accomplished for which the position exists, and what special equipment or expertise will be used to accomplish it?

4. With whom will the employee be working and to whom will they be accountable? Should questions or needs arise, workers need to know who they can turn to and who will be judging the quality of their work.

5. What time tables are involved for the job? Workers should be aware of deadlines along with an estimate of how long it will take to complete the task. Unclearly defined deadlines lead to chaotic work environments and potential conflict.

CONTENTS OF JOB DESCRIPTIONS

Literature concerning **job descriptions** consistently recommends the inclusion of specific components (U.S. Small Business Association, 2003; Wolf, 1999). These components should paint a clear picture of the expectations of a position and how it fits into the organizational structure.

1. *Job Title*—Specifically, identify what the position is. A short descriptor such as grant writer, case manager, or executive assistant is sufficient.

2. *Objective or Purpose Statement*—Include a statement consisting of about three to four sentences that describes the general nature and objective of the job.

3. *List of Duties*—List essential duties that consume at least 5% of the worker's time. This list should rank duties in order of importance and provide information regarding how the task will be evaluated. An example duty of a case management supervisor could read, "Prepares monthly caseload activity reports and submits to the director of case management."

| BOX 10.1 | CONTENT OF JOB DESCRIPTIONS |

1. Job title
2. Objective or purpose statement

3. List of duties
4. Description of relationships and roles

| BOX 10.2 | A SAMPLE JOB DESCRIPTION |

The Program Manager is responsible for administrative oversight of the project, including (a) management, guidance, and evaluation of the clinical director (who in turn manages, guides, and evaluates the clinical staff); (b) management, guidance, and evaluation of the program assistant; and (c) management, guidance, and evaluation of the program volunteers. In addition, the program manager is responsible for interaction with those outside the program including but not limited to: (a) interaction with funding sources and other stakeholders, (b) interaction with collaborative partners and other service providers, and (c) interaction with the community at large. The project director administers the budget and is responsible for all recruiting, hiring, and training. The program manager reports to the executive director of the XYZ Agency.

---

4. *Description of Relationships and Roles*—Identify the person to whom the worker reports as well as any employees the worker supervises. Also include a summary of the staff members with whom a worker will be expected to collaborate. For example, a CEO could be expected to "locate new funding opportunities through collaboration with the board of directors."

A sample job description is included in Box 10.2.

COST-BENEFIT ANALYSIS OF JOB DESCRIPTIONS

Successfully utilizing job descriptions as a tool within an agency requires a commitment of substantial time and energy from the agencies. The value of the activity has been clearly substantiated through **cost-benefit analysis** (Wolf, 1999). Some costs involved in the process include:

1. In today's task environment the demand to change is frequent. Job descriptions must be altered to reflect change when modifications are made.

2. Many documents require several drafts. The process of creation and revision requires manpower that is valuable to an agency. Some organizations hire compensation analysts to develop this system due to the time required. Experts suggest that developing an appropriate job description for one position can take as much as four hours (Winning, 2000).

3. Organizations may become overly compartmentalized in an effort to stick to the guidelines and roles identified in the job descriptions. Internalizing job roles that are too rigid will decrease teamwork and collaboration. Workers evaluate each task to determine whether the task has been listed as one of their responsibilities. For that reason, managers often add a phrase such as, "other tasks deemed necessary," which acts as a catchall.

4. The ability to engage in effective problem solving is often a casualty of over-compartmentalization. Staff who see themselves as limited by their job descriptions may fail to engage in the creativity needed to meet the needs of clients whose problems do not fall neatly into their job

CREATING JOB DESCRIPTIONS AND CLASSIFIED ADS   **175**

descriptions. In these cases, common sense problem solving approaches may be lost in bureaucracy.

Although the costs creating and maintaining job descriptions can be great, the benefits far outweigh the costs. These benefits include:

1. Comparing responsibilities across the various positions in the organization may allow administrators to shift some responsibilities to other staff members, enhancing efficiency and balancing workloads. Evaluating an employee's workload and comparing that to the load of other workers may lead to important discoveries about workload distribution. Tasks can be completed more effectively when workloads are balanced and responsibilities are given to those with appropriate levels of knowledge and skill.

2. Job descriptions protect the organization from unnecessary lawsuits. Job descriptions provide written expectations of a worker, defining what the tasks are and how they should be completed. Once those expectations are articulated, foundations for worker evaluations are created. If expectations are not met, the organization may have a right to dismiss a staff member without fear of legal actions. These descriptions allow supervisors to make objective judgments about the performance of a worker without being confronted by accusations of favoritism or sabotage.

3. Similarly, job descriptions protect employees from unlawful dismissal. With responsibilities defined in measurable terms, a worker can justify his job performance and challenge unethical treatment from managers.

4. Job descriptions also become a tool to identify the expertise and qualifications needed to effectively meet the needs of the organization (Winning, 2000). The decision to hire additional staff members has major implications on an organization's budget. The expertise a worker brings to an agency also brings a price tag. Managers can use a job description as a human resource tool to justify the type of professional needed to meet the agency's need.

Flexibility in Job Descriptions

Many of the costs of job descriptions can be offset by incorporating some Japanese management techniques. These techniques involve adding a component of flexibility to job descriptions, allowing workers to address organizational and client needs creatively and proactively. Agencies may develop defined duties among various segments within an organization but use general and flexible job descriptions to allow for overlapping activities between positions (Keys, 1998). The U.S. Small Business Administration (2003, p. 17) states that flexible job descriptions "will encourage employees to grow within their positions and learn how to make larger contributions to the organization."

WRITING CLASSIFIED ADVERTISEMENTS

The job description can also become a tool to recruit a new member of the organization. Organizational leaders and human resource managers frequently use **classified advertisements** to fill open positions in the agency. Information contained within advertisements should be taken from the job description but should be made more concise and should be adapted to grab the attention of the hungry, prospective applicant.

BOX 10.3 | CONTENTS OF CLASSIFIED ADVERTISEMENTS

1. Job activities, specifications, and requirements
2. Job location
3. Equipment needed to perform the job

4. Specialized requirements and conditions
5. Salary range

BOX 10.4 | A SAMPLE CLASSIFIED ADVERTISEMENT

Program Manager—The XYZ Agency is seeking a program manager to administer its Home and Community Counseling Initiative. Responsibilities will include management and oversight of a clinical director and staff, management and oversight of a program assistant, management and oversight of all program operations, and communication and interaction with other organizations and individuals in the community on behalf of the program. The successful applicant will hold a Master of Social Work degree and will have at least two years direct practice experience and one year management experience. The office is located in the Addiesburg community, but will require some visits to local homes, schools, and community centers. The successful applicant will possess a valid driver's license, will have or be able to obtain professional malpractice insurance, and will be proficient in the use of a word processing program. A criminal background check and drug screening are required. Salary ranges between $45,000 and $52,000 depending on experience, training, and background.

The U.S. Small Business Administration (2003) recommends using the following information in a classified advertisement:

1. *Job activities, specifications, and requirements*—Applicants should be told what activities the job will require. In addition, they should be informed of the minimum qualifications needed. Applicants should be aware of the education, experience, knowledge, and skills needed to complete tasks. Also, address any substitutions that can be made. For example, two years of experience in the field may be substituted for a master's degree.

2. *Job location*—Identify where the work will be expected to take place, whether that be in the office or an alternate location, such as during home visits with clients.

3. *Equipment needed to perform the job*—Identify any special systems an applicant will be using in the job, such as specific computer programs.

4. *Specialized requirements and conditions*—Define any terms that relate to job functions, such as membership within a professional organization or union. Some organizations require that social workers purchase their own **malpractice insurance** as a term for employment.

5. *Salary range*—Identify the salary offered for the position. Most organizations state this figure in terms of a range depending on experience of the applicant.

Classified advertisements provide an opportunity to attract qualified candidates to the organization. Whether filling a vacant position or creating a new position, organizational leaders frequently seek out self-motivated and creative staff members, often leading to a high degree of competition for desirable jobs. However, they can also serve as a method to discourage unqualified applicants from applying (Jentlie, 2003). Each time an organization receives applications from interested parties, the organization can use the contents of the advertisement to evaluate the applicant's ability to perform a job. Box 10.4 contains a sample classified advertisement.

TIPS FOR WRITING

Simple is better. Classified advertisements do not require writing full sentences. Rather, the noun can be implied to refer to the employee who will fill the position. Passive verbs should be avoided and the present tense used. It is a good rule to place the desirable and exciting tasks at the head of the list. Beginning a job description with the menial and monotonous activities will lead some job hunters to skip over the ad in effort to locate a more exciting opportunity.

USING THE MACRO PRACTITIONER'S WORKBOOK

The Macro Practitioner's Workbook for this chapter includes two worksheets, one for writing a job description and the other for preparing a classified advertisement. Use the case study associated with this unit to prepare each.

SUMMARY

In this chapter, two vital components of the hiring process have been discussed: writing job descriptions and preparing classified advertisements. The former provides not only the clarity needed to initiate the hiring process, but also an opportunity to examine the overall functioning of and relationships within the agency. The latter is an effective method of locating and evaluating prospective employees.

Activities for Learning

1. Working in a small group, select a position that one of you holds or might hold in a social service agency. Make a list of the duties required by that position. How would you describe those in a job description, in a classified advertisement, and in a job interview?
2. Ask the executive director or personnel manager at your agency or practicum site to show you the job descriptions for the agency. Ask her to explain how the descriptions were planned and written. Ask whether they fit into an overall organizational chart. Ask her how they would decide what information from the job description to use in a classified advertisement to recruit someone for that position.
3. Search the Internet for a simplified explanation of the Americans with Disabilities Act (ADA) as it applies to hiring and job descriptions. Think about a position in your agency or at your practicum site. How would you need to write a job description for that position in order to comply with the ADA?

Questions for Discussion

1. What are the advantages of preparing a job description? What are the disadvantages? What can agency administrators do to maximize the advantages and minimize the disadvantages.
2. What do you find appealing in a classified advertisement? What do you find unappealing? What kinds of things would discourage you from

applying for a position for which you are not qualified? What would encourage you to apply for a position for which you are qualified?

3. What issues can arise because of the over-compartmentalization created by too-rigid job descriptions? How could you make these descriptions more flexible?

Key Terms

Classified advertisement—a means of recruiting employees by writing a description of the position for the classified section of periodicals or online position announcement pages.

Cost-benefit analysis—an analysis that compares the expense of performing a function to the benefits derived from performing it.

Job descriptions—a summary of the responsibilities, requirements, expectations, and functions that must be performed by an individual in a specific position.

Malpractice insurance—insurance purchased by professionals to protect them against lawsuits filed because of errors or accusations of errors committed in their practice.

References

Career Search Consultants (2003). *How and why to write a good job description.* Available: www. cscrecruiters.com/ jobdescriptions.htm.

Jentlie, P. (2003). *How and why to write a job description.* Available: www.cscrecruiters .com/jobdescriptions.htm.

Rice University Human Resources. (2000). *Guidelines for writing job descriptions.* Available: www.ruf.rices.edu/ ~people/Training/How to Hire.

U.S. Small Business Administration. (2003). *What are you looking for? Writing effective job descriptions.*

Available: www. sba.gov/manage/ descriptions.html.

Winning, E. (2000). *The many uses of job descriptions.* Available: www.all-biz.com.

Wolf, T. (1999). *Managing a nonprofit organization in the twenty-first century.* New York: Simon & Schuster.

WORKSHEET 10.1 | DEVELOPING A JOB DESCRIPTION

1. Provide the job title for the position.

Associate Adminastor

2. Clearly and concisely state the general nature and purpose of the job.

To work primarly in the feild office, supenising all staff that are employed in that office, penuding direct supenusiun, budgeting and overall all responsibily to the daily actuities of the department

3. List the duties that will be performed by the person who holds the job.

Reports directly to Regional Director
Direct supenusiun
Committee partisapatiun
Leiason

4. Provide a description of the positions to which the worker will report and those the worker will supervise.

This person will report directy to the Regional Director
This person will besponsibile for the direct supenusion of P.O's
This person will also be responsible for the supenusion of the adminstative manager.

5. Describe any specialized roles the worker will be expected to fulfill.

It is a requrment that this person be able to speak tou outside organzATions and have good writing skills

WORKSHEET 10.2 | WRITING A CLASSIFIED ADVERTISEMENT

1. List the required activities and responsibilities of the employee.

Community Leason
Supervisor
public speaker
grant writer

2. List the necessary specifications and requirements for the employee.

Masters in Social work
3 yrs in management position

3. Include information about where the work will be done, including information about alternate locations, such as schools or the homes of clients.

mostly from the main office
but will be required to go to homes and
other community organization.

4. Describe any specialized knowledge or equipment that may be needed.

grant writing.
Public speaking
supervision
office machinery

5. Provide information about requirements, such as membership within a professional organization, membership in a union, or a requirement for malpractice insurance.

6. Describe the salary range for the position.

55,000 to 69,000 dependent on experence.

THE HIRING PROCESS

CHAPTER OUTLINE

Overview of the Hiring Process

Stages of Hiring

Equal Employment Opportunity and Affirmative Action

Americans with Disabilities Act

Using the Macro Practitioner's Workbook

Summary

One of the most important functions of organizational management involves finding good people to further its work. Employee turnover can be devastating to an organization, particularly in social service organizations where the turnover rate can be high. Historically managers have attempted to fill voids quickly to enable the work of the agency to continue with as little disruption as possible. Being short one employee in an organization requires that others work harder to pick up the slack. In many agencies these employees are already overextended, which increases the probability of frustration, burnout, and further turnover. However, efforts to replace departed workers or to fill new positions should not be undertaken without following proper procedures and giving each candidate due consideration. An organization will spend resources (time and money) in the process of filling positions. A failure to do so effectively can be expensive. McCarter and Schreyer state that agencies spend 50% or more of an employee's first year salary attempting to recruit that candidate (2000). In terms of money, this means it costs an agency $15,000 to hire a worker for a position that pays $30,000. Although this seems like a surprisingly large amount, it is magnified by the fact that the average employee changes jobs every two years (McCarter & Schreyer, 2000). Due to budgets and limited resources, managers and organizational leaders are realizing the benefits of effective hiring. This chapter will identify and explain the processes involved in the effective hiring of new workers. In addition, three sets of federal guidelines that regulate this process will be discussed.

OVERVIEW OF THE HIRING PROCESS

Hiring processes should follow carefully prepared procedures and guidelines. Too often, decisions to hire new employees are made haphazardly, are rushed, or are given minimal attention. Often, the decision to add an employee is made because the expense can be made to fit the budget. Although budget is a major factor, decisions based on monetary factors alone often waste resources that are needed in other areas. Before adding a new employee or filling a vacant position, leaders should determine how this move fits into the organization's strategic plan. Long-range staffing needs should correlate with the long-range vision of the agency. Once the decision is made to bring in new workers, much thought should be given as to how this person will fit into the overall operation of the agency. Some nonprofit leaders refer to this process as job analysis.

Job Analysis

A job analysis involves examining the tasks and processes that are associated with successfully performing a job (McNamara, 1999). One agency tool, the job description, facilitates this process. The job description, as has been discussed in a chapter 10, is a comprehensive list of the tasks and functions assigned to a position. If the position will be new for the agency, creating a job description should be one of the first tasks completed because it provides they key link to the agency's strategic plan. In addition to looking at the job description, the manager must consider the abilities and attributes a worker needs to do the job. This examination cannot focus solely on a single position but must consider how that position fits or will fit into the overall system of the organization. A **job analysis** must identify how jobs overlap and how one position is enabled to complete assigned tasks by interacting with another. In some situations, the evaluation may uncover the need to shift responsibilities or restructure in order to utilize resources more effectively. In other situations, the analysis may eliminate the need for either adding a new position or filling a vacant one. Grensing-Pophal (1999) suggests that organizations should consider five questions before making the decision to hire an employee:

1. Does this task need to be done to meet the organization's goals and objectives?
2. Does this task need to be done by this position?
3. Could the task be more efficiently accomplished in some other part of the organization?
4. Could the task be streamlined through technology or job restructuring?
5. Is this a long- or a short-term need?

STAGES OF HIRING

Once the analysis is complete and the decision is made to move forward with hiring, managers begin a complex and sometimes lengthy process in search of the right employee. This process should involve more than simply advertising for and interviewing a few prospects. With a competitive job market and many federal guidelines to be followed, the process should be conducted

BOX 11.1	THE STAGES OF HIRING

1. Advertising and recruiting   3. Selecting
2. Screening   4. Hiring

strategically and efficiently. As previously stated, the task of locating and hiring a qualified and dedicated employee that will remain with the organization for several years can be expensive, making it imperative to succeed the first time. A key to success involves evaluating a candidate holistically. Spragins (1992, p. 21) states that evaluating an applicant solely on the basis of education and previous work experience is "myopic—like looking at a candidate through a peephole when you could open the door for a full view." Organizations should create tailored processes with this goal in mind. Although the process should be adapted for each situation and candidate, certain stages should be present in every case. These stages include: (a) advertising and recruiting, (b) screening, (c) selecting, and (d) hiring.

Advertising and Recruiting

In the past, organizations were able to attract qualified candidates by merely listing an advertisement in a newspaper. Presently, companies that only rely on this method are finding it insufficient. The main goals of an agency's recruiting efforts are threefold: to attract a wide range of qualified candidates, to maximize compliance with EEOC regulations, and to provide information regarding the minimum qualifications of the position (Pecora, 1998). Organizations must plan a comprehensive recruiting strategy in order to accomplish all of these goals.

Recruiting from Within the Organization Some organizations make it a policy to post job vacancies internally before opening the position to the public. These agencies have defined policies in place that discuss how internal hiring will be handled. Organizations usually have an area where available positions are posted. These descriptions generally include the title, essential functions, qualifications, and salary of the position (Montana & Charnov, 2000).

This practice has both benefits and disadvantages. In many circumstances, a change in position within the organization may prevent a worker's exploration for a new position outside the organization if the worker is unhappy or seeking additional responsibilities. However, the practice may boost morale for workers as they perceive an opportunity for promotion and upward mobility within the organization. This option also decreases the time required to hire and train someone because an employee already is familiar with the agency and can begin sooner. It also decreases some of the guesswork in regards to an employee's work ethic and dependability because leaders know firsthand how the employee performs based on past performance within the organization (Grensing-Pophal, 1999).

The disadvantages must also be weighed before including this practice in the hiring policy. Although bringing new employees into the organization often presents the opportunity for an objective, fresh view of agency practices or barriers shifting employees from one position to another may mean missing out on this opportunity. Also, hiring from within the organization may limit the pool of qualified applicants that a manager has to select from. Finally, shifting a current employee to a new position still leaves one position open. Grensing-Pophal (1999) describes this as a "ripple effect" that still creates a job vacancy that must be filled through outside means.

Recruiting from Outside of the Organization   The task of attracting qualified applicants is usually accomplished through the use of advertisements. These tools should be straight and to the point because they are priced according to their length. It is important for advertisements to be brief but accurate. Misrepresentations of the position may only lead to problems in the future.

Accuracy is also important because the goal is to attract qualified people. Being contacted by a multitude of unqualified candidates costs the organization valuable resources. The advertisement should address four areas (Grensing-Pophal, 1999):

1. Qualifications of the person you are looking for include job skills, experience, and education. Any requirements such as travel or relocation should be clearly defined.

2. Pay scale, if desired. Listing the salary will discourage applicants from applying if they are looking for more but may rob the agency of the opportunity to convince a candidate of the benefits of working with the organization even if the salary is lower than desired.

3. Benefits to be included are medical coverage and retirement package. Benefits are so important to most job seekers that they may inquire about a position even though the salary is lower.

4. Location of where the application is to be sent, along with any applicable deadlines (Grensing-Pophal, 1999).

5. Advertisements should also include a disclaimer identifying that the organization is an Equal Opportunity Employer.

Recruitment no longer takes place within the pages of newspapers alone. Although newspapers remain an effective medium, organizations are capitalizing on new arenas where qualified candidates can easily be reached (McNamara, 1999; Montana & Charnov, 2000; Pecora, 1998).

Professional Organizations—An inexpensive, yet effective, method of recruiting could involve a sending a copy of the advertisement and job description to a professional organization where colleagues network and share information.

Internet—Agencies who maintain websites frequently post job announcements on either their websites or websites focused on job advertisements.

Local Universities and Colleges—Each year, new graduates eagerly seek employment opportunities to begin their professional careers. Many universities host job fairs each year at no expense to participating employers to assist new graduates in locating jobs.

Recruiting as Public Relations   Pecora (1998) suggests that recruiting always be viewed as a public relations function. Because the goal of recruiting is to attract a large pool of qualified candidates, the agency will interact with a large number of prospective employees. Agencies who communicate with candidates in a courteous, respectful manner will likely earn their appreciation even if those candidates are not hired. Those applicants who have a negative experience during the application process may not only decide to never apply to the agency again but will also share the experience with their colleagues. A negative experience could not only affect the future number of applicants but also the partnerships and referrals an agency may receive (Pecora, 1998).

Screening Applicants

This step in the hiring process involves determining which applicants meet the necessary qualifications and should further be considered for the position. Managers frequently use the application as a screening tool. The application provides an objective view of the applicants' past experience and qualifications. Although applications should be tailored to the position, parts of the application should ask some standard questions (Grensing-Pophal, 1999; Pecora, 1998):

1. Contact information that identifies an address and telephone number where the applicant can be contacted. It is helpful to obtain an e-mail address and both daytime and evening phone numbers, as a candidate may not want to be contacted at work.
2. Work experience such as dates of employment, supervisor's name, responsibilities, and reasons for leaving. It is important to look for gaps in information such as missing dates or inconsistencies.
3. Other work experience such as volunteer experiences.
4. Education or training that focuses on school, dates attended, and course of study. Training or special skills depending on the position will be important to address.
5. Other activities such as membership in professional organizations or community activities.
6. Personal references that can attest to the candidate's character. These references should not be relatives or past employers.
7. Agreement clause stating the information provided by the applicant on the employment application is accurate. The clause also gives permission for all organizations and people named in the application to be contacted. The statement could be as simply stated as: "I certify that all information contained within this application is accurate and truthful to the best of my knowledge. I further understand that any false information provided to mislead could result in my termination or refusal for employment. I authorize this organization to contact any person, organization, or educational institution to verify my work experience, character, and education."

It is at this stage that the organization begins to narrow down the field. A good practice includes allowing key employees to view the application and look for any missing information or patterns (McNamara, 1999). A **selection committee** of organization representatives often conducts the screening process. This practice can be a key to preventing discrimination in the screening process. In the past, agencies used tests as a major component of the hiring process. Governmental agencies continue this practice. The use of testing is facing increasing criticism as the validity of the tests is called into question. If used by the organization, tests should be used as "supplements" to the selection process because tests are commonly able to predict failures only, rather than predicting potential for success (Pecora, 1998).

Interviewing Candidates

Once the qualified candidates are pulled from the applicant pool, the process of gathering more subjective information through a face-to-face exchange with candidates is initiated. This process can make or break an organization. An organization should interview all applicants who meet the minimum qualifications to avoid questionable hiring practices. Conduct a good interview and the organization reaps the benefits of a highly skilled professional. Do a poor job of interviewing and the organization will be going through the entire process again to

| BOX 11.2 | STANDARD INFORMATION TO COLLECT WHEN SCREENING PROSPECTIVE EMPLOYEES |

1. Contact information such as address, e-mail address, and both daytime and evening phone numbers
2. Work experience including dates of employment, supervisor's name, responsibilities, and reasons for leaving
3. Presence of and reasons for gaps or inconsistencies in employment information
4. Volunteer or other relevant experience
5. Education or training including school attended, dates of attendance, course of study, and degree or certificate received
6. Special training or skills
7. Other related activities such as membership in professional organizations or community activities
8. Personal references that are not relatives or past employers
9. An agreement clause stating the information provided by the applicant is accurate and giving permission for all organizations and people named in the application to be contacted

Sources: Adapted from Grensing-Pophal, L. (1999). *HR Book: Human Resources Management for Business*. Vancouver BC, Canada: International Self-Counsel Press Ltd. pp. 7–34; Pecora, P. (1998). Recruiting and Selecting Effective Employees. In R. Edwards, J. YanKey, & M. Altpeter (Eds.), *Skills for Effective Management of Nonprofit Organizations* (pp. 115–185). Washington, D.C.: NASW.

replace the ineffective, unqualified employee that was just hired. Montana and Charnov (2000) contend that interviews enable leaders to answer three questions:

1. Does the prospective employee possess the qualifications to do the job?
2. Does the candidate possess the motivation to do the job and stay with the organization long enough to justify the costs of hiring and training?
3. Does the applicant "fit" with the organization's culture? This step is so important that this text will dedicate chapter 12 to discussing interviews.

Finally, here are a couple of thoughts to remember during the interview process. In order to enable candidates to adequately prepare for an interview, mangers should send a job description to a candidate ahead of time (McNamara, 1999). An important detail to address in the interview process is any personnel policies that affect the hiring process. For example, if the agency has a probation period, candidates should be given that information. Probation periods, usually lasting between three and six months, allow an organization to terminate an employee if that employee fails to demonstrate an ability to perform the job.

Screening Candidates

Job applicants are often separated into three categories. First, there are top applicants (sometimes referred to as the "short list") who are likely candidates to fill the position. Second-level applicants are those who are likely to be considered only if no top applicants are acceptable or some important additional information is received. Third-level applicants are those who are inappropriate for the position and will not be considered. Once these categories have been identified, the selection process begins.

Checking References   One component of the process of selecting top applicants often involves contacting references to verify the information provided on the job application. Contacting professionals who have firsthand experience about the candidate's abilities is crucial to getting a deeper perspective of the candidate. This step sometimes can be frustrating, however (Nonprofit Risk Management Center, 2003). Previous employers are often hesitant to provide

| BOX 11.3 | A SAMPLE HIRING MATRIX | | | |

Candidates	A	B	C	D
Degree in social work or related field	X		X	X
Work experience includes 2–3 years in the field		X	X	
Volunteer experience in a social work setting	X		X	
Exhibits good verbal skills and writing abilities	X	X	X	X
Exhibits dedication to a job as demonstrated by the length of employment	X	X		
Received good references from previous employer	X	X	X	X

many details about the candidate's past performance outside of confirming dates of employment. As employers have become increasingly concerned about the liability attached to providing references, information has become increasingly limited or less accurate. Some organizations have faced lawsuits for the information they have reported to prospective employers. In response to these fears, 25 states have now enacted legislation to protect employers that provide honest information about previous employees (Nonprofit Risk Management Center, 2003). In order to protect the organization, prospective employers should be educated about the agency's reference check policies and asked to sign a release. Providing former employers with some information about the position for which the applicant is being considered may be helpful. In addition, questions directed to former employers should be related exclusively to the job for which the candidate is being considered.

Selecting the Right Candidate

If qualified candidates are recruited, screened, and interviewed, the selection process is likely to be less difficult. It is better to have to make a decision between three qualified candidates than to be faced with selecting from among inferior candidates. Following the completion of the interview and reference checks, the selection committee should convene to discuss the final candidates. Each committee member should have the opportunity to promote the candidate he fells as qualified. Some organizations utilize selection matrixes (Box 11.3) to compare candidates (Pecora, 1998). The organization will identify the skills and qualities it feels are important for the position and grade each candidate according to how well that skill or quality was demonstrated.

Offer Letters

An offer letter is given to the candidate when she is verbally offered the position and verbally accepts the job. The letter is a formal invitation to become a member of the organization and provides the candidate the assurance to make arrangements to leave their current position to begin work elsewhere. Imagine the horror of a worker submitting their resignation to a current employer only to learn of some mix-up in the organization's hiring process. The damage is irreversible and leads to a difficult situation for all parties. This offer specifies the details about the position being filled and includes the salary, benefits, and starting date. It is a good practice to include a copy of the job description with the letter. Following the completion of this step, it is critical to notify those candidates not selected for the position. It would be bad public relations to allow applicants to wonder about their hiring status concerning the position any longer than necessary.

EQUAL EMPLOYMENT OPPORTUNITY AND AFFIRMATIVE ACTION

Every step of the hiring process is affected by equal employment opportunity and affirmative action legislation. Title VII of the 1964 Civil Rights Act was created to decrease discrimination in recruiting, screening, and selection processes. These regulations focus on eliminating discrimination based on race, color, religion, sex, or national origin. Affirmative action policies require organizations to take steps to recruit, select, and promote underrepresented minority groups. Employers must be able to establish a clear connection between the job and the requirements established by the organizations. The use of tests or screening tools must be proven as valid instruments at predicting success in a job (Grensing-Pophal, 1999; Pecora, 1998).

Because affirmative action legislation addresses practices that are both deliberate and unintentional, organizations cannot plead ignorance in their hiring processes. Failure to comply with these standards can result in a number of consequences. These consequences include loss of funding, loss of tax-exempt status, and loss of lucrative government contracts. Many organizations create an equal employment and affirmative action plan in order to comply with legislation. The organization may retain all applications and advertisements to demonstrate a diverse pool of applicants and extensive outreach efforts.

AMERICANS WITH DISABILITIES ACT

The American with Disabilities Act is the portion of the Civil Rights Act that protects workers with disabilities from discrimination during the recruiting, hiring, and promotion processes. This regulation does not mean that a person with disabilities must be hired for the job. It states that if a candidate meets the minimum requirements and can do the job with reasonable accommodations, discrimination against that candidate due to a disability is unlawful. Pecora (1998) recommends considering two questions when screening a candidate who is disabled:

1. What are the essential functions of the job? Understanding those functions, evaluate if the candidate meets the minimum qualifications.

2. Can the individual perform the functions with or without a reasonable accommodation? A reasonable accommodation is any action an employer may take to enable a worker to do the job. The action does not require changing the nature of the position or spending large amounts of money. It could be as simple as providing a piece of adaptive equipment.

Employers must be sensitive to discussing the disability. Applicants should not be questioned about the severity or origin of the disability. It is acceptable to review each essential function with the candidate to inquire about their ability to do each task (Pecora, 1998; Rocky Mountain Disability and Business Technical Assistance Center, 1992).

USING THE MACRO PRACTITIONER'S WORKBOOK

The worksheet for this chapter includes the basic stages in the hiring process. The only portion that is omitted is hiring, which will be treated in the next chapter. Use the case study for unit 3 to complete the worksheet.

SUMMARY

In chapter 11 several aspects of the hiring process have been considered. The importance of following proper procedures during the process, identifying the stages of the process, and federal legislation regarding hiring were discussed. Effective, efficient hiring is critical to the success of any organization. Following the guidelines in this chapter, along with those in chapters 10 and 12, will help ensure that agencies complete this process successfully.

Activities for Learning

1. Working in a small group, discuss the hiring experiences each person has had. Those who have been the employers should talk about times they have hired someone. Those who have been employees should report their experiences in being hired. What might have made those experiences more effective and efficient?
2. Interview the executive director of an agency about its hiring procedures. Report the results to the group.
3. Obtain an employment application from a social service agency. What would you do differently if you were developing an application? What would you not change?

Questions for Discussion

1. What additional information would you need about affirmative action to ensure that your agency complied with it? How might you obtain that information? Do an Internet search to see what you can find.
2. What additional information would you need about the Americans with Disabilities Act to ensure that your agency complied with it? How might you obtain that information? Do an Internet search to see what additional information you can find.

Key Terms

Affirmative action—federal policy that requires organizations to take steps to recruit, select, and promote underrepresented minority groups

The Americans with Disabilities Act—the portion of the Civil Rights Act that protects workers with disabilities from discrimination during the recruiting, hiring, and promotion processes

Job analysis—the process of examining the tasks and processes that are associated with successfully performing a job

Selection committee—a group of agency employees chosen to review job applicants and their associated materials and rate them according to their desirability

References

Grensing-Pophal, L. (1999). *HR book: Human resources management for business.* Vancouver, BC, Canada: International Self-Counsel Press Ltd., pp. 7–34.

McCarter, J., & Schreyer, R. (2000). *Recruit and retain the best: Key solutions for human resource professionals.* Manassas Park, Virginia: Impact Publications, p. 75.

McNamara, C. (1999). *Specifying job and role competencies.* Available: www.mapnp.org/library/staffing/specify/cmptncys/cmptncys.htm.

Montana, P., & Charnov, B. (2000). *Management* (3rd ed., pp. 216–220). New York: Barron's Educational Series, Inc.

Nonprofit Risk Management Center. (2003). *How should we conduct reference checks to minimize our liability?* Available: www.allianceonline.org/Test_FAQs/rmfaq18.html.

Pecora, P. (1998). Recruiting and selecting effective employees. In R. Edwards, J. Yankey, & M. Altpeter (Eds.), *Skills for effective management of nonprofit organizations*. Washington, D.C.: NASW, pp. 155–185.

Rocky Mountain Disability and Business Technical Assistance Center. (1992). *Nondiscrimination in the hiring process: Recruitment; applications; pre-employment inquiries; testing*. Available: www.ada-infonet.org/documents/titleI/tam1e.asp.

Spragins, E. (February 1992). Hiring without the guesswork. *Inc. Magazine*. Available: www.inc.com/incmagazine/archives/02920801.html.

THE HIRING PROCESS 191

WORKSHEET 11.1 | STEPS IN THE HIRING PROCESS

Advertising and Recruiting

1. Will there be a committee to review the applications? If so, who will be on the committee? When will it meet? *No, The agency director will decide who the top candidates are, and after this person has interviewed first the board, or a subcomittee will have a chance to meet the top 2 or 3 canditates in an interviewing process*

2. Who might be recruited to fill the position from within the organization? What means should be used to approach that person? What will the effects be on the rest of the organization from having made such a move? *Since it was realized that there are no persons sutable for this postion, the position will be filled by an outside person. The staff will recieve notice that this will be taking place*

3. What are the most likely sources of recruits from outside the organization? What are the best ways of reaching them? How can these methods of reaching them be used? *Contact MSW program @ universty, NASW Local papers afflication papers for people w/ MSW*

4. What information do you need to share in order to recruit successfully? What should you not include? When will the deadline for applicants occur? *Name of postion agency. Requirments deadline is 3wks after ads are run*

Screening Applicants

1. What qualities on the application are important to this position? Which are the most critical?
    - what this person has done since graduation
    - work related opportunities
    - people skills
    - supervision responsiblites

2.   Does the prospective employee's work history appear to be acceptable? Are the supervisor's name, responsibilities, and reasons for leaving acceptable? Are there any gaps or inconsistencies? If so, are they disqualifying or will you simply want to ask about them? If you want to ask about them, what questions will you ask?

Why did you leave or leaving your past or present job.

May we contact you previous employer.

3.   Does the applicant have other experiences such as community or volunteer work that might contribute to her ability to perform this job?

what have you done outside of your prensent job

4.   Are the applicant's education and training suitable for this job? Has she had special training that might be significant?

Do you have any other trainings that might inhance you in this position

5.   Are there other special qualities such as membership in professional organizations or community organizations?

are you a member of any proffesional organizations

Why did you choose those organizations

6.   Are there personal references that can attest to the applicant's past behavior and character?

I will be contacting the references that have given us, are you comfortable with that.

Interviewing Candidates

1. Who will conduct the interviews? How many interviews will there be? If there will be more than one interview, what will be the goal(s) of each?

> *Top 3 chooses made, 3 First interviews Director of Dept who will supervise this person will do the interviews. There will be a call back to top choice for second interview or an interview by the board*

2. Using the application, the job description, and other available information, prepare an interview guide that considers the following issues.

    1. Does the prospective employee possess the qualifications to do the job?

    2. Does the candidate possess the motivation to do the job and stay with the organization long enough to justify the costs of hiring and training?

    3. Does the applicant "fit" with the organization's culture? This step is so important that this text will dedicate chapter 12 to discussing interviews.

4.   Are there personnel policies that affect the hiring process?

5.   What will you tell the prospective employee about the job?

6.   Allow the prospective employee to ask questions.

Screening Candidates

1.   Use the information gathered above to identify three categories of applicants: a "short list," a group of second-level applicants, and a group of third-level applicants.

2.   Prepare a list of questions you will want to ask the applicants' personal references.

1. How was this person received by other employees
2. Any issues or conceens
3. People skills
4. What positive impact did this person have on your agency.

3. Prepare a list of questions you will want to ask the applicants' professional references.

How long + in what capasity do you know this individual what do you think this person can do for our organization

4. Call each personal and professional reference and record the answers to your questions.

Selecting the Right Candidate

1. Meet with the selection committee to discuss the applications, interviews, and references for each of the "short list" applicants. Rate the applicants in terms of the committee's preferences.

2. Schedule a meeting with the committee's first choice applicant and make the offer. If the offer is accepted, prepare and present an offer letter.

12

CHAPTER

CONDUCTING INTERVIEWS

CHAPTER OUTLINE

Overview of Interviews

Purposes of Interviews

Stages of Interviews

Types of Interviews

Federal Guidelines for Interviews

Preparing for Interviews

Using the Macro Practitioner's Workbook

Summary

Researchers have long debated the value of using interviews as a tool to predict a candidate's capacity and willingness to perform a job. Interviews present opportunities for applicants to impress interviewers in an attempt to convince organizations of their abilities and talents. Many managers have later found themselves wondering how the new employee, who appeared very competent and motivated during an interview, was ever chosen for the position. An interview presents the first picture of an organization. A well-conducted interview can win the organization a new asset. A poorly conducted interview may force the organization to choose the new employee from a pool of less-desirable candidates. Preparing and conducting interviews consumes organizational resources in the form of staff time. An interview often lasts 30 to 45 minutes. Some time is generally spent contacting references along with follow-up calls to all applicants. Walking away from the process without anything less than a new, qualified member of the organization is costly. For these reasons, leaders in the fields of human resource and organizational management have spent a great deal of time describing how effective interviews should be conducted. In addition, the federal government has provided some parameters regarding what can and cannot be addressed within the course of an interview. This chapter defines tools to structure interviews that will ensure achieving the most benefit from these interactions while complying with federal regulations.

OVERVIEW OF INTERVIEWS

Interviews are structured conversations between members of the organization and applicants. They are human resource tools used to screen and select new workers by providing a view that cannot be seen on paper. Organizations can evaluate both the prospective employees' writing abilities through resumes and cover letters and also their their interpersonal and communication abilities through the interviews (Montana & Charnov, 2000). These conversations are initiated and facilitated by the organization. Although interviews are generally viewed as opportunities for agencies to learn more about the candidate, candidates should similarly use the meeting as a chance to get a feel for the potential employer. Interviews require the use of active listening skills, where all participants are required to listen, reflect, respond, and evaluate capacities (Rutgers University, 2003). Conversation should be reciprocal, with the exchanging of questions and ideas between all participants. According to Rutgers University, an effective interview usually finds applicants doing 75% of the talking (2003). Organizations should view themselves as having just as much to prove to applicants as the applicants need to impress the organization.

PURPOSES OF INTERVIEWS

Interviews are conducted with specific goals in mind. Through the exchange between interviewers and applicants, interviews are intended to answer three specific questions (Montana & Charnov, 2000):

1. Does the applicant have the necessary qualifications, education, experience, and skills to complete the tasks?
2. Does the applicant possess the motivation both to perform the job and to remain employed for a long enough period of time to justify the expense of hiring and training?
3. Does the prospective employee fit in with the existing company culture and possess the values that align with the mission of the organization?

Edwards, Yankey, and Altpeter (1998) assign additional purposes to conducting interviews. One purpose includes working on public relations and outreach to future employees. An interviewer may be the first representative of the organization that a potential employee meets; interviewers should approach interviews with optimism and therefore positive energy. A poor impression may stifle a candidate's current or even future interest in becoming a member of the team. An organization's negative reputation may spread quickly and be difficult to change once established. Another purpose for the interview is to clarify any aspects of the position that appear unclear from the job description.

STAGES OF INTERVIEWS

Although we have recommended conducting the interview as a conversation with an applicant, it is important that the conversation have some structure. Interviews are intended to gather much information in a limited amount of time. Observing the stages of an interview will ensure that participants

| BOX 12.1 | STAGES OF INTERVIEWING |

1. Opening or greeting phase
2. Questions for the applicant

3. Questions for the organization
4. Closing phase

Source: Matrix Resources, Inc. (2003). *Conducting the Interview*. Available www.matrixres.com/
matrix/website.nsf/Framesets/AboutMATRIXSiteSearchFrames?OpenDocument&LID=HNFA002

remain on track while addressing all questions. Although outlines may vary, researchers generally agree on four key components: (a) opening or greeting, (b) questions for the applicant, (c) questions for the organization, and (d) the closing (Edwards, Yankey, & Altpeter, 1998; Montana & Charnov, 2000).

1. *Opening or Greeting Phase*—The purpose of the greeting phase is to begin to establish rapport. Interviewers must work to lessen the effects of anxiety and nervousness experienced by both the candidate and the interviewer. Engaging in small talk can begin to paint a multidimensional picture of the applicant. Good candidates not only possess the knowledge and professional skills but also the ability to build a strong, working relationship with the team. The applicant should be introduced to all participants in the interview and offered simple refreshments. This phase may include an overview of the position or information about the history of the organization and generally lasts between five to ten minutes.

2. *Questions for the Applicant*—This phase is usually led by the interviewer and is focused on gathering information about the candidate's background. Questions focused on an applicant's previous work experiences, skills, and anticipated contributions to the organization are common. For example, an interviewer may ask about projects that an applicant enjoys doing or a past project that was successful. Some topics are off-limits and will be discussed later in the chapter. This phase also provides a glimpse of the applicant's critical thinking and communication skills.

3. *Questions for the Organization*—Applicants should always be given the opportunity to ask questions about the responsibilities of the position or organization's mission and leadership. Providing an invitation to clarify any gray areas about the job responsibilities or the organization will decrease the potential for future problems. This stage of the interview may provide an indication of how interested an applicant is in working with the organization. Interviewers should volunteer to follow up with the candidate and answer any questions that cannot be answered during the interview.

4. *Closing Phase*—This stage should offer the opportunity to gather any missed information from all parties. Interviewers generally use this time to fill in any missing information from the candidate's application or résumé. The interviewer may also verify the contact information for the applicant's references. Some attention should be paid to educating the applicant about the organization's hiring process and what will be happening next. The applicant should be given the date the organization plans to make a decision. Sharing this information may also prevent multiple calls from anxious applicants. Some organizations offer short tours of the facilities to final candidates. This strategic move should be designed around positive, upbeat members of the organization, as they will score points for the organization (Matrix Resources, Inc., 2003).

TYPES OF INTERVIEWS

A good practice for conducting interviews involves preparing an interview guide. This guide will contain questions that will be asked of each applicant. These questions will be uniformly shared with each applicant. Questions following the response will be ad-lib as interviews begin to probe for clarification or additional information. This practice presents at least two advantages. First, it allows interviewers the opportunity to summarize the responses of all applicants and compare the results between candidates. Asking different questions to each applicant or even asking the same question but phrasing it differently does not allow interviewers to compare the responses in a fair, balanced manner. Second, it protects the organization and interviewer from drifting off into a panel of questions that are illegal to ask any applicant. Every interview guide is unique, however best practices involve structured interviews with some of the following types of questions.

1. **Situational Questions**—Situational questions focus on identifying capacities related to a specific skill set (Matrix Resources, Inc., 2003). The question presents a hypothetical situation that may occur on the job and allows the candidate to provide an explanation as to how he would react. Although these questions are not exactly scientific, the premise is that the candidate may behave in a manner similar to the one described (Edwards, Yankey, & Altpeter, 1998). Because there are no wrong answers, interviewers should spend some time evaluating what the best practices would be in these situations in order to evaluate competency prior to the interview. For example, when making a home visit with a family you observe a mother shaking her 4-year-old son when he spills her drink. How would you handle the situation? A good answer could include ideas such as making sure the child is safe and providing a toy or some distraction for the child in order to have a private moment with the parent to discuss the situation. A poor response could include leaving the home because it is obviously not a good time for the visit.

2. **Background and Job Knowledge Questions**—Background questions focus on the applicant's prior work experience, education, or other past activities that relate to the position being applied for (Montana & Charnov, 2000). For example, what talents could you bring to the organization as a member of the team? What are your professional goals for the next ten years? These questions are based on information from the application and résumé. This category of questions tests a candidate's communication skills and ability to articulate ideas but may lack the opportunity to ask the candidate's professional skills or knowledge base (Matrix Resources, Inc., 2003). They are effective in filling in gaps in an application or résumé. Questions about the reasons for leaving multiple jobs may identify negative behavior patterns. General background questions alone may not reveal a great deal of information. The follow-up, probing questions are the ones that dig below the superficial responses.

3. **Patterned Behavior Description Questions**—Behavior questions focus on looking at the candidate's activities in prior positions. The goal is to identify how the applicant actually reacted in a real situation rather than how he would react in a hypothetical situation (Edward, Yankey, & Altpeter, 1998). These questions are specific about past functions in a job. For example, "describe a situation in a previous job where you felt you handled conflict with a client effectively." Behavior questions are important because past behaviors are a predictor to future behaviors. Obviously, an applicant may recreate situations in a manner that portrays her in a

| BOX 12.2 | TYPES OF INTERVIEW QUESTIONS |

1. Situational questions
2. Background and job knowledge questions

3. Patterned behavior description questions

positive manner. In order to neutralize this risk, ask questions that involve describing failures in their past work histories, for example, "describe a situation where you felt you did not handle conflict appropriately and what you learned from that situation."

FEDERAL GUIDELINES FOR INTERVIEWS

In order to protect vulnerable groups from discrimination during the screening, selection, and hiring process, the Equal Employment Commission of the federal government has identified some topics that should not be asked about in an interview. According to the U.S. Department of Labor, as a general rule, questions should be relevant to the job and activities that will be performed rather than focused on the applicant's personal life (1999). Anyone who may be involved in the interview process should be familiar with the regulations of the Civil Rights Act and the Americans with Disabilities Act to avoid agency liability. Some questions that should not be addressed are identified in Box 12.3. Generally, they concern personal areas of the applicant's life, such as race, religion, gender, national origin, age, pregnancy, and disability (Matrix Resources, Inc., 2003; Mississippi State University, 2003; U.S. Department of Labor, 1999; U.S. Small Business Administration, 2001). Examples of the kinds of questions that may not be asked include: "How old are you?" "In what year were you born?" "What kind of arrangements will you make for child care while you are working?" and "Do you plan to have any more children?" The suggestions for complying with federal guidelines offered in this chapter should neither be regarded as comprehensive or as any form of legal advice. Interviewers should educate themselves regarding the law. When in doubt, it is better to avoid a question or consult with an agency attorney before asking.

PREPARING FOR INTERVIEWS

Interviewers should spend some time in preparation in order to get the maximum benefit from an interview. Most applicants who are moderately intuitive can sense when inadequate preparation has occurred. The following steps should ensure that interviewers are in the correct frame of mind and create the physical setting appropriate for most interviews (U.S. Department of Labor, 1999):

1. Spend some time reviewing the job description for the position. A clear understanding of the responsibilities of the position will help identify the characteristics and capacities that are needed to complete the job well.
2. Make sure that human resources clarifies all aspects of the job. Offering a candidate a $35,000 position that is intended to pay only $25,000 could lead to disastrous consequences and misunderstandings.
3. Review the applications and résumés for missing information and inconsistencies prior to the interviews in order to ensure that all information is complete.
4. Review the interview guide with the questions that will be posed to the applicant. If conducting interviews is an uncomfortable or new process, hold a mock interview with a coworker to practice.

BOX 12.3 | QUESTIONS TO AVOID DURING INTERVIEWS

Civil Rights Act, Title VII (Prohibits employment discrimination based on race, color, religion, sex or national origin)

1. Are you a U.S. citizen?
2. What is your national origin?
3. What church do you attend?
4. What is your credit record?
5. Do you own your home?
6. Have you ever been arrested?
7. What is or was your spouse's name or place of employment?

Age Discrimination in Employment Act

1. What is your age or date of birth?
2. Don't you feel you may be overqualified for this position?

Civil Rights Act, Title VII; Pregnancy Discrimination Act

1. Has your salary ever been garnished?
2. How many children do you have? What are their ages? Have you made child care arrangements?

3. What is your marital status? What is your maiden name?

Americans with Disabilities Act

1. Have you ever filed a workers' compensation claim?
2. Do you have any physical impairment that would prevent you from performing the job for which you are applying?
3. Have you ever been hospitalized? If so, for what condition?
4. Have you ever been treated by a psychiatrist or psychologist? If so, for what condition?
5. Is there any health-related reason you may not be able to perform the job for which you are applying?
6. How many days were you absent from work because of illness last year?
7. Are you taking any prescribed drugs?
8. Have you ever been treated for drug addiction or alcoholism?

---

5. When confirming the meeting time, discuss how the interview will be conducted with the candidate along with any reasonable accommodations that will be needed during the interview process.
6. Manage the length of the interview without rushing the process. Allow the candidate time to gather thoughts, answer questions, and ask questions without feeling pressured by interviewers.
7. Rely on those interview techniques and communication skills used with all clients and coworkers. Maintain eye contact and ask open-ended questions to get the most information.
8. Create a quiet and inviting environment to meet with applicants. Avoid receiving calls or other distractions in order to focus full attention on the applicant.
9. If interviews are planned with multiple applicants, take some time between interviews to review responses and score applicants rather than doing it all at the end.

USING THE MACRO PRACTITIONER'S WORKBOOK

Worksheet 12.1 is designed to lead you through the process of developing an interview guide. Use the case study from unit 3 to obtain the information you will need to do so. As you complete the worksheet, keep in mind that every guide will vary to some extent, but the guide developed for any one series of interviews should be followed closely.

SUMMARY

The process of interviewing is critical to the success of any organization. In order to interview effectively, practitioners must understand the purpose of interviewing, design the interview to accomplish specific goals, develop an interview guide, and conduct the interaction in an effective manner. For every group of interviews, a guide should be developed and followed closely. Further, interviewers should be aware of federal guidelines for interviewing and should be careful to comply with the guidelines.

Activities for Learning

1. Working in a small group, develop an interview guide for hiring a therapist for a mental health center. Then role play the interview and discuss the results.
2. Talk with the personnel manager at a local agency. Ask her questions about the interviewing process at her agency. How do their procedures differ from those described in this chapter? What have you learned from the discussion that you will be able to use in your own practice?
3. Conduct an Internet search for information about the kinds of questions you cannot ask during interviews. Report the results to the class.

Questions for Discussion

1. How could you tell whether a person you were interviewing was sincere? How could you gauge their interest in the position? What might be some signs that the candidate was exaggerating experience and qualifications?
2. How would you react if a person you were interviewing suddenly and without any prompting from you volunteered information about one of the forbidden areas? Would you warn them, refuse to listen, or say nothing and record their comments? Would you have an ethical responsibility to handle that situation in any particular way?
3. What are some situational questions you might ask a potential case management supervisor? What are some patterned behavior questions?

Key Terms

Interviews—structured conversations between members of the organization and applicants for positions with the organization

Patterned behavior description questions—a type of interview question that examines the candidate's activities in prior positions by asking how he reacted in a real situation rather than how he would react in a hypothetical situation

Situational questions—a type of interview question asked of an applicant that focuses on identifying capacities related to a specific skill set. For example, asking how a potential employee might deal with an emergency situation.

References

Edwards, R., Yankey, J., & Altpeter., M. (1998). *Skills for effective management of nonprofit organizations*. Washington, D.C.: NASW, pp. 164–169.

Matrix Resources, Inc. (2003). *Conducting the interview*. Available: www.matrixes.com/ matrix/website.nsf/Framesets/About MATRIXSiteSearchFrames?Open Documents&LID=HNFA002

Mississippi State University. (2003). *The interview and background check: Support staff*. Available: www.hrm.msstate .edu/employment/HiringToolKit/ Interviewing101.htm.

Montana, P., & Charnov, B. (2000). *Management* (3rd Ed., pp. 216–220) New York: Barron's Educational Series, Inc.

Rutgers University. (2003). *Conducting the interview*. Available: uhr.rutgers.edu/ conducting-the-interview.html.

U.S. Department of Labor. (1999). *Preparing for and conducting an effective job interview*. Available: www.dol.gov/odep/pubs/ek99/ jobinter.htm.

U.S. Small Business Administration. (2001). *The interview process—how to select the "right" person*. Available: www .onlinewbc.gov/doc/manage/ interview.html.

WORKSHEET 12.1 | DEVELOPING AN INTERVIEW GUIDE

Opening or Greeting Phase (approximately 5–10 minutes)

1. Determine where you want to meet the candidate. Do you want a formal setting or a casual setting? Where do you want her to sit? Where will you sit?

    Canidate will come to agency. Will meet in Directors office around a conference table. Close enough but on corner or across table

2. What kinds of refreshments will you offer. If the candidate accepts, who will bring them?

    Will offer coffee or water, and assistent will bring them in.

3. Prepare a repertoire of casual questions you can ask or comments you can make to ease the rapport-building small talk.

    Did you have any problems finding the agency? Glad you could come in today. I was @ your agency yesterday. Great Bldg.

4. Do you want to include a description of the job and the agency at this point? If so, what do you want to say?

    Let me take a few minutes to inform up about our agency. And if you like we could have a tour

Questions for the Applicant (approximately 10–15 minutes)

1. Based on your review of the candidate's job application and résumé, what questions do you want to ask?

    Why would you like to come and work here. What would you say is your greatest accomplshnt at your last agency.

2. Based on other interactions with the candidate, what questions will you ask?

- What do you think you could accomplish working @ this agency.

3. Based on the requirements of the job and the conditions within the agency, what questions do you wish to ask?

Questions for the Organization (approximately 5–15 minutes)

1. How will you let the candidate know that it is time to ask questions?

Explain that the interviewing process is a two-way street, and that you would like the candidate to to have the opportunity to interview you.

2. Will you find ways to encourage questions? If so, what will they be?

- Ok what would you like to know. Would you like to see an agency organizational chart.

Closing Phase (approximately 5–10 minutes)

1. Fill in any questions or information you have failed to cover during the earlier phases of the interview. Allow an opportunity for the candidate to ask additional questions.

2. What information will you provide about the organization's hiring process and what will be happening next?

Explain the process of the 3 interviews, and how the candidate will be contacted.

3. By what date will the agency inform the candidates of their decision? How will candidates be informed?

The candidate will receive a letter if they are not selected for the next processes.

UNIT 4

Effective Financial Management and Fundraising

INTRODUCTION

Unit 4 focuses on the financial management of organizations and initiatives. Because both the information is most often used in agencies and also the procedures described in each chapter are nearly identical for community work, the chapters are addressed primarily to organizational practitioners. Where information specific to community practitioners is needed, boxes provide that information.

Chapter 13, "Basics of Financial Management," provides an overview of the financial processes that take place in agencies and funded initiatives. Primary attention is given to budgeting, with secondary discussions of the methods of preparing other types of financial documents. The worksheets are designed to help develop a simple budget for either an organization or a community initiative.

Chapter 14, "Writing a Government Grant Proposal," provides step-by-step instructions on completing a grant proposal to submit to federal, state, or local governments. Although many government agencies now provide templates, and those templates sometimes between agencies, the principles and procedures are usually similar. These principles and procedures are discussed in chapter 14.

"Writing a Foundation Inquiry Letter," chapter 15, describes the process involved in obtaining funding from philanthropic foundations. Beginning with a description of the various types of foundations, the chapter proceeds to offer advice on locating a likely candidate to approach, developing a letter for the approach, and following up after the letter has been sent.

Chapter 16, "Planning a Fundraising Event," discusses the basics of yet another important way of obtaining financial support for an agency or initiative: holding special events designed specifically to raise money. Selecting a type of event, recruiting assistance for the event, and budgeting for the event are all included.

The final chapter, chapter 17, "Writing a Fundraising Letter," describes the basics of developing an effective direct mail campaign. The positives and negatives of direct mail are described, methods of identifying a target audience are discussed, and the process of developing the direct mail kit are outlined. Following these steps should enable the reader to initiate a successful campaign.

Each chapter includes the worksheets from the Macro Practitioner's Workbook. As for the previous units, use the case study from this unit to find the needed information. If necessary, feel free to refer to the case studies from previous units as well.

EFFECTIVE FINANCIAL MANAGEMENT AND FUNDRAISING CASE STUDY

You are in the sixth month of your tenure as regional director for the Department of Human Endeavors. Your efforts at improving services and stabilizing the organization have shown some success, and you have the right people in place to ensure that the organization is managed properly. Despite the progress, the organization still faces many serious challenges. However, the Addiesburg project has made significant strides and you have received funding to hire a part-time employee, to pay volunteer expenses, and to cover additional office expenses.

Organizational Practice Information

You have one program that is struggling financially. The Housekeeping Assistance Program (HAP) provides assistance to troubled families whose children are in or are in danger of entering state custody. Its services include house cleaning, light maintenance, nutritional counseling, and cooking lessons. The program has a full-time director who manages a staff of community volunteers. The volunteers do most of the actual work with the families. You discover the financial problems because you receive frequent requests for additional funds for the program. You ask for a copy of the program budget and are told that there is no budget.

You meet with the program director to calculate expenses and develop a budget. You are aware that the program receives $50,000 from your organization and an additional $10,000 from the local Department of Human Services. This $60,000 represents the total funding for the program.

HAP also has a number of expenses. These include the salary and benefits of the director that cost a total of $47,950, volunteer travel costs totaling about $5,700 per year, cleaning and repair supplies costing about $15,000, and the program expends approximately $5,000 on training materials. Its only other expenditure is for office supplies, which cost about $750 per year.

Your innovations in the Protective Visitations portion of your agency have ensured that allegations of abuse and neglect are being investigated much more quickly and effectively. The benefit of this improvement is that children who are being abused or neglected are identified and removed to safety more quickly than in the past. This has generated a problem, because the already overburdened system of foster homes and temporary shelters is now burgeoning. It has become clear that you must do something to lighten this load.

One of the solutions proposed in a meeting with your direct service staff is that a new program be put in place that will provide intensive services to families where it is believed the child could be made safe with the proper supports in place. The worker who suggests the idea refers to an intervention known as the Vandenberg Model that has been successful in a number of other settings. You recognize an opportunity to reduce the demand on your agency's system of care. If the removal of children from some homes could be prevented by putting appropriate services in place, fewer children would enter custody.

You decide to create a new program to deliver this service to families recognized by Protective Visitations workers as being appropriate. You estimate that about 25 families per month could benefit from the program. This would require the addition of 3 supervisors, 15 direct service workers, and 3 secretarial staff. Because you have no available resources of your own, you decide to seek external funding to develop the program.

You consider several alternatives. One is to seek the total amount needed from the federal government. A second is to approach a philanthropic foundation. A third possibility is to obtain a portion of the funding from the government or a foundation and the balance through a fundraising event and direct mail campaign.

Community Practice Information

Your work as the chair of the Disadvantaged Communities Subcommittee has uncovered a need for a special program in the Addiesburg community. Although the elementary and middle schools in the area have agreed to create after school programs for their own youth, there remains no alternative for the high school students who are transported out of the area to attend school. It has become apparent over the months that the only possibility for such a program is for the community work group to help start a program at some alternative location in Addiesburg. You want the program to include recreational activities, tutoring, and on-site counseling for about 30 juveniles. Your work group decides to seek outside funding and engage in fundraising activities to fund the program.

Your group decides that the program can operate with a full-time director, a part-time clinical director, and a group of community volunteers. The clinical director will supervise the activities of four Master of Science in Social Work (MSSW) therapists provided by one of the local mental health agencies. Each therapist will work eight hours a week at no cost to the program. Volunteers will provide tutoring and supervise the recreational activities.

The program will be able to use the recreation center at a local park at no cost, but will have to pay one-half the cost of the utilities (about $250 per month). It will need to invest in tutoring materials (about $125 per month), recreational supples (an initial cost of $1,500 plus about $100 per month), and office supplies (about $45 per month). A single telephone will cost about $50 per month. Computers will be provided by one of the member agencies.

Your own agency can provide $25,000 per year to support the program. You and your work group then develop a budget to determine how much additional funding you will need. You consider several alternatives for obtaining the additional funds. One is to seek all the necessary funds through a federal grant. The second is to request support from a foundation. Yet another possibility is to get partial funding through a government or foundation grant and supplement those dollars with a fundraising event and a direct mail campaign.

BASICS OF FINANCIAL MANAGEMENT

CHAPTER 13

CHAPTER OUTLINE

Steps in the Financial Management Process

The Budget

Cash Flow

Accounting Methods

Financial Statements

Audit

Using the Macro Practitioner's Workbook

Summary

Although budgeting is a critical activity for every agency, this chapter will not be limited to budgeting. Rather, it will consider budgeting within the overall context of financial management. This implies a strategy of planning and being in control of a budget rather than being controlled by it. Solid financial management requires the input of both administrators and program staff, as well as members of the board of directors. It is important to understand the necessary steps in order to engage in the process, as well as to plan an effective and manageable budget.

Although the bulk of the narrative in this chapter is written as though it were for organizational practitioners, its principles are equally applicable to community practitioners who manage a budget for an initiative. Although these budgets are likely to be simpler, the processes of developing budget and financial reports are nonetheless critical. In many cases, the funding for an initiative will pass through one of the partner agencies so that a large part of the responsibility for financial management resides within the agency. Even in these situations it is important that the community practitioner understand and be able to participate in the financial management process.

STEPS IN THE FINANCIAL MANAGEMENT PROCESS

Steps in the financial management process include: (a) preparing the budget, which involves estimating revenue and expenses; (b) identifying restricted and unrestricted funds; (c) developing a cash flow statement; and (d) identifying an agency's mission and priorities (Gross, Larkin, & McCarthy, 2000; Henke, 1980). Although teaching the in-depth techniques necessary to perform all these tasks is beyond the scope of this chapter, it is necessary to understand what they are and how they fit together in order to grasp the budgeting process. Some aspects of the process may differ for community practitioners. These are discussed in Box 13.1.

THE BUDGET

Programs and finances should continuously be reviewed and evaluated. Agencies should do a final evaluation of program goals and achievements at the end of each fiscal year. Administrators need to evaluate programs for their effectiveness, measure how well the agency stayed within or went over budget, analyze how much was spent on each client, and see how many clients the agency served. Administrators should also review the agency's mission and consider what its goals will be for the upcoming year. All these processes play into the critical decision about how incoming revenues will be distributed in the coming year, in essence, planning next year's budget.

Types of Budgets

Two types of budgets will be considered here: line-item and program. The line-item budget will be given the lion's share of the attention and will be the subject of the Macro Practitioner's Workbook. This is because the line-item budget is most frequently required by funders. Program budgets have a role to play in agency financial management and are therefore also included in the discussion.

Line-Item Budgets   In a line-item budget, each expense is entered on its own line. For example, if an agency expects to spend $7,000 on its telephone service for a year, that amount will be recorded on a single line that is labeled "telephone service." These individual lines are generally grouped into categories such as travel, equipment, and office supplies. In addition to these "direct" expenses, agencies may also list "indirect" expenses, that is, expenses that are not directly tied to a line item, but which must be included in the budget in summary form.

During the planning and review stages of budget management, common expenses on line-item budgets should be examined and their true cost considered. The categories mentioned above (travel, equipment, and office supplies) are typically divided into two larger categories: personnel and nonpersonnel. Personnel expenses are the costs of staff wages, salaries, and benefits. Personnel costs may also include consultants and other contract services. Nonpersonnel expenses are those expenditures not directly related to the compensation of employees or contractors. One example is "equipment," often a large line-item expense. Equipment includes items such as copy machines, computers, furniture, and similar articles. Each of these articles has a value, representing its initial cost or expense. The value of each depreciates, or diminishes, every year. Other nonpersonnel expenses include "facilities" (the cost of office space used by the agency), and "supplies" (articles used almost daily in an office, such as paper, pens, and printer toner). Whether facilities are purchased, leased, or rented, the cost is included in the single line item. Budgets

| BOX 13.1 | FINANCIAL MANAGEMENT FOR COMMUNITY PRACTITIONERS |

Community practitioners may or may not manage their own budgets. When the initiative is funded directly, they may have a simple budget to manage that covers their own salaries and benefits plus some operating expenses. When an initiative is newly funded, particularly when funding was obtained from nonlocal sources, the funders are likely to be more willing to commit funds to an established agency that has proven its stability and its capacity for responsible money management. In these cases, community practitioners must still understand budgeting basics. The agency may choose, for example, to treat initiative funding as a "pass-through" in which dollars are transferred into an account on a regular basis so that they will be available for the practitioner's use. In other cases, the agency may completely manage the budget, yet require regular interaction between the community practitioner, the agency's finance department, and the agency leaders. In either case, a community must understand and be able to utilize budgets.

---

may also include "indirect costs," meaning those costs that cannot be directly attributed to any line item. Indirect costs refers to expenses that cover services and other expenses that are shared between multiple budgets. For example, if a single agency had five separate programs that shared a single office staff, then administrative staff time and electricity might be shared by the programs. In this case, the shared items would be "indirect expenses." The amount of these expenses (also referred to as overhead) is agreed to ahead of time and is based on a formula (percentage of total budget or percentage of personnel costs) (Gross, Larkin, & McCarthy, 2000; Hankin, Seidner, & Zeitlow, 1998).

Program or Functional Budgets   Program budgets refer to budgets that describe the income and expenses of individual programs that operate within an agency structure. They may be written in a line-item form or may be simply summary numbers, with individual expenses recorded in the agency's overall budget. For example, an agency might determine how much of each line item (personnel, supplies, equipment, and printing) will go into certain activities in a program. This type of budget can help produce effective staffing patterns. For instance, costs may be broken down into the cost of developing parenting classes, the cost of conducting the classes, and the cost of evaluating the classes (Gross, Larkin, & McCarthy, 2000; Hankin, Seidner, & Zeitlow, 1998).

Predicting Expenses

Budget preparation requires estimating the monetary amount needed to achieve the goals and objectives in the upcoming year. This must include every aspect of agency and program operations. Agency administrators should work with program directors and department managers to understand and help determine their goals, resources, and needs. It may be wise to overestimate costs to account for unforeseen expenses.

There are two methods for estimating expenses: zero-based and incremental budgeting. Most agencies use a mix of both of these. **Zero-based budgeting** sets each item of the budget at zero until it is justified for a specific dollar amount. **Incremental budgeting** uses past information to make predictions about future expenses. Increases due to inflation and other factors can simply be added to past costs (Gross, Larkin, & McCarthy, 2000; Hankin, Seidner, & Zeitlow, 1998).

Predicting Revenue

After estimating costs, administrators must calculate revenue or income. Past figures are used to estimate future revenue. In other situations future revenue may be known. When this is the case these figures should be used. Income from grants and fundraising activities can be difficult to predict. Planners should be realistic and have a contingency plan for what might be done should funding be considerably lower than expected. Planners should use the most accurate information available, but should underestimate income by at least 10%. They must also plan ahead for emergencies. For example, they should prioritize programs and services in case budget cuts occur. This is simply the reality of the modern economy. The inability to choose between programs may result in the failure of an entire agency. Administrators should develop a plan for what to do should severe income cuts occur. It is also wise to plan alternatives for what might be done should funding be higher than expected. The important thing is to be prepared for a variety of scenarios.

Restricted and Unrestricted Funds

When planning a budget, it is also critical to identify restricted and unrestricted funds. Restricted funds are constituted by income that is given to the agency for a specific purpose which is not to be used on any other type of expense. Unrestricted funds are dollars that are given that have no specific rules or restrictions attached.

Restricted funds should be placed in an appropriate category and marked in such a way that it is clear that this money cannot be moved. Unrestricted money is generally used to cover administrative costs, as well as any program costs that are not covered by the proposed budget (Gross, Larkin, & McCarthy, 2000; Hankin, Seidner, & Zeitlow, 1998).

The next step is to compare expense and revenue predictions. If there are gaps, administrators must make serious programmatic decisions. There are alternatives. More time and energy might be committed to fundraising. It might be possible to collaborate with another agency to cut costs. Program expenses might be cut or costs to clients might be increased. The budget must be balanced, and the priorities set by the administrators will determine the final product.

Final responsibility for approval of the budget falls on the agency's board of directors. The board must feel certain that the agency will be able to generate the revenue that is needed to cover their expenses.

The finalization of the annual budget is only the beginning of the process. Budgets should be reviewed periodically. They must be modified when new information is received. If, for example, a local businessperson makes an unexpected large contribution, the agency may be able to make budgetary increases in some areas. If, on the other hand, some funding source cuts agency income, tough decisions may need to be made. Budget review also involves determining whether agency guidelines for adhering to budgets have been followed. It is particularly important that the guidelines of government, corporate, and foundation funders be followed.

CASH FLOW

Budgets must be monitored on a monthly basis to ensure that income and expenses are on track with the plan developed in the annual budget. While an annual budget is a critical tool, it doesn't provide information about what resources and expenses are at any given point during the year. It is often

BOX 13.2

A LIST OF EXPENSE CATEGORIES
FOR VICTIM-OFFENDER MEDIATION
OF MADISON COUNTY

Project director's salary	Internet access
Office manager's salary	Office furniture
Rent	Office equipment
Utilities	Office supplies
Transportation for employees and volunteers	Postage
Travel to conventions	Training materials
Telephone	Professional dues and memberships
Computer (hardware)	Accounting fees
Computer (software)	Appreciation banquet

impossible to defer expenses when income fails or is delayed. The electric company, for example, may not care that next month's gala event will raise the revenue to pay the bill. A cash flow chart can help to plan for such contingencies. It is possible to foresee which months will bring gains and or losses by writing down monthly income and expenses. This information can be used to determine how much cash must be drawn from reserves obtained from other sources.

Sample Expense, Revenue, Budget, and Income Statement

Boxes 13.2 through 13.4 include a sample expense, revenue, budget, and income statement for an imaginary agency: Victim-Offender Mediation of Madison County (VOMMC). In order to understand the budget, it is necessary to understand the breakdown of expense and revenue (also referred to as "income") for the agency. The following description provides the necessary information.

VOMMC is a small not-for-profit agency serving a single county. The county is composed of both urban and rural areas, containing a town of about 85,000 and a surrounding rural community of about 20,000. The agency provides services to any resident of the county who is referred by the juvenile or circuit courts. It offers a single service, victim-offender mediation, to juveniles and adults who have been arrested for assault or property crimes and have been determined to be suitable candidates for diversion by the court system. The agency sees approximately 600 cases per year relying on a combination of direct services by the program director and the work of a large group of volunteers, all of whom she has recruited and trained. The agency has a small budget, needing to cover only a full-time project director, a part-time office manager, the travel expenses of its volunteers, and its operating costs. It combines small amounts of income from a variety of sources in order to cover its expenses.

The agency's expenses include two salaries, that of the project director ($40,000 per year plus $14,800 in benefits) and that of the office manager, who works 20 hours per week at the rate of $15 per hour. She works 50 weeks per year, resulting in a total expense to the agency of $15,000.

In addition to these personnel expenses, the agency has a number of non-personnel expenditures. It pays $500 per month ($6,000 per year) in rent for a modest office space and an average of $125 per month for utilities ($1,500 per year). VOMMC pays the travel expenses of its volunteers, most of which are incurred in visits to the county's various communities to visit with clients.

BOX 13.3 | A LIST OF REVENUE CATEGORIES FOR VICTIM-OFFENDER MEDIATION OF MADISON COUNTY

Contract with the Department of Juvenile Services

Contract with the Department of Correctional Services

Grant support from the United Way

Grant support from the Madison County Police Confiscation Fund

Easter basket sales

Annual fundraising dinner

Direct mail campaign

Local donations

BOX 13.4 | A SAMPLE BUDGET: VICTIM-OFFENDER MEDIATION OF MADISON COUNTY

Expenses

Personnel

Project director	$54,800
Office manager	15,000

Nonpersonnel

Rent	6,000
Utilities	1,500
Transportation	3,200
Travel	1,500
Telephone	2,860
Computer purchase	540
Software licenses	144
Internet access	420
Office furniture	300
Office equipment	300
Office supplies	1,500
Postage	300
Training materials	600
Professional dues and memberships	600
Accounting fees	240
Appreciation banquet	500
Total Expenses	$92,304

Revenue

Contracts

Department of Juvenile Services	$30,000
Department of Correctional Services	18,000

Grants

United Way	10,000
Madison County Police Confiscation Fund	10,000

Fundraising

Easter basket sales	5,000
Annual dinner	7,500
Direct mail	10,000
Local donations	5,000
Total Revenue	$95,500

This costs approximately $3,200 per year. About $1,500 in out-of-state travel expense is typically incurred annually, to allow the executive director to attend conferences and training.

Telephone costs run about $155 per month, a total of $2,860 each year. The agency recently purchased two computers, two printers, and a scanner, resulting in a $40 per month ($540 per year) expense. Software licenses cost $144 and Internet access is $420 per year. Other office-related expenses include office furniture ($300 per year), office equipment ($300), office supplies ($1,500), and postage ($300). Materials for training volunteer mediators average $50 per month, and professional dues and memberships cost the agency about $600 each year. It spends $240 per year in accounting fees and $500 on a volunteer appreciation banquet. Box 13.1 contains a list of agency expense categories.

BOX 13.5	FINANCIAL MANAGEMENT FOR COMMUNITY PRACTITIONERS

Just as it is important for community practitioners to understand budgeting, it is also important that they understand other types of documents related to financial management. If they manage their own budgets, they may be required to produce documents such as the balance sheet and income statements offered as examples in Boxes 13.6 and 13.7. If they do not manage their own finances, they may need to understand these processes for other reasons. One example might occur if a community practitioner is involved in helping recruit a partner to the initiative that is unknown to the other partners. In such a situation, the practitioner might need to help review the new participant's financial documents in order to determine the degree of the agency's stability.

VOMMC's revenues include two contracts. The Department of Juvenile Services purchases services for 25 clients each month at $100 per client. The Department of Correctional Services (DCS), which serves adult offenders, pays $100 per month for each of 15 referrals. It also receives two $10,000 grants, one from the United Way and one from the Madison County Police Confiscation Fund. It also has four sources of fundraising revenue: (a) Easter basket sales that net about $5,000, (b) an annual fundraising dinner that brings in about $7,500, (c) a direct mail campaign that produces approximately $7,500, and (d) local donations from a variety of sources that total about $5,000 each year. The agency is prohibited by state statute from accepting payment from its clients. For a summary of the agencies categories of revenue, see Box 13.3.

The agency budget (in this case a simple one) is little more than a tally of expenses and revenues and a comparison of the results. A sample budget is included in Box 13.4. Please note that several modifications are possible. For example, many of the categories in this budget might actually be condensed into several subcategories. Office supplies, computer costs, office furniture, office equipment, postage, and telephone costs might become subheadings grouped under a single category of office expenses. This would not be particularly important in a small, simple budget such as the one illustrated here. However, it might be the only way to manage a vast tangle of multiple categories in a large, complex budget.

The budget may be prepared by the treasurer, the executive director working with the treasurer, or an accountant working with information provided by the agency. The annual version is typically broken down into monthly versions, and the results of each month's expenses and expenditures are reported to the board of directors at each meeting. This both allows both agency leaders to have a strong sense of where the finances stand and also provides a basis for planning adjustments when they must be made. There are many additional financial documents that agencies may or may not use depending on the complexity of their finances and the expectations of their funders. Some of these are discussed in "Financial Statements" below.

Nonprofit Does Not Equal Broke

Some practitioners misunderstand the meaning of nonprofit. Nonprofit agencies may have more revenue than expenses. Excess revenue can be saved for times when expenses are excessive. Endowments and other reserve funds can be developed for future use. Whenever possible, agencies should plan to set some portion of their revenue aside each year. This should be no more than 5% of the agency's total budget. Many experts recommend doing this until approximately 25–50% of the annual budget is set aside in a reserve fund (Gross, Larkin, & McCarthy, 2000; Hankin, Seidner, & Zeitlow, 1998).

Notice that VOMMC projects extra money in its budget. The term "projects" is used because the levels of expense and revenue are subject to change. Expenses can be more or less depending on a variety of external and internal conditions. Excess income might be saved against future deficits or used in some other productive manner.

ACCOUNTING METHODS

Accounting methods are systems of tracking the actual income and expenses experienced by the agency. There are two basic types and a third type that is a combination of the first two (Gross, Larkin, & McCarthy, 2000; Hankin, Seidner, & Zeitlow, 1998; Henke, 1980).

Accrual-Based Accounting

Accrual-based accounting systems include what an agency owes and what is owed to it, in addition to its actual income and expenses. In **accrual-based accounting,** an expense is recognized as soon as the purchase order is written. It is labeled as a payable until the money is actually received. Similarly, when a foundation indicates it is awarding $10,000 in grant money, that money is counted as income. It is labeled in the budget as a receivable until the money is physically deposited into the account. Accounts should be examined frequently when using this system to ensure that outstanding revenues are being received as expected.

Cash-Based Accounting

In **cash-based accounting,** financial expenses and revenues are only recorded when the money is deposited or a check is written. Money actually must move in order to be recorded. Cash-based accounting is familiar to most people because it is the way in which their personal checking account records are kept.

Modified Cash Basis Accounting System

Many agencies use some modification of a cash-based accounting system. Although the cash-based system is simpler, it leaves out important information about an agency's financial status. For this reason, agencies often keep some accounts on a cash system and others on an accrual system. For example, funds which require that federal and state taxes be paid are often kept on the accrual-based system.

FINANCIAL STATEMENTS

Financial statements summarize the overall financial status of the agency. Agencies keep varying levels of detail in these documents. The two most critical documents are the balance sheet and the income statement.

The Balance Sheet

The balance sheet is a statement detailing assets and liabilities on a particular date. Some analysts liken the balance sheet to a snapshot illustrating a company's financial health. A balance sheet gets its name from the fact that the assets and liabilities need to balance. Assets include all money that an organization has: land, buildings, cash in the bank, equipment, and all money that

| BOX 13.6 | A SAMPLE BALANCE SHEET FOR MEDIATION SERVICES OF MADISON COUNTY |

	June 30	
	2002	2003
Assets		
Cash	$3,500	$6,100
Equipment	2,100	1,900
Accounts receivable		
DOJ contract	5,000	5,000
DCS contract	3,000	1,500
Total assets	$13,600	$14,500
Liabilities		
Computer equipment contract	0	2,300
Lease on office space	3,000	3,000
Total liabilities	$3,000	$5,300

is owed to that organization. Liability is what the organization owes. This includes revenue that will be collected in the next fiscal year, also known as deferred revenue. It also includes any outstanding loans (Gross, Larkin, & McCarthy, 2000; Hankin, Seidner, & Zeitlow, 1998).

A simple balance sheet using MSMC as an example is included in Box 13.6. Notice that, despite its simplicity, several things about the organization's financial status can be learned at a glance. First, notice that there is considerably more cash on hand ($2,600) than was the case a year earlier. This is despite a $1,500 deficit in the contract payment from DCS. This deficit may exist for a number of reasons. Given the fact that $1,500 is exactly the amount of a monthly payment from DCS if the contracted number of clients are seen, it is likely that this figure represents one of three possibilities: (a) that no clients were referred for a month, (b) that DCS is one month ahead of the previous year in its payment schedule, or (c) DCS is one month behind the previous year in its payment schedule. There is, of course, the possibility that other factors, such as an irregular pattern of referrals over several months, has produced exactly a $1,500 deficit, but this is the least likely possibility.

The presence of such a discrepancy in a balance sheet should cause agency administrators and board members to investigate. Regardless of the cause of the income deficit there is an excess over the previous year in terms of assets despite a $300 decrease in the value of the agency's equipment category (probably due to depreciation). This is, of course, a positive development. It is even more positive if there is a monthly payment from DCS still outstanding.

Those who have dealt with state government will recognize that it is unlikely that DCS is ahead in its payment schedule. It is more likely that the agency is running behind or that fewer referrals have been received. Administrators and board members would find this a crucial distinction. Because the DCS contract represents almost 19% of the agency's income, organizational leaders would need to know whether referrals had decreased. If referrals had decreased, leaders would need to intervene with DCS administrators to remedy any problem that might have caused the agency to refer fewer clients. Further, because the majority of the referrals are court-ordered, agency leaders might want to check with the judge and the court staff to determine whether problems existed there. If referrals have followed the usual pattern and the $1,500 simply represents a lag in the payment schedule, administrators and board members might want to determine whether some problem exists in DCS's compensation system that may also delay future payments.

The Income Statement

The income statement, or statement of activities, shows an agency's income and expenses and taxes associated with those expenses for some financial period such as a month or a year. It is used to understand the way in which funds have come to the agency as well as to project future income and financial status (Gross, Larkin, & McCarthy, 2000; Hankin, Seidner, & Zeitlow, 1998). A sample income statement is included in Box 13.7.

Notice that the example is from 2003, the year before the balance sheet was developed. Therefore some of the numbers are different. A comparison of the figure from both documents reveals two interesting facts. First, many of the expenses and revenues for the organization have been remarkably consistent over a three-year period. This may mean that agency leaders should expect an increase in some categories such as rent and utilities in the near future. Second, it suggests that the executive director, the treasurer, or whoever is managing the funds is an excellent money manager, holding costs consistent over a three-year period.

You will remember that in the budget for 2004 there were more categories related to office expense and travel. In the 2003 income statement these expenses are condensed into single categories: office materials and transportation. Similarly, the salaries for both employees are grouped into a single category: salaries and benefits. Please note that despite the fact that this method simplifies the sheet, it provides substantially less information. Agency leaders are unable to learn how money was spent within each category without seeking additional information.

AUDIT

Social service organizations need to have an independent certified public accountant (CPA) who will prepare a formal report or audit of the organization annually. In general, nonprofit agencies with budgets over $100,000 are required to undergo an audit. However, it can be a useful tool to smaller agencies that are seeking additional funding. Funders, the government monitors, and other stakeholders often require a copy of the agency's most recent audit. An audit gives information about an organization's history, activities, and financial status, and usually compares the agency against the previous year. The audit contains components such as a balance sheet (or statement of position), an income statement (or statement of activities), and a statement on cash flow. Other important issues might also be reported in the audit, such as fundraising activities and functional or program expenses (Gross, Larkin, & McCarthy, 2000; Hankin, Seidner, & Zeitlow, 1998).

Reporting Requirements

Several forms need to be filled out every year so that a nonprofit agency can maintain its 501(c)(3) status. There are both federal and state forms to be filled out. Where states require that some form other than the federal forms be filed, each has its own that must be completed. The following is a list of the basic federal forms that are required:

| BOX 13.7 | A SAMPLE STATEMENT OF CASH RECEIPTS, DISBURSEMENTS, AND BALANCE: VICTIM-OFFENDER MEDIATION OF MADISON COUNTY |

	2003	
	Actual	Budget
Receipts		
Contract with DJJ	$30,000	$30,000
Contract with DCS	18,500	15,000
United Way grant	10,000	10,000
Police Confiscation Fund	10,000	10,000
Fundraising	28,800	27,500
Total receipts	$97,300	$95,500
Disbursements		
Salaries and benefits	$69,800	$69, 800
Rent	6,000	6,000
Utilities	1,500	1,500
Travel and transportation	5,060	5,060
Office materials	3,504	3,504
Dues and memberships	600	600
Accounting fees	240	240
Training materials	600	600
Appreciation banquet	500	500
Total disbursements	$95,500	$95,500
Excess of receipts over disbursements	$1,800	

1. Annual return: Most all nonprofit organizations are required to complete and file a 990. This gives the IRS information regarding the activities to show that the organization qualifies as tax-exempt. This form also reports income and expense data.
2. Employment taxes: Income tax, social security, and Medicare are withheld from salaries and paid to the IRS.
3. Other tax information returns: For someone who is not employed by an agency but is paid over $600 per year requires the agency to fill out Form 1099-MISC along with Form 1096. There are other forms that may need to be filled out regarding donations (Gross, Larkin, & McCarthy, 2000; Hankin, Seidner, & Zeitlow, 1998).

USING THE MACRO PRACTITIONER'S WORKBOOK

The Macro Practitioner's Workbook for this chapter will include the basic steps necessary to formulate a budget. This will help practitioners in three ways: (a) it will help middle- and lower-level administrators understand budgeting and allow them to explain their agency or program's budget to their staff, (b) it will help administrators interact with the consultants or staff who actually do the preparation, (c) it will help administrators in small-budget programs gain an understanding of what they must do in order to create and follow a budget. Use the case study for this unit to complete the worksheets.

SUMMARY

This chapter reviewed financial management. It is a process that goes beyond budgeting, but the process must be understood in order to grasp the way in which a budget fits into the overall financial picture of an organization. The chapter discussed the three types of budgets and described the steps to be taken when a budget is prepared. Methods of accounting were also reviewed. Finally, audits and reporting requirements were discussed. Practitioners must maintain a financially healthy agency in order to bring in funding, gain the support of the community, and most of all, further their agency's mission. This requires wise and careful budgeting as part of a sound overall financial plan.

Activities for Learning

1. Obtain a budget from a local agency or program. Look at the categories of income and expense. Is everything easy to recognize? Is anything difficult to understand? How detailed is the budget? What would you have done differently had you prepared it?
2. Obtain a local agency budget and a local program budget. Compare the two. How are they different? How are they similar? If they are from the same agency, are you able to see how the program's figures are incorporated into the agency's numbers? Why do you think this is the case?
3. The text discussed two types of accounting: accrual and cash based. Hold a debate in your classroom. One side should argue that accrual-based accounting is better. The other should support the use of cash-based accounting.

Questions for Discussion

1. The text stated that agencies typically use some combination of zero-based budgeting and incremental budgeting. Why do you think they choose to do this? Do you think it is a good idea, why or why not?
2. What advantages might there be to having an audit performed even if your agency budget is small enough that it is not required by law? What are some ways you might get this done on a pro bono basis? What are some ways you might use the results of an audit after it has been completed?

Key Terms

Accrual-based accounting— includes what an agency owes and what is owed to it, in addition to its actual income and expenses

Cash-based accounting— financial expenses and revenues are only recorded when the money is deposited or a check is written

Incremental budgeting—uses past information to make predictions about future expenses

Zero-based budgeting—sets each item of the budget at zero until it is justified for a specific dollar amount

References

Gross, M. J., Larkin, R. F., & McCarthy, J. H. (2000). *Financial and accounting guide for not-for-profit organizations*. New York: John Wiley and Sons.

Hankin, J. A., Seidner, A., & Zeitlow, J. (1998). *Financial management for nonprofit organizations*. New York: John Wiley and Sons.

Henke, E. O. (1980). *Introduction to nonprofit organization accounting*. Boston: Kent Publishing Company.

WORKSHEET 13.1 | PLANNING A BUDGET

1. List the categories of expense you expect to receive during the coming year (remember the sample list included in Box 13.2).

   Directors Salery
   Adminstative staff Saleey
   Rent
   utilities
   Telephone
   Computers

   Office supplies
   Postage
   Training materials
   Accounting Fees
   Program Expenses

2. Fill in the dollar amount of the expenses you expect to experience in each category.

3. List the categories of income you expect to have during the coming year (remember the sample list included in Box 13.3).

   dues
   Grants from United Way
   annuel Fund raiser
   direct mail campaigns
   Local donations
   Contract with other agencies

4. Fill in the dollar amount of income you anticipate receiving in each category.

5. Record the figures you have obtained into a form like the example provided in Box 13.4.

14 CHAPTER WRITING A GOVERNMENT GRANT PROPOSAL

CHAPTER OUTLINE

The Grant Process

Where to Find Government Grants

What Are They Looking For?

Preparing to Write a Grant Proposal

Essential Parts of a Proposal

After the Proposal Has Been Written

Using the Macro Practitioner's Workbook

Summary

In this chapter, methods of finding announcements of government grants and writing proposals to receive funding from them will be covered. Finding government grants is not an easy task, but the rewards can be tremendous. They involve a great deal of preparation, a tremendous amount of paperwork, and a challenging amount of teamwork. They do, however, offer substantial sums of money that may continue over a period of several years. These dollars and the continuity associated with them can help to ensure the stability of the agency or community initiative and the services they provide over a period of several years.

Grant awards in which the government is **grantor** are typically more substantial than for other grants, but this comes at a price. The contracts that result from these grants often require substantial paperwork and frequent monitoring. Before writing a proposal, it is important to be certain that your agency or initiative is a good fit for both the grant and the **grantor**, and also that you have a full understanding of what will be required if you receive the award. Agencies have been known to apply for funding, be delighted to be notified that they have received the award, and then be dismayed when they realized that they would have to pay hundreds of thousands of dollars in

BOX 14.1	GOVERNMENT GRANT WRITING FOR COMMUNITY PRACTITIONERS

Community practitioners should be cautious in their selection of partners in the process of application for federal grants. First, and perhaps obviously, it is important that they choose organizations that have a high probability of success. For example, agencies that have received prior funding and have managed it well are known to funders and have a greater likelihood of receiving funds than those who have not. Additionally, agencies that have demonstrated a long record of competent financial management and who utilize volunteers and collaborative partnerships are particularly well regarded by federal funding sources. A second important consideration is the ease of working with a sponsoring organization. Because the government is likely to require that an established 301(c)(3) corporation or some unit of government receive the funds directly, a positive working relationship between the practitioner and the finance department of that organization can be critical. A third consideration is whether an organization's bureaucratic structure may make it difficult to receive funds in a timely manner. These situations should be avoided whenever possible.

---

advance due to the quarterly reimbursement system under which the grant would be operated. These factors have particular significance for community practitioners and are discussed in greater detail in Box 14.1.

Government agencies offer strict sets of instructions in the documents they use to announce their offerings. These documents are known as Requests for Proposals (RFPs) and typically provide a full explanation of the requirements and expectations of the agency. There is usually a person at the agency who can provide verbal or written responses to questions applicants may have.

This chapter contains basic information on the grant process, locating government grants, the work that should be done to prepare a proposal, and the actual preparation of a proposal. Many, if not most, government agencies now provide either a physical application form or an electronic template that can be followed to complete the application. The worksheets to the exercises in this chapter are based on those guidelines. When applying for an actual grant, however, it is important to determine precisely what the funder is looking for and to follow its guidelines. If you fail to do so, you may automatically disqualify your agency.

Government grants are usually very exacting. Guidelines must be closely followed. Deadlines must be met precisely. Every required form must be included and must be submitted along with the application. Many RFPs contain lists of "fatal flaws," or problems in the application that result in its immediate rejection by the funder. These must be avoided at all costs. Even though funding has declined in recent years, the federal government continues to be the largest resource for external funding (Brody & Nair, 2002). It therefore represents an important source of potential revenue for agencies, making it critical that practitioners understand and be able to participate successfully in the funding process.

THE GRANT PROCESS

When government funds become available, the agencies that control them put out a notice of their availability, which is typically referred to as a funding announcement. The announcement contains a brief description of the activities for which the funding is available, the name of the agency from which it will be distributed, and information on how to obtain a RFP. The RFP is an application packet that contains instructions and all the forms that must be completed and submitted in order to be considered for funding. RFPs may contain different types of information, but almost always include the following: (a) the details of the grant, (b) the amount of the grant award, (c) the period of time for which the funding will be offered, (d) information about who is eligible to receive funding, (e) a format or template for the proposal, and (f) a list of the restrictions involved in submitting a proposal.

WHERE TO FIND GOVERNMENT GRANTS

Government grants come from all levels of government: local, state, and federal. There are several different resources that provide information about when grant money becomes available. A few of the sources that can help you locate available funds include:

1. Funding Directories: These directories offer up-to-date information on grants.
2. Federal Register: The **Federal Register** is a publication that announces selected grant programs, among other things.
3. Catalog of Federal Domestic Assistance: The **Catalog of Federal Domestic Assistance** is a reference on federal programs that assists the American public. This database gives a variety of information about funding that has been awarded, contact names, deadlines, and how to apply for funding. It can often be found at the public library or through government offices.
4. Federal Assistance Programs Retrieval System (FAPRS): FAPRS is a computerized service that provides immediate access to information from the Catalog of Federal Domestic Assistance.
5. The Commerce Business Daily: The Commerce Business Daily lists contract awards and RFPs. Based on information from this publication, federal agencies can be identified and application packets can be requested.

WHAT ARE THEY LOOKING FOR?

All funders, including government agencies, are looking for specific items in a grant proposal. They are entrusted with large sums of money and will, in turn, entrust that money to others. They want to be sure that those who receive the funds will be capable of using the funds in an effective, efficient, and responsible manner. Typically, funders look for several characteristics in those to whom money will be granted. In this section we will talk about each of those characteristics and the ways in which agencies can demonstrate that they have them.

One of the characteristics funders seek in potential grant recipients is a *thorough understanding of the problem* the grant funds are intended to address. The problem statement should include information about what the problem is, how it affects those who experience it, how pervasive the problem is, and how the problem impacts the community or society at large. An applicant, for example, who explains child abuse as solely the result of broken families is unlikely to receive support. That applicant will have failed to demonstrate a grasp of the multiple, interrelated factors that contribute to the abuse of children.

A second feature applicants must demonstrate is a *knowledge of interventions that have been shown to be effective in addressing the problem.* Creativity is often welcome in grant applications. However, that creativity is rarely welcome in a vacuum. If a creative program is offered and a rational explanation for why it might work is included, the proposal has a reasonable probability of being accepted. The most appealing intervention will be one that has been empirically tested and shown to be effective in some other venue.

Today virtually every government funder places a heavy emphasis on *outcomes*. It is not enough to simply deliver services. The services must produce positive

GOVERNMENT GRANT WRITING
FOR COMMUNITY PRACTITIONERS

Community practitioners who are preparing a grant proposal in support of their initiative must remember that they need to convince funders that both the agency through which they apply and their initiative are attractive. It may be easy to focus on one or the other, neglecting to provide critical information that might sway decision makers. When writing a proposal, make a checklist of the factors that make applications attractive to funders. Then review your proposal to ensure that each factor is addressed for both the agency that will manage the funds as well as for the initiative as a whole.

---

changes in the lives of those who receive them. The changes must be clear, measurable, and theoretically and observably connected to the intervention.

Sustainability is another important characteristic of a desirable funding applicant. Sustainability has at least two important dimensions. One of those has to do with the stability of the agency. Funders will not initiate a grant process with an organization that is likely to vanish before the funding period is over. The second dimension has to do with the degree of support that exists in the community. Many government grants are designed to help a program get started. The funders want to know that financial support is likely to be available from the local community to support the proposed program once the state or federal funding period has ended.

Yet another factor in funding decisions is *fit*. Funders look for a fit between their mission and that of applicants. Fit also includes the philosophical and theoretical approaches of the potential partners, that is, whether the general approach to service delivery of the agency is consistent and compatible with those who make decisions within the funding agency.

Agencies should be honest and straightforward in representing their position in each of these areas. It is critical, however, that the applicant submit its request in a *language* the funder will appreciate and understand. "Language," of course, is not meant literally. Rather, it refers to the group of terms and expressions commonly used by the employees of the funding organization when they talk about the problem, interventions, outcomes, and other aspects of the grant. It is important, for example, when interacting with a funder that strongly believes in community-based intervention and evaluation, that the terms related to those activities are used liberally but appropriately in the grant proposal (Brody & Nair, 2000; Karsh & Fox, 2003; U.S. Government, 2003).

As with other aspects of federal grant funding, community practitioners must look at the factors described in this section in a slightly different way. Tips regarding applicant attractiveness to funders are included in Box 14.2.

PREPARING TO WRITE A GRANT PROPOSAL

There are several things to do before actually writing your proposal. Many first-time writers hope to win the confidence of funders with good intentions and hard work. Although both are important, they are unlikely to be adequate to win a grant award. However, several other steps can greatly enhance your probability of success.

1. *Learn to write like successful grant writers.* Creative writers have a special way of expressing themselves, as do journalists and scientists. If any member of one of those groups wishes to write for another group (for example, a scientist for a newspaper), he must change the way in which he writes to accommodate that audience. Funders also expect to hear

ideas expressed in a certain way. Prospective grant writers must learn to write in that manner. There are several ways to learn to write grants. Local colleges and universities may offer classes or workshops. Books that offer helpful hints are available. Experienced grant writers are often willing to offer mentoring and advice.

2. *Research your area.* There is little that is more embarrassing in the world of funding than to propose an idea that has already failed or else to make a broad statement about a problem that has already been proven to be untrue. Either is likely to be the death of a proposal. Research should include a review of the scientific literature, an investigation of reports from government sources, and information gained from Internet searches.

3. *Explore possible funding resources.* Use the resources mentioned earlier in this chapter to identify possible sources of support. Compose a master list of potential funders including the requirements and deadlines of each. Determine the funders that would be realistic possibilities to which you might target a proposal.

4. *Network in your community.* Funders will want to know several things about your community. They will want to know how badly the services you are recommending are needed and wanted there. They will want to know the degree to which your agency is respected and supported locally. By getting to know others in the community, you will be able to garner their support for your proposal.

5. *Identify collaborative partners.* You will need to identify agencies within your community who will participate with you in the grant. These agencies may actually partner with you in service delivery, share in the funds from the grant, or provide some sort of ancillary services. You will need letters of agreement from those who will share in the grant funds and letters of support from others. If you are a community practitioner, draw heavily on your partnerships and seek others who might bring new strengths to the initiative.

6. *Develop your proposal ideas and practice writing them.* It will be important that your grant proposal be written clearly and succinctly. You can facilitate this process through practice. Write your ideas again and again until they become clear. Don't hesitate to ask for the help of others. They may be able to help you clarify your thoughts.

It is vital that your proposal is professional and shows an understanding of the contributions of science to the problem area. It should also be concise and easy to follow. Separate the sections with attractively labeled tabs where it is possible and appropriate to do so. Be sure to reference supportive materials in appropriate places in the text (Brody & Nair, 2000; Karsh & Fox, 2003; U.S. Government, 2003).

ESSENTIAL PARTS OF A PROPOSAL

This list was developed by Coley and Scheinberg (2000) for their book, *Proposal Writing.*

Cover Letter and Opening

The cover letter is a summary of the entire proposal. It briefly introduces you and your agency and communicates the basics of your project to the funder. The cover letter is also a chance to demonstrate the professionalism of your agency and show that it is capable of achieving its goals and objectives. This letter should indicate interest in being funded and give the funder contact

| BOX 14.3 | SAMPLE PROGRAM DESCRIPTION |

Goal 1

The "Transitions" program will enable youth in state custody in Doe County to have the skills that are needed to live independently once they have "aged out" of the foster care system.

Objective 1.1

Forty-five youth, ages 16 to 18, in foster care, who participate in the "Transitions" program will increase their knowledge of independent living skills by 40% as measured by the Casey Life Skills Assessment between September 1, 2002 and August 31, 2003 through participation in independent living classes.

Program Design 1.1

To accomplish this objective, each of the 45 youth living in foster homes will attend two 90-minute life skills classes each month over the course of the year,

resulting in 36 annual hours of formal classroom learning per youth. Classes will be taught to groups of 15 at each of the congregate adolescent homes by the assigned independent living specialist. The 24-lesson curriculum that will be used is the Casey Life Skills Curriculum, published by the Casey Foundation. This curriculum covers six domains of independent living: daily living skills, housing and community resources, money management, self-care, social development, and work and study skills. In the first month of the project, independent living specialists will administer the Casey Life Skills Assessment to determine the current knowledge of each participant. Independent living specialists will work with each youth to create a Personal Development Plan (PDP) based on assessment scores and client input to determine participant strengths and goals.

---

information for the agency. The cover letter should be concise and powerful. It is important to remember that it should provide a summary that will interest its reader in going further.

Needs Statement/Problem Statement

The first major section of a grant proposal is typically a discussion of the problem or needs that the proposed project will address. This section should describe the problem, the people who experience the problem, the ways in which those people are affected by the problem, the pervasiveness of the problem, and the ways in which the problem affects the community as a whole. It should also identify the geographical area in which the problem occurs, providing a description of the boundaries (for example, streets, rivers, or county lines) that will define the service area.

The problem statement should use scientific and professional literature to support the claims it makes. Statistics should be available regarding the number of people in the community who experience the problem and the degree to which they are affected by it. There should also be information available about the factors that cause or contribute to the problem. These factors should be cited in the problem statement and the relationship between them explained. This will lay the groundwork for the initiative that will be proposed in a later section of the proposal.

In summary, the problem or needs statement should carefully and succinctly define the issue the applicant wants to change. It should indicate exactly who the target audience is, the specific issue that will be addressed, and the geographic location that will benefit. It should also clearly explain why the problem exists. It is insufficient to say, "Child Abuse exists in X County because there are no child abuse prevention services." It should explain what is known about the source of the problem. In the case of child abuse, factors such as poverty, lack of education, and teen pregnancy contribute to the problem. Whenever possible the statement should also describe the way in which the problem affects the community as a whole, for example, increased tax money, increased juvenile crime, or excessive medical care rates.

Project Description

The project description is the explanation of the project the applicant is proposing. It provides the details of the intervention, a description of the manner in which it will be implemented, the goals and objectives of the project, and a time line showing when the various tasks of the project will be completed. Although this section must be thorough, it should also be brief and to the point. It is often helpful to include staffing diagrams and flow charts. These visual aids can help the funder see how the plan fits together, demonstrating that it has been thought through carefully.

Goal Statement and Objectives

The goal statement should be broad and should incorporate the ideals of your mission. Objectives should be measurable increments that will lead to the accomplishment of each goal. The objectives should then be tied to the program description, which will clearly demonstrate how the program will accomplish the objectives and thus cause the goal to be met. More extensive information about developing goals and objectives can be found in chapter 1.

The goal statement may include more than one type of objective. The two most likely types are process objectives and impact objectives. These are sometimes known under other names. For example, process objectives may also be called service objectives and impact objectives may be referred to as outcome objectives.

Process objectives are standards that must be met in terms of the activity of either agency or initiative employees or clients. One example would be the number of new clients that will be seen during a year or during the grant period. Another might be the number of units of service to be delivered. Other examples include the number of classes conducted, the number of training sessions provided, and the number of referrals an agency hopes to achieve. Process objectives do several things. Process objectives: (a) explain the expected changes in agency procedures, (b) calculate the utilization of services, and (c) project how much of each service will be received. Process objectives do not describe the change that will occur in the target population.

Impact objectives are typically more important than process objectives. Although it is necessary to see an adequate number of clients and to ensure that the projected change is sufficiently broad enough to justify the grant award, the more critical issue to many funders is the degree to which the recipients of the funded services will experience positive life changes. Impact objectives describe the specific outcomes that will be achieved due to the intervention that the applicant's program will provide. These usually start with statements such as "to reduce" or "to increase." An example might be "to reduce the teenage pregnancy rate among African American females ages 12–17 in X county by 15% in 2 years." The goals must be realistic and must be supported by objectives that are in turn supported by program activities. Impact objectives are typically directed toward: (a) change in attitudes or beliefs, (b) increase in knowledge, (c) increase in skill, or (d) improvement in behavior.

Program Activities

In this section the plan of action should be detailed. The steps to implementation, such as hiring, training, establishing office space, and marketing must be clearly explained. Each of these steps should be associated to a time line. The people responsible for each activity should also be identified as well as the method that will be used to ensure that the tasks are completed. You should carefully lay out how many hours each staff person (or, for community practitioners, each collaborative partner) will dedicate to the program. In addition, show how this program fits in with all programs at your agency or those of partner agencies.

Evaluation Plan

Funders require grant recipients to furnish evidence that their goals have been met. To do this, it is necessary to describe exactly how the success or failure of each objective will be measured. The evaluation plan must include a data collection strategy, a discussion of the projected methods of data analysis, and a plan for disseminating the results. An evaluation plan is a highly technical process that may be beyond the expertise of the person preparing the proposal. If this is the case, the applicant may want to include an outside person or organization who will be able to both design and implement the evaluation.

Budget Request

The budget request itemizes the expenditures of the project and includes a justification for the expenses. The applicant must decide what type of budget to use: line item or function. The processes of budget development described in chapter 13 should then be followed. A budget narrative is then written to explain and justify the budget.

Capability of the Agency

This section is intended to satisfy the concerns of the funder regarding the sustainability of the project, the stability of the agency, and the competency of the agency to perform the proposed tasks. It explains who the agency is and why it is qualified to implement the project successfully. It uses the applicant's past performance and current situation to demonstate its stability and capability. A good capability statement includes: (a) history and background of the organization, (b) significant accomplishments, (c) resources available, and (d) strengths of the organization or initiative.

Future Funding Plans

The statement regarding future funding plans indicates the agency or initiative's ability to continue the project beyond the requested funding project. Grantors want to know that their investment will be sustainable. Support from such organizations as the United Way, local governments, foundations, or corporations will be helpful. The applicant should provide a detailed plan, or contingency plan (see chapters 2 & 3), to explain how the program will be funded after the grant period.

Letters of Support

This section should include letters from prominent people and organizations in the community that reflect support for the proposed project. These letters should come from a variety of stakeholders, such as program recipients, community leaders, agencies, schools, and faith-based organizations. Some should show in-kind (nonmonetary) support. If working with other agencies, memoranda of understandings should be included to show that the relationships exist and that the roles of each are clearly understood.

| BOX 14.4 | ESSENTIAL PARTS OF A PROPOSAL |

1. Cover letter and opening
2. Needs statement/problem statement
3. Project description
4. Goal statement and objectives
5. Program activities
6. Evaluation plan
7. Budget request
8. Capability of the agency
9. Future funding plans
10. Letters of support
11. Appendix materials

Source: Coley, S. M., & Scheinberg, C. A. (2000). *Proposal Writing.* Thousand Oaks, CA: Sage.

Appendix Materials

Funders may request a variety of other materials such as an audited financial statement, insurance, or other documentation. Applicants should develop and use a checklist to ensure that they include everything that the funders ask for. Not doing so could make all the difference in getting funding and may well constitute a fatal flaw in the application. In addition, omitting a required item may been seen as a negative statement with regard to an applicant's professionalism and competency.

AFTER THE PROPOSAL HAS BEEN WRITTEN

Be sure to have several people read over the proposal. Ask them to make comments and suggestions, as well as correct grammar and spelling. If the proposed project is a collaborative effort, each of the partners should have the opportunity to comment. It is also often helpful to have a proposal read by someone who knows little about the problem area. A novice can often point out places where meaning has become lost, or where the writer has been unclear for other reasons. The proposal should be simple to read, easy to follow, and free from grammatical errors.

USING THE MACRO PRACTITIONER'S WORKBOOK

The Macro Practitioner's Workbook for this section will require more creativity and invention than it has in other chapters. In this case, you should use the case study for this unit for basic information about the agency that will be applying for the grant, but then you must imagine the problem, come up with a program to address it, and provide other information in order to complete a sample grant application. Worksheet 14.1 will lead you through the process.

SUMMARY

In this chapter the government grant process was reviewed. Most grantors issue RFPs that detail what must be included in a proposal. Finding grants as well as what government funders are looking for was also discussed. In addition, the process of preparing to write a proposal was examined. Time spent in careful and strategic planning will save you time in the long run. Finally, the essential parts of a proposal were reviewed, including: (a) the cover letter and opening, (b) the needs/problem statement, (c) the project description, (d) the evaluation plan, (e) the budget request, (f) the agency capability statement, (g) future funding plans, (h) letters of support, and (i) appendix materials. Future chapters will discuss the submission of other kinds of grant proposals.

Activities for Learning

1. Working in a small group, search the Federal Register for funding announcements. What kinds of announcements does it contain? How did you find the announcements that relate to your area of interest? How could you use this document to find funds for your agency? Report the results of your work to the class.
2. Practice your problem description skills. Referring back to chapter 1 for guidance, write problem descriptions for three social problems that affect people in your area. Then use the steps in the Macro Practitioner's Workbook to complete a problem description for each that you might choose to include in a grant proposal.
3. Have a discussion in class about writing the evaluation portion of a grant proposal. Who would be qualified to write the section? How might you find such a person? Would you want the same person who wrote the section to actually perform the evaluation, why or why not?

Questions for Discussion

1. Why would agencies want to seek outside funding to create additional programs? What are the advantages to doing so? What are the disadvantages?
2. What state-level grant opportunities are available in your community? How might you find out about others?
3. Who are some people in your community that you should get to know in order to help you develop grant proposals?

Key Terms

Catalog of Federal Domestic Assistance—a database of information on federal programs including funding that has been awarded, contact names, deadlines, and how to apply for funding

Federal Register—a publication that announces selected grant programs, among other things

Grantor—the agency that provides grant funding

References

Brody, R., & Nair, M. D. (2000). *Macro practice: A generalist approach* (5th Ed.). Wheaton, IL: Gregory Publishing Company.

Coley, S. M., & Sheinberg, C. A. (2000). *Proposal writing*. Thousand Oaks, CA: Sage.

Karsh, E., & Fox, A. S. (2003). *The only grant-writing book you'll ever need: Top grant writers and grant givers share their secrets*. New York: Carrol and Graf Publishers.

U.S. Government. (2003). *2003 guide to federal grants and government assistance to small business—Catalog of federal domestic assistance, loans, grants, surplus equipment, SBA, GSA, SEC information for entrepreneurs, startup kit, loan programs, financing, law, regulations, reports, workbooks—Applying for federal assistance* (CD-ROM). New York: Progressive Management.

WORKSHEET 14.1 | WRITING A GRANT PROPOSAL

Cover Letter and Opening

1. Prepare a letter in proper business form addressed to the funder.

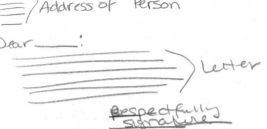

2. Compose a paragraph introducing your agency.

3. Compose a paragraph summarizing the program you will be proposing.

4. Compose a paragraph indicating your interest in being funded and providing contact information for yourself and your agency.

    We are very interested in learning more about funding that may be provided by your organization; I would greatly appreciate and information you may be able to provide to me. My mailing address is ———

Needs Statement/Problem Statement

1. Write a brief description of the problem. (See the guidelines for problem statements in chapter 1.)

2. List the groups that experience the problem. If your project will focus on a subgroup, identify that subgroup.

> Hispanic
> African American
> Elderly

3. Explain the ways in which those who experience the problem are disadvantaged.

> Because our clientel is composed mostly of immgrants of Hispanic orgin and African American

4. Describe the pervasiveness of the problem.

> most all unemployed, with little or no education

5. Describe the ways in which the problem affects the community as a whole.

> Because we work with families who have many needs.

6. Identify the geographical area in which the problem occurs.

> Aoldesburg is a small rural community, that is isolotated, and there is no public transporation

7. Use the information gathered in this section to write a two or three paragraph problem description.

Project Description

1. Write a brief summary of the initiative being proposed.

2. Write a description of the manner in which the project will be implemented.

3. Determine what visual aids might be helpful to your proposal and prepare them.

Goal and Objective Statement

1. What are your goals for the project?

2. What process objectives will be needed to reach those goals?

3. What impact objectives will be needed to reach those goals?

4. Describe the way in which the program activities will support the goals and objectives.

5. Organize the above information into an outline or matrix form.

Program Activities

1. Identify the steps that must be taken in order to implement the proposed program.

2.   Generate a time line that includes each of those activities.

3.   Identify the person who will be responsible for each activity and the way that person will report the results of his work.

Evaluation Plan

1.   Identify the person or agency that will be responsible for completing your evaluation.

2.   Explain your research plan and design for completing your evaluation.

3.   Describe your plan for disseminating the results of your evaluation.

4. Describe your plan for reporting the results to your grant monitor.

Budget Request

1. Use the information in chapter 13 to prepare a budget for the proposed project.

2. Write a four or five paragraph budget narrative justifying the items in your budget.

Capability of the Agency

1. Describe the history of the agency including the number of years it has been operating, the types of programs it has offered, and the types of collaborative relationships it has developed.

2. Describe the key personnel of the agency, including those who will be responsible for overseeing the activities of the proposed program. (For a real-world proposal you would include a copy of the résumé of each of these people.)

3. List any significant accomplishments of the agency.

4. Describe the size of the agency, its budget, and its resources.

5. Identify the strengths of the organization.

Future Funding Plans

1. Include information about local reaction to the proposal from such organizations as the United Way, local governments, foundations, and corporations.

2. Develop and record a contingency plan for continuing to fund the program after the grant period has ended.

Letters of Support

1. Attach letters of support from prominent local people and organizations.

2. Attach memoranda of understanding from agencies with which you will partner.

Appendix Materials

1. Prepare a checklist of every item required by the prospective funder.

2. Collect and include the required items as appendices.

15 CHAPTER

WRITING A FOUNDATION INQUIRY LETTER

CHAPTER OUTLINE

What Is a Foundation?

Trends in Foundation Giving

Finding the Right Fit

Doing Preapproach Research

Writing the Letter of Inquiry

What to Do after Submitting the Letter of Inquiry

Using the Macro Practitioner's Workbook

Summary

Writing an effective letter of inquiry can be even more difficult than writing a full grant proposal. This is because there is so much to be done in just a few pages. First, you have to capture the funder's attention. You must demonstrate that you have done your homework. You must convince the decision makers that they are a good fit for your organization. You must also demonstrate a need for funding and cause them to believe that your organization or initiative can achieve its goals. Of course, along with all this you must describe the program. All this needs to be achieved in 2–3 pages. A challenging task it is indeed!

In this chapter, philanthropic foundations are introduced and how to approach them will be discussed. Seeking foundation funding can be a time-consuming process, and time is a precious commodity in social service management. Many sections of this chapter will explain ways to enhance your search, minimizing the time requirement and maximizing the results. This chapter examines how to narrow your search to find the funders that are most appropriate for your agency and its mission. Finally, how to write an approach letter to a foundation and what to do after the letter has been sent will be discussed. Foundations are an excellent way to bring in money to support your agency's mission. Understanding how to approach a foundation can enhance your probability of success.

WHAT IS A FOUNDATION?

A foundation is a nongovernmental, nonprofit organization whose purpose is to make grants to nonprofit organizations with a 501(c)(3) designation. There are nearly 62,000 grant making foundations in the United States. A board of trustees or a board of directors manages the funds and programs of each. Foundations assist in charitable, social, religious, educational, or other activities in a community by providing financial support and technical assistance.

There are different types of foundations. It is important to understand the various nuances of each in order to determine which funding sources might be most appropriate for your organization (The Foundation Center, 2004a).

Private/Independent Foundation

A private or independent foundation manages a fund or endowment identified by law. The primary function of a private foundation is funding grants. Funds in a private foundation generally come from a gift of an individual or family. For this reason, these foundations are sometimes referred to as family foundations. Private foundations generally narrow their giving to a specific field such as public health, early childhood education, science and technology, the environment, or similar causes.

Corporate Foundation

Corporate foundations have a tendency to award grants in the geographic areas where their businesses are located. Often a grant needs to be tied to an employee. For example, an employee of the business needs to be on the board or volunteer for the organization in order for an organization to receive consideration for funding. By law, a corporate foundation is a private foundation that gets its funds from a corporation or company.

Community Foundation

Community foundations are not classified as a foundation under IRS standards. Instead, they are categorized as a public charity. Community foundations tend to receive and administer funds in a specific geographic area and tend to have various sources of income from a wide variety of donors. A community foundation is organized for the benefit of a specific geographic area. Rather than focus on a specific cause, community foundations focus on the needs of a specific local area.

TRENDS IN FOUNDATION GIVING

Government funding for programs has been on the decline due to recent economic conditions. However, foundation funding has stayed at relatively the same level. According to The Foundation Center's Foundation Growth and Giving Estimates: 2003 Preview, grant awards have taken only a slight drop over the last two years. At the time this book was written the Center expects an improving economy to result in increases during 2004. The Foundation Center (2004a) also found other interesting data:

1. There was a 9.2% increase in the number of active foundations. There were 5,200 new foundations created in 2001.
2. Funding by community foundations increased by 2.6% in 2002. While this is positive, it was the smallest growth in giving by community foundations since 1994. This was a direct result of the decline in donor gift levels.

3. Funding by corporate foundations increased by 2.2% in 2002. Corporate foundations donated $3.4 billion to organizations in 2002.
4. Funding by private foundations decreased by 1.5% in 2002. These types of foundations make up a majority of the number of foundations and comprise the majority of funding. While private foundations gave $23.7 billion in 2001, funding dropped to approximately $23.3 billion in 2002. Considering the drop in the stock market and the assets for these organizations, this decline in funding was less than anticipated.

It is important to understand these trends in order to make good decisions about what sources of funding should be approached. Understanding the level of competition for funds and the ability of specific foundations to donate can help practitioners strategize to ensure that their efforts have the greatest probability of being rewarded.

FINDING THE RIGHT FIT

As was discussed earlier, obtaining foundation funding can be a time-consuming process. If it is not done properly, it can waste valuable time and exhaust and disappoint staff. In order to avoid these problems, practitioners must determine which foundations would be most likely to fund the proposed project (Brody & Nair, 2000; The Foundation Center, 2004c). Foundations tend to award grants based on three primary categories.

Geographic Proximity

Many private foundations only award grants in specific parts of the country. For example, a foundation may focus on the southeastern United States. They may only fund programs in a certain state or other geographic area. It would be a complete waste of time, energy, and postage to send proposals to foundations that do not fund in your geographic area. Corporate foundations also tend to award money in those areas where they have large numbers of employees. Community foundations are set up specifically to fund services in their community.

Similar Mission or Goals

All foundations should have a mission statement. Before you approach a foundation, read its mission statement carefully and examine what types of organizations and programs have been funded in the past. You must determine whether your proposal would assist the foundation in furthering its mission. Many foundations fund specific causes such as the environment, women's issues, or HIV/AIDS awareness and prevention. It is important to be sure that your agency's mission is consistent with that of the foundation before proceeding.

Natural Connections

A foundation may have a natural connection to a certain organization by the nature of what they do. A foundation funded by a business that provides products for mothers may be naturally inclined to fund programs related to children or women. A relationship with someone at the foundation is not a guarantee, but it can certainly help to lend credibility to the proposal. Many foundations do not accept unsolicited letters. In these cases, the foundation actually seeks out organizations it is interested in funding.

DOING PREAPPROACH RESEARCH

One of the most critical parts of seeking foundation funding is the preapproach research. There are thousands of foundations who provide funding to thousands of causes. Many of these foundations, however, are exacting with the projects they fund. The most wonderful proposal to prevent child abuse is likely to be rejected by a foundation committed to funding projects for elders. Others may be willing to fund only building projects or may forbid any portion of their award to be used for salaries. Failure to understand the guidelines under which foundations operate can result in repeated frustration and failure for even the most persistent of applicants.

To ensure that their efforts are as efficient as possible, practitioners should learn as much as possible about the way foundations they will approach do business. Because of the plethora of foundations and the variety of standards each uses, it is often a good idea to develop a form on which the critical information about each can be recorded. The completed forms can be used to help the applicant identify those foundations that are the best match and therefore are the most likely to be receptive to the applicant's proposal. There are excellent examples of these forms available in several places. An excellent form can be found on The Foundation Center's website (fdncenter.org/). This form should contain basic information about the foundation, such as the name, address, and the person to whom the letter of inquiry should be addressed. It should also consider the range of funding the foundation typically awards, as well as the time line for proposals. The form should also have space for the foundation's areas of interest, the geographical areas in which it funds, and the type of support it typically provides. A space for additional comments will allow the researcher to note whether the foundation has application forms, the date of its deadline, and other important information (Brody & Nair, 2000).

There are several options for locating foundations and for finding the information needed to complete the research form. These options include:

1. Foundation websites.
2. The Foundation Center's online directory: fconline.fdncenter.org.
3. 990-PFs—every private foundation is required to file a 990-PF by the IRS every year. This form will give you basic financial information, information on the foundation and their board of directors, and some data on the grants they have funded. For several foundations, this may be your only source of information. This information can be found on The Foundation Center's website and at www.Guidestar.com.
4. Foundation directories often give information about the foundations but do not tell as much about the programs that they have funded. In addition, there are often directories that are specific to certain fields, such as the arts or the environment.
5. Public libraries offer a wealth of information about grants, and many libraries have specific sections on this topic.
6. Annual reports of foundations.

WRITING THE LETTER OF INQUIRY

You can prepare to write the letter of inquiry once you have done your homework and identified the foundations that are a good fit for your organization. First you will need to see if there are any guidelines for letters of inquiry and gather any data and attachments needed by the foundation. The letter of inquiry will give foundations an opportunity to see whether they are interested in the proposal.

Things to remember when writing a letter of inquiry:

1. Make every word count: don't use jargon or flowery language
2. Be specific and thoughtful
3. Follow their guidelines, make a checklist and review it several times
4. Avoid grammatical errors, these take away from your credibility and make your agency seem unprofessional
5. Use the active voice
6. Keep sentences simple
7. Have several people proofread your letter for grammar and content, and be sure to have someone read it who is unaffiliated with your organization to see if someone with no background with your organization's goals can understand your program

Format for the Letter of Inquiry

Following the appropriate format will enhance your proposal's probability of acceptance. Many foundations have their own format or template that will be sent on request. The following is a modification of the format proposed by The Foundation Center (2004a).

Salutation   Be sure to address your letter to an individual and not to "To Whom It May Concern." This will immediately show reviewers that you have researched their organization and have put time into learning about them.

Overview of the Organization   This is your first paragraph. Your opening statement needs to grab their attention and let them know why they should be interested in giving time to your request. It is important to answer the foundation's questions up front. Let them know how much you are requesting, when you will have the program operational, and why they should be interested. Show why your proposed initiative will further the mission of the foundation. Show them that you and your program are a good fit.

Needs Statement   A needs statement explains what the problem is and why it needs to be addressed. You should clearly articulate who will benefit from this program and explain what society as a whole will gain. The foundation needs to know that your agency has a clear understanding of the problem and must be convinced of the severity of the need.

Project Description   The project description is where you give the funders a general overview of your project. The project description summarizes the solution to the problem described in the needs statement. This is the time to explain why your program is unique and what evidence you have that it will be successful. The project description should also briefly state the desired outcomes and explain the evaluation plan.

Budget   This section should include a budget summary that describes the amount of money being requested and the general ways in which it will be applied. Unlike a government grant in which the budget and budget narrative may consume two to three pages, the budget summary in an inquiry letter to a foundation should not exceed a single paragraph. This section should also include information about others who support the program, particularly those who provide financial support or will in the future.

WRITING A FOUNDATION INQUIRY LETTER

Agency Credibility   This section, composed of about one paragraph, is designed to demonstrate that your agency is capable of achieving the stated goals and outcomes. Foundations want to make a good investment with their money. It may be helpful to list awards or other honors that showcase the agency's competence. You may also want to mention the partnerships and collaborative ventures in which you have participated.

The Grand Finale   In your closing statement, ask permission to submit a full proposal to the foundation. Ask for their guidelines and an application. Be sure to give them a contact name and information for a follow-up. Let the foundation know that you will be available to answer any questions. Finally, express your appreciation for the opportunity to work with the foundation and thank them for their time.

Attachments   If the foundation does not require attachments with an approach letter, they should be kept to a minimum. At most you might include a brochure or some other promotional material. You should include a copy of your letter of determination from the IRS certifying 501(c)(3) status. Some foundations may request specific attachments, such as an audit or other items. Be sure to submit everything that is requested. If you do not follow the instructions of the foundation, you risk immediate rejection of your proposal.

WHAT TO DO AFTER SUBMITTING THE LETTER OF INQUIRY

If your letter receives a negative response, ask the foundation for suggestions on how to improve your work in the future. If your letter of inquiry results in the foundation's request for a formal proposal, this will be your next step. The foundation should provide basic guidelines to follow in the development of your proposal. The information provided in chapter 14 on writing government grant proposals should also be useful here. Some foundations will not require a full proposal. Instead, they may schedule a visit to your agency to discuss, explore, and plan.

USING THE MACRO PRACTITIONER'S WORKBOOK

The Macro Practitioner's Workbook for this chapter focuses on the development of an inquiry letter. Use the case study for this unit to complete the worksheet. When you prepare the letter, assume that you have identified a foundation that is a good fit for your agency and your proposal. Write the letter as though it is being submitted to that organization.

SUMMARY

In this chapter, foundations as a source of income for nonprofit organizations were discussed. Foundations were defined and the various types of foundations were described. Next, the process of searching for foundations that are a match for the applying agency were reviewed. Fourth, the components of a letter of inquiry were discussed. Finally, the steps to follow after a letter of inquiry has been submitted were outlined.

Activities for Learning

1. Go to the foundation section of your local library. Peruse the foundation directory or a similar publication. Look at the policies and requirements of the organizations that are listed. How would these organizations fit into your agency's plans? How would you find out more about them?

2. Ask around in your community about agencies that have received foundation funding. Make an appointment with someone from the agency who was involved in the application process. Talk with them about how they identified the foundation to which they applied. Ask them about the letter they developed and the ways in which they interacted with the foundation after the letter of inquiry had been sent.

Questions for Discussion

1. What are the advantages of seeking foundation funding? What are its disadvantages?

2. Compare foundation funding to government funding. Which seems easier to do? Why does it seem easier? Which seems more likely to be successful and why?

3. What characteristics of a foundation would make it a good fit with your agency or practicum site?

Key Terms

Community foundation—an organization, not strictly a foundation, that receives and administers funds in a specific geographic area and that typically has various sources of income from a wide variety of donors

Corporate foundation—a foundation created through the financial support of a corporation

Private/independent foundation—an organization that manages and distributes money from a fund or endowment under the laws for creating private foundations (the funds are frequently from a gift of an individual or family)

References

Brody, R., & Nair, M. D. (2000). *Macro practice: A generalist approach* (5th Ed.). Wheaton, IL: Gregory Publishing Company.

The Foundation Center (2004a). *The Foundation Center's foundation growth and giving estimates: 2003 preview*. New York: The Foundation Center.

The Foundation Center (2004b). *Online orientation: The grant-seeking process*. Available: fdncenter.org/learn/orient/intro1.html.

The Foundation Center (2004c). *Proposal writing short course*. Available: fdncenter.org/learn/shortcourse/prop1.html.

WORKSHEET 15.1 | WRITING A FOUNDATION INQUIRY LETTER

Salutation

1. Identify the person at the foundation who should receive the letter of inquiry.

Dear Mr. Smith

2. Address the letter to that person.

Overview of the Organization

1. Explain who your agency is and what it is requesting.

We are a non profit social service organ. that operates a region for child abuse and child neglect, and also operate a mobilization program in the communities

2. Explain how your proposed initiative will further the mission of the foundation.

Needs Statement

1. Explain what the problem is, who it affects, and how they are affected by it.

Our needs are financial, Since we are located in a rural community we are very limited to are receiving funds. We have exhausted all of our local agency and organizations funds and are now needing to enquire elsewhere. Most of our clients are poor immigrants, who depend on our services daily.

2.   Explain how the problem affects the community and society as a whole.

Project Description

1.   Describe what the proposed project will do to solve the problem.

We would like to start a mobil communications van that would allow us to travel to the outlining rural area, in order to meet with our clients that are in need of our services

2.   Explain how these things will be done.

We would hire a full-time case manger who would daily reach out to the surrounding areas, to meet with clients

3.   Describe how you will know whether or not the project is working.

We would be able to monitor and track our clients through this project better because we would be meeting the needs of client face to face on a daily basis

Budget

1.   Explain how the money being applied for will be used.

If granted the funds would be used to pay for the full time case manger, gas, and the mobil unit

2. Identify other groups that are providing support for the project and the amount of support they are
    providing.

    We are receiving support thru United Way, and from a private foundation who's funds pay for the daily operations of the organization,

Agency Credibility

1. Provide basic information about your agency.

2. Explain the factors that make your agency sufficiently capable and stable to complete this project
    successfully.

    We have sustained our organization in this rural community for the past 25 years.

The Grand Finale

1. Ask permission to submit a full proposal to the foundation.

    We would like to submit a full proposal for you foundation to review.

2. Ask for their guidelines and an application.

    It would be greatly appreciated if we could receive the guidelines and a application form, so that we may submit them to you in the time frame set forth by your organization

3. Give them a contact name and information for follow-up.

    _____
    _____
    _____
    _____

    _____

4. Let them know that you will be available to answer any questions.

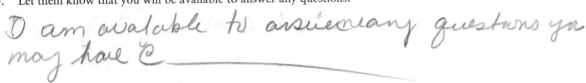

I am available to answer any questions you
may have @ _____

5. Express your appreciation for the opportunity to work with them and thank them for their time.

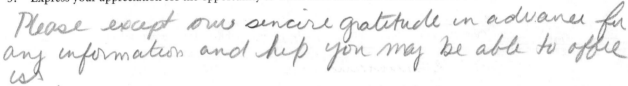

Please except our sincere gratitude in advance for
any information and help you may be able to offer
us .

Attachments

1. Add a brochure about your agency and evidence of your tax status.

2. Add any additional documents requested by the foundation.

PLANNING A FUNDRAISING EVENT

CHAPTER 16

CHAPTER OUTLINE

Planning a Fundraiser

Determining the Target Audience

Selecting a Type of Event

Setting Goals for Events

Time Line and Responsibilities

Advertising for Your Event

Evaluation

Using the Macro Practitioner's Workbook

Summary

Fundraising events are a great deal of work, but they also offer a variety of opportunities. **Fundraisers** are a great way to gain publicity, increase volunteer support, and of course, raise funds! In addition, these funds are generally unrestricted, meaning that they can be used in any way the agency needs them. Fundraising events can offer social service agencies an important means of funding their services and achieving their missions in an era where grant and foundation money are becoming tighter and the number of restrictions on those funds is increasing.

Despite all the positive benefits of fundraising events, these occasions can be financial and public relations disasters. An event that runs over budget and fails to attract a sufficient number of supporters can strain the agency or initiative's overall budget. Similarly, a poorly conceived event can be a public relations nightmare. People want to support organizations that are successful. Fundraising events are seen as a reflection of the quality and competence of the agencies that sponsor them. It is important to remember that you are selling a "product." In this case, the product is twofold: a good time at the event and the opportunity for the donor to support the mission of the agency.

BOX 16.1 FUNDRAISING FOR THE COMMUNITY PRACTITIONER

Community practitioners may become involved in fundraising activities in a number of ways. In most cases, it will involve the participation of some organization or organizations who help sponsor the activity. Partners in collaborative fundraising ventures do not need to be nonprofit agencies, however. Successful dinners, sporting events, and other activities have been held on behalf of community initiatives by members of the for-profit community who have philanthropic interests. For example, a large grocery chain might sponsor a Science Fun Fair for children in its parking lot during a busy weekend. The grocer might offer some personnel assistance (expecting community members and others to participate as well), the cost of equipment rental, technical advice from one of its activity planning experts, and advertising in its stores. The proceeds would be donated to the initiative. In this case, the initiative might need to furnish several things, such as some volunteers to work the fair, physical labor for set up and take down, and the preparation of public service announcements to publicize the event in the media. Partnering with other organizations can help fund community initiatives, but such efforts require that practitioners be knowledgeable about the strategies and techniques of fundraising.

PLANNING A FUNDRAISER

Planning a fundraising event is a challenging activity. It involves many of the other functions of macro practice, including goal setting, planning, budgeting, and committee development. For example, the following things must be taken into consideration (Ciconte, Ciconte, & Jacob, 2001; Stallings & McMillion, 1999):

1. What is the financial goal? How much money does the event need to raise?
2. Who is the target audience?
3. How much can the agency afford to spend on this event?
4. How much staff and volunteer time will be required? Is that amount of time available?
5. Who will be responsible?
6. What type of fundraising event will be held?
7. What would make this event be considered a success. Why would this event be a success?
8. How will the success of the event be evaluated?

DETERMINING THE TARGET AUDIENCE

Before deciding what type of fundraising event you will hold, you must determine the audience you hope to attract. Is it a well-established crowd of historical donors or perhaps a new group of young professionals? Do you want to attract a group with a specific interest, such as runners or golfers? The event should be carefully designed to appeal to the attendees you hope to attract. In addition to donors, your event can be the occasion for the recruitment of volunteers and board members, so you may want to consider these groups as you evaluate your target audience.

SELECTING A TYPE OF EVENT

Your fundraising event should be an enjoyable activity. Few people will attend simply because they support your cause. It is important to design an event that will attract potential attendees from their busy schedules. Many agencies find that a brainstorming session with key employees, board members, and

| BOX 16.2 | FUNDRAISING IN COMMUNITY PRACTICE |

Community practitioners may find that they have less occasion for involvement with fundraising events than do organizational practitioners. Although this chapter should help them prepare for times when they will participate in events, they may still find it helpful to draw on the expertise and experience of others. The following tips should help guide their collaborative efforts.

1. Identify a specific benefit to the community. The assistance of many people, particularly event sponsors and individual volunteers, can be more easily attracted to an event with a specific outcome, for example, "to purchase medical supplies for the Addiesburg Clinic" rather than the more general appeal, "to raise money for the Addiesburg community initiative."

2. Develop a work group using the guidelines for task force development offered in chapter 8 of this text.

3. Ask someone with a high level of expertise in event planning to facilitate the group.

4. Ensure that all participating and contributing agencies and organizations receive recognition and publicity.

---

volunteers can be helpful in identifying the type of event that will be successful. One of the authors of this book worked in a small, new nonprofit agency that was considering an annual fundraiser. During a brainstorming session, a group such as the one described above agreed on a single idea: dessert. From this key theme they developed a plan to get area caterers, restaurants, and cooks to participate in a dessert competition. This quickly grew into a gala event complete with donated appetizers, a bar, a live and silent auction, and music. In the first year, their "Taste of the Town" netted about $10,000, and it now is a major annual event that brings in over $50,000. The techniques for brainstorming were discussed in chapter 1. It can be a powerful technique for planning fundraising events.

There are other issues to be considered when planning a fundraiser. The culture of the community in which it will be held must be considered. What works in a large city may not be successful in a rural town. Take a careful look at other events and activities in the community and decide if you want to compete with an established event or come up with a new, creative alternative. In addition, you will need to examine your agency's calendar to determine how other activities may affect event planning. If the December holidays are particularly hectic at your agency, a holiday fundraiser might be unrealistic (Freedman & Feldman, 1998; Stallings & McMillion, 1999).

Examples of Fundraising Events

Agencies have been successful with many different types of events. The following list should be seen as examples rather than as a comprehensive summary. There may be other possibilities. Some agencies, for example, have considered purchasing and operating fast-food restaurants. Others have begun to explore participation in online auctions and marketing through their Web pages. The following is a partial list of possible fundraising events.

1. Dances
2. Dinners
3. Fairs
4. Auctions
5. Art shows
6. Home tours
7. Wine tastings
8. Raffles

   9. Food festivals
  10. Phone drives
  11. Sports tournaments
  12. Sales, such as bake or donated items.
  13. Yard sales
  14. Race, marathon, or walking events
  15. Concerts

SETTING GOALS FOR EVENTS

It is important to set goals when planning any event. Agencies should have goals about the amount of money to be made, volunteer involvement, board involvement, public relations, and support of local businesses (Ciconte, Ciconte, & Jacob, 2001; Kirst-Ashman & Hull, 1997). Please reference the information on developing goals and objectives included in chapter 1.

Financial Goals

When setting financial goals, aim high, but avoid predisposing the effort to failure. It is important that all the participants feel a sense of success and accomplishment. Although the goals for the first year of an event may be modest, success in attaining those goals may provide a foundation for even greater success in the future. The following guidelines can help planners identify realistic financial goals.

The first step involves tasks similar to those discussed in chapter 13. Both income and expenses must be estimated, and the sums of these compared. Gathering information about potential expenses will help determine whether the event is a good investment for your agency. When in doubt, it is important to underestimate income and overestimate expenses.

Remember that some estimates will be fixed and others will be dependent on the number of participants in the event. It is important to determine the point at which the event will break even. For example, how many tickets must be sold in order to cover all expenses? How much money can be realistically expected from an event's sponsors?

The goal, of course, is to maximize profit. There are two ways to do this for any event. One of those ways involves increasing the income the event generates. The other involves decreasing expenses.

Ways to Increase Income   One way of increasing income is by *adjusting the price of participation*. More tickets might be sold at a lower price. Alternatively, the cost of tickets might be increased, assuming that it would not negatively impact participation. Any decision to change the cost of participation must be balanced against the probability of affecting attendance.

A second means of increasing income is by *obtaining outside sponsorship*. For example, if you are holding a 10K race, a health food store, gym or sports injury clinic may be willing to underwrite the cost in exchange for publicity. For every prospective sponsor, a package of benefits should be developed that can be offered in exchange for specific monetary amounts. For example, a "Platinum" donor might contribute $10,000 and get its name and logo on event banners, its logo on all event favors, and its name mentioned in advertisements publicizing the event. A "Gold" sponsor might donate at the $7,500 level and get its name on the T-shirt and brochure with smaller signs only in selected areas of the event. The "Silver" sponsor might donate $5,000 and have its name on the T-shirt only.

There are many *other options* for increasing income at events. These may include the sale of donated items, silent auctions, games of chance, and identification of individuals who will contribute at smaller levels as "patrons" of the event. Any decision to attempt to increase income should be weighed against the additional staff or volunteer time that will be required to make that attempt successful.

Ways to Decrease Expenses

Get Things Donated   Get local businesses involved by having them donate items for free or at cost. This is a great way to build relationships with local businesses and open them up to the possibility of participating in corporate campaigns in the future. Offer publicity or tickets in exchange for donations. You can often get food, drinks, decorations, and entertainment free if you utilize the connections of your staff, board, and supporters. You may get restaurants to donate food, a florist to donate centerpieces, or a local band to donate their talent to your cause.

Spend Less   Determine what things are truly necessary to make the event a success. It sounds simple, but putting on a gala event can be exciting, and budgeting can sometimes fall on the back burner. Make decreasing expenses a goal and continuously evaluate the planning to determine whether this is being accomplished.

A budget for the event should be prepared and adhered to strictly. (Please see chapter 13.) Whenever possible, expenditures should be reduced. If, for instance, the agency expects to spend $1,500 on food but finds a donor for half that amount, the expenditure can be reduced to $750.00. This would be reflected in a revised budget that is prepared by the planners and submitted to the executive director of the agency. Costs can also be cut by involving volunteers, recruiting assistance from corporate sources, and encouraging participation by board members.

Identifying Financial Goals

Financial goals should be clearly identified and discussed. These can simply be listed until dollar amounts have been established. They should then be rewritten into full goal statements as described in chapter 1. A sample summary of financial goals might be as follows:

1. Financial goal: raise $25,000
2. Sell 250 tickets at $50/ticket $12,500
3. Make $7,500 on auction items sold
4. Get $5,000 in underwriting from 10–15 businesses

Volunteer Goals

Just as agencies should have financial goals for their events, they should also have goals for volunteers. **Volunteer goals** should include a measure of the degree to which they want current volunteers to participate as well as a goal for the number of new volunteers that should be recruited. Volunteer goals might include such categories as:

1. Specific number of volunteers
2. Number of volunteer hours
3. Increase in new volunteers

BOX 16.3 SAMPLE BUDGET: DECORATIONS SUBCOMMITTEE

Income	Estimated	Actual
Donated items	$2,000	$1,500
Underwriting	$3,000	$3,500
Total Income	**$5,000**	**$5,000**
Expenses	**Estimated**	**Actual**
Flowers/centerpieces	$2,000	$250
Tablecloths	$300	$800
Total Expenses	**$2,300**	**$1,050**
Net income	**$2,700**	**$3,950**

4. Number of repeat volunteers
5. New volunteers gained after the event as a result of participation/attendance

Board of Directors Goals

Another category of goals that should be set for fundraising events is board of directors goals. As with volunteer goals, these should include both level of participation by current members and either the number of new members or the number of new prospects to be gained from the event. Sample board of directors goals include:

1. Number of board members that donate to the event
2. Number of board members that participate on committees
3. Number of tickets sold by board members
4. Amount of donations brought in by board members
5. Amount of underwriting dollars secured by board members

Public Relations Goals

Yet another category of goals to be considered has to do with the public relations opportunities afforded by the event. Sample public relations goals include:

1. Number of articles in paper concerning fundraising event
2. Number of times the event is mentioned in other forms of media
3. New attendees to the event

Local Business Involvement

The final category of goals has to do with the involvement of local businesses in the event. Sample **business goals** might include:

1. Amount of underwriting dollars
2. Value of donations by businesses
3. Number of businesses who repeat their donation
4. Number of new businesses that donate

TIME LINE AND RESPONSIBILITIES

Taking care of details is a key to the success of your event. Committees will need to be established to oversee these details. A staff member should be appointed to oversee the process, and it will be helpful to include a volunteer or board member to serve as the cochair of this committee. This person should be extremely committed to and a good spokesperson for the agency (Ciconte, Ciconte, & Jacob, 2001; Freedman & Feldman, 1998; Stallings & McMillion, 1999).

Committee Composition

Determine what skills, talents, and connections are needed to make the event a success, and then develop the committee based on those needs. You will need people with a variety of skills. For example, you will want some people who can help with decorating, others who are skilled in publicity, and perhaps someone who is skilled in construction. You will need individuals who are creative, talented, and hardworking. In addition, you will need people on this committee who can encourage other people to attend the event. Consider the connections that members of the committee might have. Does someone's brother run a golf course? Does someone's aunt own a restaurant? How might those connections help you to increase income or decrease your expenses? How will your committee help you reach your target audience? Be sure to refer to chapter 8 of this book for an overview of this process.

Possible Subcommittees

The planning committee will oversee the process. It will also need to form subcommittees to perform specific tasks. Examples of subcommittees that might be formed include:

1. Auction
2. Entertainment
3. Food and drinks
4. Decorations
5. Publicity
6. Programs
7. Set up/clean up
8. Budget
9. Evaluation
10. Volunteers

ADVERTISING FOR YOUR EVENT

Strategic advertising will be essential to the success of your event. You will need to determine the best way to reach your target audience and direct your advertising to them. Public relations strategies for a men's golf tournament would likely be very different than advertising for a fashion show. You may decide to use the newspaper for marketing. You should consider, for example, whether your target audience would be more likely to read the society pages or the sports pages. You might also consider what stores your target audience might frequent so that you can place flyers or brochures in strategic places. It is also important to consider the types of invitations that might be used, whether the approach will be selective or mass market, and what type of media advertising has the greatest probability of success. Use the chapter 6 of this book to help make these decisions.

 | SAMPLE TASK LIST DECORATIONS
SUBCOMMITTEE

What	When	Who Is Responsible	Date Completed
Solicit florist for centerpieces	July 1	Amy—her aunt is a florist	June 28; flowers donated
Recruit 30 volunteers to help set up decorations	July 15	Jason	July 15; list of volunteers attached
Pick up centerpieces	Day of event: August 1; 1 P.M. at Emily's Flowers	Ellen	August 1; 1 P.M.

EVALUATION

Before holding the event, it is important to have a plan in place for evaluating its success. Soon after the event has occurred, preferably within a week, the fundraising committee, staff, and board members should fill out an evaluation. The evaluation should gather information about what things went well and should be repeated and also what things need work. It should also gather suggestions on ways to improve the fundraiser. The budget will also serve as an important data source in evaluation (Kirst-Ashman & Hull, 1997).

USING THE MACRO PRACTITIONER'S WORKBOOK

The Macro Practitioner's Workbook for this chapter includes a worksheet for identifying goals for the event. The other functions, such as budgeting and committee development, are discussed in other chapters of this book. Preparing goal statements is also discussed in other chapters, but these worksheets refer to the processes that must be undertaken before developing the statements. The worksheet in this chapter will help you with those processes.

SUMMARY

Planning a fundraising event is a serious decision, and it is one that should not be taken lightly. You will need to determine what you want to accomplish and the degree to which your organization has the capacity to support the effort. It is critical to determine financial goals and find creative ways to maximize your profit. Your agency must set clear and quantifiable goals and set up a committee structure to ensure success. Tools such as budgets, time lines, and task lists will be crucial to easing the workload of the event. In addition, evaluation is a critical component that can help to ensure that the event can be replicated and made even more successful in the future.

Activities for Learning

1. Contact local agencies and ask about their fundraising activities. Ask them to explain the process they use in planning events. Report the results of your research to the class.
2. Think about the types of fundraisers that might be effective for your agency or practicum site. Which would be the most likely matches? What kind of financial commitment would they require? What kind of commitment of agency personnel would they require? How would you determine the likelihood of success for each?

3. Attend a fundraiser for a local agency. Was the event done well? How might it have been done better? Report the results of your visit to your class.

Questions for Discussion

1. What potential ethical issues do you see arising with fundraisers? How would you handle those conflicts?
2. How might you recruit volunteers to work at a fundraising event? How would you identify potential volunteers? How would you approach them?
3. How might you recruit board members to work at a fundraising event? How would you identify potential new board members at that event? How might you go about approaching them?

Key Terms

Fundraiser—an event designed to raise money that will go toward the operation of an agency

Board of directors goals—goals that an agency hopes to accomplish at a fundraiser that concern its board of directors (these might include both participation by current board members and recruitment of future board members)

Business goals—goals that an agency hopes to accomplish at a fundraiser that concern the business community (these are typically related to providing some sort of support either in the form of employee participation or financial sponsorship)

Volunteer goals—goals that an agency hopes to accomplish at a fundraiser that concern volunteers (these might include both participation by current volunteers and recruitment of future volunteers)

References

Ciconte, B. L., Ciconte, B. K., & Jacob, J. G. (2001). *Fundraising basics: A compete guide.* Boston: Jones and Bartlett Publishers.

Freedman, H. A., & Feldman, K. (1998). *The business of special events: Fundraising strategies for changing times.* Sarasota, FL: Pineapple Press, Inc.

Kirst-Ashman, K. K., & Hull, G. H. (1997). *Generalist practice with organizations and communities.* Chicago: Nelson-Hall.

Stallings, B., & McMillion, D. (1999). *How to produce fabulous fundraising events: Reap remarkable returns with minimal effort.* New York: Building Better Skills.

WORKSHEET 16.1 | IDENTIFYING GOALS FOR A FUNDRAISING EVENT

Financial Goals

1. What is a realistic amount you can expect in gross revenues for this event?

   $25,000

2. How can the gross revenues be increased?

   – Thru private donations
   – sale of tickets

3. What is a realistic amount you can expect in expenses for this event?

   –$10,000

4. How can the expenses be reduced?

   donated items
   – volunteer hours.
   – bartering
   – shopping around

5. Use the information in chapter 1 to guide your development of goals and objectives for your fundraiser.

Volunteer Goals

1. Specify the number of volunteers you need to make this event successful.

   25

2. Specify the number of volunteer hours you need to make this event successful.

3. Specify the number of new volunteers you would like to recruit from the event.

   the would about 5-10,

Board of Directors Goals

1. Specify the number of board members that will donate to the event.

   all it is a requirement of board policies

2. Specify the number of board members that will participate on committees.

   all it is a bi-law

3. Specify the number of tickets that will be sold by board members.

We are looking for tickets to be sold in groups of 4.

4. Specify the amount of donations that will be brought in by board members.

There needs to be as many. There is not specified amounts

5. Specify the amount of underwriting funding that will be secured by board members.

6. Specify the number of prospective board members that will be identified through the event.

Public Relations Goals

1. Identify the number of articles that will appear in newspapers about the event.

- Media will be used weekly 2 month prior to the event. The week before event it will be in local paper.

- Maybe be able to have advus using rado stations

2.   Identify the number of times the event will be mentioned in other forms of media.

— mailer - postcard
— Church papers
— radio
— community center

Local Business Involvement

1.   Specify the amount of underwriting funding that will be received for the event.

5,000 from local communy member

2.   Specify the value of the nonmonetary donations that will be received for the event.

3.   Specify the number of businesses who will repeat their donation from previous years.

We had 15 the year before, so we are
hoping for at least the same this year.

4.   Specify the number of new businesses that will donate.

There are 25 new business we are hoping
for 10 out of this list

17 CHAPTER

WRITING A
FUNDRAISING LETTER

CHAPTER OUTLINE

Why Use Direct Mail?

What to Do Before Writing the Letter

The Psychology of Fundraising Letters

The Direct Mail Kit

Using the Macro Practitioner's Workbook

Summary

Over $39.3 billion dollars were spent in **direct mail** marketing campaigns alone in 1998. Advertisers are skilled in the science of getting people to part with their money. A direct mail campaign is a **marketing** strategy that is used to get people to buy a product through a letter and other enclosed materials. In the world of social services, the improvement to society that results from the work of an agency is the product, and donors can "buy" this product by donating to the cause.

An annual direct mail campaign can be an important part of both your public relations and fundraising efforts. You must first decide whether it is possible for your agency to take on a direct mail campaign. The campaign will require the use of staff time and resources. As with any fundraising effort, a direct mail campaign is a public relations effort and failure can mean not only loss of funding, but also loss of credibility and staff morale. On the other hand, a successful direct mail campaign can be critical to the future of your agency. Your agency must strategically plan for fund development and determine what resources can be invested and what outcomes are desired. Your staff and board must be supportive of this campaign, and the board should show their support by being the first ones to donate.

| BOX 17.1 | DIRECT MAIL FOR COMMUNITY PRACTITIONERS |

The following are tips to help community practitioners deal with the benefits and restrictions of direct mail campaigns.

1. Direct mail campaigns to benefit disadvantaged neighborhoods may have limited effectiveness because the target audience for the mailing is unlikely to include many community members, and therefore they may not see the initiative as a donation priority. If you choose to use direct mail, do so judiciously to ensure that your costs do not exceed the return.

2. Be sure to pick a specific cause that donors outside the community will find appealing. Projects to benefit children, such as educational or recreational alternatives, may be particularly effective.

3. To minimize the investment of cost and time as well as to take advantage of expertise, ask agencies involved in your initiative to assist with the campaign.

4. Try to find an individual or group that will donate toward the cost of the campaign so that the initiative does not need to bear the expense.

WHY USE DIRECT MAIL?

Direct mail campaigns have a number of benefits. These benefits include:

1. Building a base of regular donors that will grow and increase donating over time.
2. Providing positive public relations by increasing awareness of the agency.
3. Bringing in regular money.
4. Providing unrestricted income.
5. Helping agencies gain volunteers and other supporters.

What Can Be Expected?

Although direct mail campaigns have a number of benefits, they also have a number of restrictions. For tips on dealing with the benefits and restrictions of direct mail as a community practitioner, see Box 17.1.

1. Generally, direct mail gets only a 3–5% response rate.
2. Direct mail campaigns that target potential donors who have a relationship with the agency have a higher response rate.
3. The contributions are often small. Most fall into the $10 to $20 range.
4. Most of the work is done before the letter goes out.

WHAT TO DO BEFORE WRITING THE LETTER

Several things must be done before the letter is written. These are preparatory steps, involving research similar to that which is undertaken for other fund raising activities.

Defining Your Direct Mail Concept

Direct mail is a major form of marketing. Marketers know the power of words, images, and ideas to move us to action, be it buying, donating, or volunteering. We should take advantage of their expertise when developing our direct mail concept. Understanding packaging and your donor's motivations are key concepts. There are several questions that must be answered before you can begin a direct mail campaign (Lister, 2001; Voegle, 1969).

Why Are You Writing a Letter? You must help donors understand that their contribution is needed in order for you to fulfill the mission of your agency. In order for you to convince them of this, you must first decide why you are writing this letter. You must be able to articulate clearly and succinctly why you need the donation. For example, are you hoping to?

> Build a new donor base or new membership?
>
> Increase the support of past donors?
>
> Begin or continue an annual direct mail campaign?
>
> Gain large donations from a few donors?
>
> Raise money for a specific program or project?
>
> Seek support for a benefit event?

Who Is the Audience? Before you can begin writing your letter, you must know to whom you will send the letter and you must be able to identify the characteristics potential donors have in common. For instance, you **target audiance** might all be members of the same community or all supporters of a specific cause. They could have a family member that suffers from a particular disease. You will also want to know the demographics of your target audience: what is their age and gender and where do they live? One of the most important questions that must be answered is what relationship the potential donors have with your organization. If they are familiar with the agency, it is important to understand how they know about you and what they know.

To maximize income, you should develop a variety of letters based on the different audiences you will approach. A letter that is perfect for a long-time supporter would not be appropriate for a new prospect. You will have to do your homework on this. You will need an updated list of past donors and volunteers who are likely to give again and increase donations when asked. In addition, you may want to develop a new prospect list. This can be done in a variety of ways. Asking staff, board members, and volunteers to assist with this can be crucial. Friends, relatives, fellow club members, and others that you feel will share the values of your agency are all potential prospects. Those who have benefitted from your services, including clients, may be potential donors. Think about why these various groups of potential donors would respond to your letter and construct your appeals accordingly. Some examples of potential donor groups include: (a) major donors (those who give large amounts), (b) loyal donors (those who give often), (c) volunteers, and (d) new prospects.

What Am I Asking For? What Do I Want Them to Do? Budgeting will be discussed in more detail later, but you need to determine how much money you plan to raise and what your minimum requested contribution is. The majority of donors will send in the minimum amount requested, so think carefully about how much you ask for. To simplify this process, a reply card should be developed that tells the reader how much you would like and where to send it. You must be very specific about what you want prospective donors do and make it as easy as possible for them to donate.

Why Right Now? Explain to your donors why you need for them to respond right away. It may be that you have a match on any funds that are raised. You may need it for a specific program that has lost funding, or your donation may be related to a specific holiday. Explain to the reader why it is urgent that they send the donation immediately. It is highly recommended that you give the reader a deadline and repeat this deadline several times.

Why Should They Do This?   You must clearly and succinctly explain how their donation will benefit the organization. You will want to use anecdotal information and touching stories. Remember that most decisions are made on an emotional level, and you must show the potential donor the benefits of their donation. The story must be combined with a call to action. The recipient of the request must feel that their donation will truly make a difference and lead to change.

Once you have answered all of these questions, you should be ready to develop your direct mail package. Try to link all the pieces of your package together. The envelope, letter, reply card, and any inserts need to have common symbols and themes. Think about magazine ads and commercials and how symbols can to move us to action. Pictures and photographs used in your materials need to be linked to the reason for sending the letter. For example, if you are requesting money for a children's program, you might want to consider a picture of children or a symbol that represents children, such as a child's toy.

Another important decision that must be made is who will sign the letter. This will be most effective if there is a connection between the signer and the social problem. The signer may be a pet owner asking for donations for the local humane society or a star quarterback asking for donations to a school. It is best to have someone outside of the staff sign this letter, such as a volunteer, supporter, or member of the board of directors. Ideally, there will also be a connection between the signer and the recipient of the letter. They might be members of the same community, from the same school, or share the same faith. It is important that the person who signs this letter also be a donor to show their true support of the cause.

THE PSYCHOLOGY OF FUNDRAISING LETTERS

Successful fundraising letters are written in specific ways to accomplish specific purposes. People respond for some personal reasons. It is important to understand those reasons so that the probability of success can be maximized.

Understanding How People Read Direct Mail

When developing your direct mail package, you must first understand how people read direct mail. Before the reader can respond, they have to open and read the direct mail. Siegreid Vogele, author of *Handbook of Direct Mail*, has done the research to help us understand how people read direct mail. His "eye camera" studies tracked how long people spent looking at various components of direct mail and how their eyes traveled across the mail. Dr. Vogele found that an average of seven seconds is devoted to the envelope, including the removal of the contents. The average time spent in reviewing the envelope contents was 11 seconds. If the reader opens the envelope, they generally start at the top of the letter, reading their name in the address and salutation (if the letter is personalized) and then move to the signature to see who is writing to them. After this, they will read the P.S. before continuing to the bold and underlined words in the first paragraph. Those who have read this much may begin reading the text of the letter.

From these studies, we can conclude that we must carefully design each piece of our direct mail package, starting with the envelope. What could be on the envelope that will entice the recipients to open it? Again, you must think about your audience. If they have a relationship to the agency, use that to get them to open it. Just seeing that it is from your organization may be enough.

Next you will want to develop your P.S. Many readers will go directly to the P.S. Use this opportunity to entice them to read the letter and to let them know how important and needed their support is. The P.S. may actually offer a lead into your opening story or tease the reader with a question. The P.S. may be your last opportunity to engage the reader.

Finally, you would begin the text of the letter. In doing your research, you should have gathered stories and anecdotal information to show what your agency is doing. Make a case for why the reader's help is needed. Underline or bold your most important points and be clear and concise. Dr. Vogele refers to his method of writing direct mail as the "dialogue method." Vogele suggest that we view a letter as what he terms a "silent dialogue." The writer must anticipate and answer all of these questions within the text of the letter.

Why Do People Donate Money?

When thinking about your audience, try to anticipate their motivation for donating to your organization. Some people will donate because they support your organization and share your beliefs and values. They want to know that their donation makes an actual difference. Others donate for recognition. These donors need to be recognized in some tangible way. Some people donate because they want to belong to something and be part of an organization. Some donate because of the tax benefits associated with their donations. Most importantly, don't forget the cardinal rule of fundraising: the number one reason why people donate is because they are asked to do so.

Appealing to Their Hearts

Begin the text of your letter with a brief, inspirational story that summarizes how your organization meets its mission. Remember why people donate and let them know how their money is going to help someone. Describe what will result from their donations: lives will be saved, children will clothed, women can be safe from domestic violence. You want to create strong feelings and emotions before proceeding to the statistics and details of your appeal.

THE DIRECT MAIL KIT

We have reviewed many of the ideas you must think about before developing your direct mail package. Now we will begin the work of actually putting all the pieces together. You will need to develop your marketing concept. You must answer several questions. To whom is the letter directed? How are they connected to you and why would they give? What are you offering in return for their support? Who is signing your letter and what impact will that have on the reader? What is your goal and how much can you spend on this effort?

Budget

You must set a fundraising goal when developing your budget. One popular mechanism for helping you predict your income is called the "gift pyramid." With the gift pyramid, it is estimated that one-third of your goal will come from the top 10–15 donations, one-third from the next 25 donations, and the final one-third of your goal will come from all other donations (Edwards, Yankey, Altpeter, 1998).

Potential expenses:

Mailing

Printing

Envelopes, letterhead, reply card

Brochures and other inserts

Anything extra you may want to give

Data entry

Staff time

Computer needs

Database to manage labels, letters, and keep track of donor information/ history

The Reply Device

Next you will develop your reply device, which includes a reply card and stamped return envelope. Tell your reader how much to donate. Determine your "ask levels" (options for amounts to donate) and establish the minimum donation. To appeal to those who like recognition, certain labels can be linked to the various levels of donation. For instance, a friend gives $50, but a benefactor gives $1,000. Their donation could be linked to something specific, but remember that this will restrict how you can spend these funds. Personalize the reply card: "Yes, I will help support the Family Center so that children will be safe from the cycle of abuse. I have enclosed my tax-deductible donation of _____." For the maximum reply, send a return envelope with the postage paid. If possible, place the recipient's name and address as a signature on the reply card to encourage a response. Rather than the agency, list the person at the agency who is making the request on the return mailing address. This lets the reader know who is waiting for their reply.

Make the directions as simple as possible. Make sure the reader doesn't have to search for information. Dr. Vogele has helpful tips for developing effective reply cards. He found that a separate response devise is three times more effective than one that must be cut or torn. Anything that can be done to make it easier for the reader to donate should be done.

The Envelope, Please

Your next step is to create the envelope. The importance of the envelope has been discussed earlier since this is often the point at which people will decide if they will open your mail. Decide what will be on your envelope and decide if you want to use a teaser. While a teaser might entice some people to open, it may alert others that you are asking for money and prevent them from opening the letter. There may be no need to add a teaser if you are writing a personal letter. If you decide to use a teaser, find something that will increase the likelihood that reader will open the envelope (examples include "news for our most important supporters" and "did you know"). Studies have found that using stamps rather than metered mail on the outside envelope increases response. Be sure to personalize the letter by sending it to an individual, not "Dear Friends" or "Dear Supporters". Again, understanding your target audience will help you make the best decisions on where to invest your money and energy.

The P.S.

The P.S. is another important piece. Because most people will read the P.S. before reading the text of the letter, it should summarize your strongest points. Say what you need, why it is urgent, and how it will help. You will want to emphasize the deadline. If they don't respond in the next few weeks, they probably won't respond. "Support from generous supporters like you will help us to find safe and loving homes for children like Emily this Christmas." The P.S. will be your last opportunity to get them to donate, and you should think carefully about what it should say.

The Body of the Letter

Finally, begin writing the text. Your first task will be to write the lead. The introductory paragraph really needs to capture the reader's attention. This is an opportunity to let your agency shine. Give a short, inspiring story about a client or situation that shows why your agency deserves their donation. Your next step will be to determine what your headings and subheadings will be. You should underline and bold those words and phrases that you want the reader to remember and that would encourage them to donate.

Remember what we learned from the psychology of fundraising letters when writing the body of the task. Be focused on the reader. Talk directly to them. Make the letter as personal and conversational as possible. Use "I" and "you", but use "you" more than any other word. Let them know that you need them to make this happen. Remember why people give and make sure the potential donor feels valued and important. Phrases such as "with your generous support" or "thanks to generous people like you" praises the donors for being generous and loyal.

A good fundraising letter needs to be professional but personal. Keep the letter conversational: write how you speak and read it out loud. It should be easy to read. This means you should keep sentences short (8–11 words) and paragraphs concise (3–5 lines). Find ways to break up paragraphs and use simpler language. The goal is to make reading the letter easy for the donor. This means your language should be clear and uncomplicated. Use good grammar, but don't be restricted by conventional rules. You can use contractions, "I hope you'll join us" is more personal than the more rigid, "I hope you will join us." Much of the research says that longer letters are better, but this will be determined by your agency and the group to which you are appealing. Try to describe your program in just a few lines. Finally, you will develop a compelling ending. Once you have drafted this, revise and rewrite several times. Get feedback from others to find out what questions and concerns they have and find ways to answer those concerns in the letter.

Tips to Remember When Writing the Letter

Don't forget to ask for the donation

Don't be unethical, lie, or promise things you can't deliver

Plan to personalize as much as possible: Review the list of past donors and have board members or supporters sign letters or write notes on letters. Have them develop new donor lists and commit to sending these personalized letters.

After the Letters Have Been Mailed

Don't forget to say thank you. Donors will need a letter for tax purposes, but you may also want to send a handwritten letter to larger donors to express your appreciation. You should also follow up with recipients with a postcard reminder or by phone to see if they got the letter and if you can answer any questions. Evaluate how the fundraiser went and begin your plans for the next direct mail campaign. Did you reach your goal? What will you do differently next time? Who responded best? What worked? Is there a way to narrow who you send the mailing to in order to increase effectiveness? As it has been emphasized throughout this text, continuous evaluation is key to an agency's success and growth.

USING THE MACRO PRACTITIONER'S WORKBOOK

The Macro Practitioner's Workbook for this chapter includes step-by-step guidelines for planning a direct mail campaign. Use the case study for unit 4 to obtain the basic information.

SUMMARY

A good fundraising letter can be a critical piece of an overall development plan. In this chapter what should be done before writing the letter, the psychology of direct mail, and how to develop the direct mail package were all discussed. Although the majority of the work is done before the campaign, there is a lot to do once the letters have been sent. Direct mail can be an important way to build new support and increase the support of donors over time. It is a popular way to raise funds while spreading the word about the beneficial work of your agency.

Activities for Learning

1. Working in a small group, collect several direct mail marketing letters. Examine the letters. Which of the techniques discussed in this chapter were used? Which were not used? What have you learned about the things you would or would not do in a direct mail campaign from this experience?
2. Make an appointment with the executive director or development director of an agency. Ask them about the direct mail campaign that they use. How often do they mail? To whom do they mail? What do they hope to accomplish when they mail?

Questions for Discussion

1. What ethical dilemmas might arise from a direct mail campaign? How would you deal with those dilemmas?
2. The text recommended making your request for funds immediate. How could you do that without being unethical or dishonest?

Key Terms

Direct mail—a method of reaching prospective donors through the mailing of materials directly to them

Marketing—the process of making your story and request known to others and asking them for a supportive response

Target audience—those to whom you hope to direct your request for support

References

Edwards, R. L., Yankley, J. A., Alterpeter, M. A. (1998). *Skills for effective management of nonprofit organizations.* Washington, D.C.: NASW Press.

Lister, G. J. (2001). *Building your direct mail program.* San Francisco: Jossey Bass.

Vogele, S. (1969). *Handbook of direct mail.* New York: Prentice Hall.

WORKSHEET 17.1 | PREPARING A FUNDRAISING LETTER

The Reply Device

1. Will you use a reply card? If so, what will it say?

    Please join us for our fundraising Frenzy.
    Please reserve _____ seats for me and _____ frieds.
    ✠

2. Will you include a stamped, self-addressed envelope? If so, what will it cost?

    28¢
    ×550 mailers
    140.00

3. What levels of contribution will you use?

    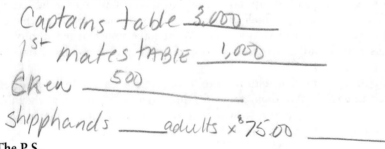
    Captains table 3,000
    1st mates tABle 1,000
    Crew   500
    Shipphands _____ adults × $75.00 _____

The P.S.

1. Will you use a P.S.?

    NO

2. If you choose to use a P.S., what will it say?

    _____

The Letter

1. How will your letter begin? What story will you include in the initial paragraph?

Dear John,
    I need your help and so do our neighbors living in Annisburg. As you are aware federal funding for all social service organ has been cut or deduced dracticly —

2. Will you use headings and subheadings? If so, what will they be?

3. What do you want to communicate to potential donors?

We and the people of Annisburg need help.
— Where we get our funding
— what's in it for them, and how there donation would help
— How appreciative we would be.
—

INDEX

Accounting methods, 218
Accrual-based accounting, 218
Action system, 16
Ad hoc committees, 145
Advertising
  for employees, 183–184
  for fundraisers, 259
  on the Internet, 184
  with local universities and colleges, 184
  with professional organizations, 184
  See also Classified advertising
Affirmative action, 188
Age Discrimination in Employment
    Act, 201
Agreements, preparing and signing, 75
Alliances, 89–92
Alternatives. *See* Contingency planning
Alternatives for Children, 55–57
Americans with Disabilities Act, 188, 201
Annual return (990 form), 221
Assessments, 7–28
  Macro Practitioner's Workbook, 18,
    20–28
  preparing a report, 17–18
  reasons for, 8–10
  step 1: creating work groups, 10–11
  step 2: understanding the problem,
    11–14
  step 3: understanding the participants,
    14–16
  step 4: understanding the resources, 16
  step 5: understanding resistance to
    change, 16
  systems, 14–16
Audiences, 102. *See also* Target audience

Audits, 220–221
  reporting requirements, 220–221

Background questions, 199
Backup plans, 58. *See also* Contingency
    planning
Balance sheets, 218–220
  sample, 219
  See also Financial management
BAP. *See* Boosting Academic
    Performance
Barriers, to communication,
    130–131
Beliefs, 86. *See also* VIBES
Board members. *See* Board of directors
Board of directors, 156–167
  board structures, 159–160
  collaborating with the executive
    director, 159
  fundraising, 158–159, 161–162, 258
  Macro Practitioner's Workbook, 162,
    164–167
  overview of, 157–158
  reviewing the activities of the
    organization, 158
  reviewing the mission, 159
  selecting, 160
  skills required of, 160
  training, 161
Boosting Academic Performance
    (BAP), 76
Bottom-up communication, 129
  methods, 136
Boundaries, 76–77
Brainstorming, 53

Budgets, 3, 212–217
  for fundraising, 258, 260
  for fundraising letters, 270–271
  grant proposals and, 231
  incremental, 213
  letters of inquiry to foundations and, 246
  line-item, 212–213
  predicting expenses, 213
  predicting revenue, 214
  program or functional budgets, 213
  restricted and unrestricted funds, 214
  sample, 216
  zero-based, 213
  See also Financial management
Business goals, for fundraising, 258

Case studies
  assessment, planning, and preparation,
    2–6
  communication, 122–124
  financial management and fundraising,
    208–210
  homeless task force, 145
  recruiting and hiring, 170–171
Cash-based accounting, 218
  modified, 218
Cash flow, 214–218
  excess revenue in nonprofits, 217–218
  sample expense, revenue, budget, and
    income statement, 215–217
  See also Financial management
Catalog of Federal Domestic
    Assitance, 226
Certified public accountant, 220
Change
  drivers for, 8
  resistance to, 16, 18, 26
  See also Opposition
Change agent system, 14
Change agents, 7
Classified advertisements, 175–177
  contents of, 176
  Macro Practitioner's Workbook, 177,
    179–180
  sample, 176
  writing tips, 177
  See also Advertising; Job descriptions
Client system, 15
Collaborative partners, grant proposals
    and, 228. *See also* Recruiting collabo-
    rative partners; Task forces
Committees
  ad hoc, 145
  for fundraising, 259
  See also Task forces
Communication, 121–143
  bottom-up, 129, 136
  case study, 122–124
  in community work, 126–127, 130,
    132, 135

developing the message, 127
electronic, 133
emotional interference, 131
face-to-face, 132
filtering and distortions, 131
horizontal, 129–130, 136
improving, 135–136
internal and external noise, 130
Macro Practitioner's Workbook, 136,
    138–143
meetings, 133–135
principles of effective, 126
process of, 126–127
receiving the message, 127–128
top-down, 128, 135
written, 132–133
Communities, work groups for, 10–11
Community foundations, 243
Community practice
  assessment, planning, and preparation,
    5–6, 17–18
  communication in, 123–124, 126–127,
    130, 132, 135
  financial management and fundraising,
    209–210, 213, 217, 254–255
  fundraising letters, 267
  government grants and, 225, 227
  public relations and, 108
  recruiting and hiring, 171
  See also Assessments
Competence, 146–147
Contingency planning, 8, 50–67
  composing a work group, 52–53
  generation and prioritization of alterna-
    tives, 57–58
  identifying processes and trends, 53–54
  internal scanning, 54–56
  Macro Practitioner's Workbook, 59,
    62–67
  need for, 51–52
  reports, 58–59
Controlling system, 15
Core values, 34
Corporate foundations, 243
Cost-benefit analysis of job descriptions,
    174–175
Cover letters, grant proposals, 228–229
Crisis planning, public relations and,
    107–108

Data collection, 40
Department of Labor, 200
Direct mail, 266–275. *See also* Fundrais-
    ing letters
Direct services, 56
Discrimination, 84
Distortions, 131
Donations
  for fundraisers, 257
  reasons people donate, 270

East Oceanside, FL, 12
Editorials, 107
Effective communication. *See* Communication
Electronic communication, 133
Emotions, as barriers to communication, 131
Employment taxes, 221
Equal Employment Commission, 200
Equal employment opportunity, 188
Ethics, 86
  public relations and, 108
  See also Social Work Code of Ethics; VIBES
Evaluation plan
  for fundraisers, 260
  grant proposals and, 231
Executive director, 158
  board of directors and, 159
Executive summary, 17
Expenses, 215–217
  decreasing fundraising, 257
  predicting, 213
  sample categories of, 215
Experts, 88
External noise, 130
External scanning, 34–35, 46, 56–57
External threats, 57

Face-to-face communication, 132
Facilitators, 32
FAPRS. *See* Federal Assistance Programs Retrieval System
Federal Assistance Programs Retrieval System (FAPRS), 226
Federal funding, 3
Federal guidelines, for interviewing job candidates, 200–201
Federal Register, 226
Feedback, 18, 59
Fiduciary responsibility, 157
Filtering, 131
Financial goals, for fundraising, 256–257
Financial management, 211–223
  accrual-based accounting, 218
  audit and reporting requirements, 220–221
  budgets, 212–214
    incremental, 213
    line-item, 212–213
    predicting expenses, 213
    predicting revenue, 214
    program or functional budgets, 213
    restricted and unrestricted funds, 214
    zero-based, 213
  cash-based accounting, 218
  cash flow, 214–218
    excess revenue in nonprofits, 217–218
    sample expense, revenue, budget, and income statement, 215–217

  for community practioners, 213, 217
  financial statements, 218–221
    balance sheet, 218–220
    income statement, 215–217, 220–221
    Macro Practitioner's Workbook, 221, 223
    modified cash basis accounting system, 218
Financial statements, 218–221
  balance sheet, 218–220
  income statement, 220–221
Fiscal management, 10
501c3 agencies, 220, 257
Focus groups, 53
Forecasting, 53
Foundation Center
  format for letters of inquiry, 246–247
Foundation Growth and Giving Estimates: 2003 Preview, 243
Foundations, 242–252
  community foundation, 243
  corporate foundation, 243
  defined, 243
  grants awards
    based on geographic proximity, 244
    based on mission or goals, 244
    based on natural connections, 244
  Macro Practitioner's Workbook, 247, 249–252
  preapproach research, 245
  private/independent foundation, 243
  trends in giving, 243–244
  writing the letter of inquiry, 245–247
    after submitting, 247
    format for, 246–247
Functional budgets, 213
Funding, 3, 54
  identifying sources, 228
  See also Foundations; Government grants
Funding directories, 226
Fundraisers, 253–265
  advertising for, 259
  board of directors goals, 258
  committee composition, 259
  community practice and, 254–255
  decreasing expenses, 257
  evaluation, 260
  financial goals, 256–257
  local business involvement, 258
  Macro Practitioner's Workbook, 260, 262–265
  public relations goals, 258
  sample budget: decorations subcommittee, 258
  sample task list: decorations subcommittee, 260
  subcommittees, 259
  target audience and, 254
  time line and responsibilities, 259

Fundraisers (continued)
  types of events, 254–256
  volunteer goals, 257–258
  See also Fundraising; Fundraising letters
Fundraising, 158–159, 161–162
Fundraising letters, 266–275
  as marketing strategy, 266
  for community practice, 267
  defining the direct mail concept, 267–269
  direct mail kit, 270–273
    after letters have been mailed, 272–273
    body of the letter, 272
    budget, 270–271
    envelopes, 271
    the P.S., 271–272
    reply device, 271
    tips for letter writing, 272
  Macro Practitioner's Workbook,
    273–275
  psychology of, 269–270
  target audience, 268
Funds
  restricted and unrestricted, 214
  See also Budgets; Financial management

Gentrification, 12
Goal statements, 102–103, 230
Goals, 29, 33–34, 44, 47, 102–103
  for fundraising, 256–258
Government grants, 224–241
  community practice and, 225, 227
  grant process, 225–226
  items grantors want in a proposal,
    226–227
  locating, 226
  Macro Practitioner's Workbook, 232,
    234–241
  program description sample, 229
  requests for proposals (RFPs), 225–226
  summary of, 232
  writing, 227–232
    1. preparing to write a grant
       proposal, 227–228
    2. cover letter and opening, 228–229
    3. needs statement/problem state
       ment, 229
    4. project description, 230
    5. goal statement and objectives, 230
    6. program activities, 230–231
    7. evaluation plan, 231
    8. budget request, 231
    9. capability of the agency, 231
    10. future funding plans, 231
    11. letters of support, 231
    12. appendix materials, 232
    13. after the proposal has been
        written, 232
Government records, 16
Grantor defined, 224. *See also*
  Government grants

Grants. *See* Government grants;
  Foundations
Groups
  types of and VIBES, 87–88, 90
  types of political alliances, 90–92

Halfway houses, 85–86.
Handbook of Direct Mail (Vogele), 269
HFT. *See* Hope for Teens
Hiring, 181–195
  affirmative action, 188
  Americans with Disabilities Act, 188
  checking references, 186–187
  cost of, 181
  equal employment opportunity (Title
    VII of the 1964 Civil Rights Act), 188
  hiring decisions, 182
  hiring matrix, 187
  information to collect when screening,
    186
  interviewing candidates, 185–186
  job analysis, 182
  Macro Practitioner's Workbook, 188,
    191–195
  offer letters, 187
  recruiting as public relations, 184
  recruiting from outside the
    organization, 184
  recruiting from within the organization,
    183–184
  screening applicants, 185
  screening candidates, 186–187
  selection, 187
  See also Recruiting
Homeless task force case study, 145
Hope for Teens (HFT), 33
Horizontal communication, 129
  methods, 136
Host system, 15

Implementing system, 15
Impressions, managing, 92–93
Impropriety, 158
Income statements, 215–217, 220–221
  sample, 221
  See also Financial management
Incremental budgeting, 213
Influence, 147
Information, collecting, 40
Initiator system, 14
Interests, 85–86. *See also* VIBES
Internal noise, 130
Internal scanning, 34–35, 46, 54–56
Internet
  foundations and, 245
  recruiting and, 184
Interventions, 8
  and grant writing, 226
Interviewing job candidates,
  185–186, 196–205

background and job knowledge
    questions, 199
federal guidelines, 200–201
interviews defined, 197
Macro Practitioner's Workbook, 201,
    203–205
patterned behavior description
    questions, 199–200
preparing for, 200–201
purposes of interviews, 197
questions to avoid, 201
situational questions, 199
stage 1: opening or greeting phase, 198
stage 2: questions for the applicant, 198
stage 3: questions for the
    organization, 198
stage 4: closing phase, 198

Job analysis, 182
Job descriptions, 3, 173–175
    benefits of, 175
    contents of, 173–174
    costs of, 174–175
    flexibility in, 175
    Macro Practitioner's Workbook,
        177, 179–180
    sample, 174
    See also Classified advertisements
Job knowledge questions, 199
Juvenile offenders, services to, 33

Key informants, 16
Key people or positions, 146

Language, grant proposals and, 227
Letters of inquiry, 245–247. See also
    Foundations
Letters of support, 231
Letters to the editor, 107
Line-item budgets, 212–213
Literature reviews, 54

Macro assessments. See Assessments
Macro Practitioner's Workbook
    assessments, 18, 20–28
    board of directors, 162, 164–167
    communication, 136, 138–143
    contingency planning, 59, 62–67
    financial management, 221, 223
    foundation inquiry letter, 247, 249–252
    fundraisers, 260, 262–265
    fundraising letters, 273–275
    government grants, 232, 234–241
    hiring, 188, 191–195
    interviewing job candidates,
        201, 203–205
    job descriptions and classified
        advertisements, 177, 179–180
    overcoming opposition and, 94, 96–99
    public relations plans, 108, 111–119

recruiting collaborative partners,
    77, 79–82
    strategic planning, 37, 40–49
    task forces, 149, 151–155
Malpractice insurance, 176
Management styles, 55
Managing impressions, 92–93
Marketing strategy, 266
Matrices
    hiring, 187
    strategic planning, 37, 49
Media, 16
    public relations plans and, 105–107
Meetings, 126
    advantages and disadvantages of, 133
    agendas for, 133–134
    guidelines for holding, 133–135
    in community work, 135
Messages, 102–104
    developing, 127
    receiving, 127–128
    See also Public relations plans
Micropractice, 7–8
Mission statements, 33, 34, 42–43, 159
Modified cash basis accounting
    system, 218
Motivation, 146–147
Multidisciplinary committees, 69

Narrative, of a report, 17
National Association of Social
    Workers, 86
Needs statements, 229, 246
Networking, 88–89, 228
Newspaper articles, 106–107
990 form, 221
990-PFs, 245
Noise
    external, 130
    internal, 130
Nonprofit organizations, 157
    excess revenue in, 217–218

Objectives, 29, 47, 102–103
    developing, 35
    grant proposals and, 230
OC. See Organizational chart
Offer letters, 187
Office of Juvenile Justice and
    Delinquency Prevention, 144
Opposition
    Macro Practitioner's Workbook, 94,
        96–99
    minimizing, 83–99
    political alliances and, 89–92
    stakeholders and, 88–89
    VIBES (values, interest, beliefs, ethics,
        slants) and, 84–88, 90
    See also Resistance
Oppressive conditions, 84

Organizational chart (OC), 3
Organizational practice
  assessment, planning, and
    preparation, 3–5
  communication, 122–123
  financial management and fundraising,
    208–209
  recruiting and hiring, 170–171
  See also Assessments
Organizations, work groups and, 10–11
Outcomes, 226–227

Participants, 14–16, 23–24
  defined, 14
Patterned behavior description questions,
  199–200
Personnel management, 9–10
Planning, 8–9. *See also* Contingency
  planning; Public relations plans;
  Strategic planning
Political alliances, 89–92
  dimensions of, 90
  types of, 90–92
Predicting expenses, 213
Predicting revenue, 214
Pregnancy Discrimination Act, 201
Prejudice, 84
Press kits, 105–106
Press releases, 106
Private/independent foundations, 243
Problem statements, 11–13, 58–59, 229
Problems
  assessing, 21–22
  and government grants, 226
Professional organizations, recruiting
  through, 184
Program activies, grant proposals
  and, 230–231
Program budgets, 213
Public records, 89
Public relations, 56
  definition and levels of, 100–101
  ethics and, 108
  for community practitioners, 108
  goals for fundraising, 258
  importance of, 101
  recruiting employees and, 184
Public relations plans, 100–119
  crisis planning, 107–108
  editorials and letters to the editor, 107
  Macro Practitioner's Workbook, 108,
    111–119
  newspaper articles, 106–107
  press kits, 105–106
  press releases, 106
  public service announcements, 104, 106
  sample of, 103–105
  steps for creating, 102–103, 109
  types of activities, 101, 108
Public service announcements, 104–106

Publicity campaigns, 93, 101. *See also*
  Public relations plans

Recruiting, 10
  as public relations, 184
  from within outside the organization,
    184
  from within the organization, 183–184
  in the Internet, 184
  through local universities and
    colleges, 184
  with professional organizations, 184
  work groups, 32–33
  See also Hiring; Recruiting collaborative
    partners
Recruiting collaborative partners, 68–82
  challenges of collaborations, 70–71
  criteria for engaging in collaborations,
    71–73
  Macro Practitioner's Workbook, 77,
    79–82
  partner selection, 73
  reasons for collaborations, 69–70
  recruitment steps, 74–75
  roles, responsibilities, and boundaries,
    76–77
References, checking, 186–187
Report summary, 17
Reporting requirements, 220–221
Reports
  contingency planning, 58–59
  parts of, 17–18
  preparing, 27–28
Requests for Proposals (RFPs), 69,
  225–226. *See also* Government grants
Resistance to change, 16, 18, 26. *See also*
  Opposition
Resources
  availability of, 16, 25
  in reports, 17
  types of, 16
Responsibilities, 76–77
Revenue, 215–218
  predicting, 214
  sample categories, 216
Revisions, in reports, 18
RFPs. *See* Requests for Proposals
Roles, 76–77

Salutations, letters of inquiry, 246
Scanning, internal and external, 34–35,
  46, 54–57
Screening prospective employees,
  185–187. *See also* Hiring
Service delivery, 4
Situation analysis, 102–103
Situational questions, 199
Skills, of board members, 160
Slants, 86. *See also* VIBES
Small Business Administration, 175–176

Social Work Code of Ethics, 13, 70, 84, 86, 108
Stakeholders, 30, 54
  defined, 85–86
  identifying, 88–89
Strategic planning, 8, 29–49
  composing work groups, 31–33
  defined, 29–30
  developing objectives, tasks, and strategies, 35–36
  internal and external scanning, 34–35
  Macro Practitioner's Workbook, 37, 40–49
  matrix for, 37
  mission statements, 33
  reasons for, 30–31
  values, vision, and goals, 33–34
  writing the plan, 36–37
Strategies, developing, 35–36
Subcommittees, for fundraising, 259
Summarizing reports, 17–18
Support gaining, 83–99. *See also* Opposition
Support system, 15
Sustainability, grants and, 227
Systems, 14–16

Target audience
  fundraisers and, 254
  fundraising letters, 268
  public relations plans and, 102–103
Target system, 15–16
Task environments, 30, 156
Task forces, 144–155
  action plans for members, 149
  defined, 144
  defining the problem, 146
  homeless case study, 145
  Macro Practitioner's Workbook, 149, 151–155
  member descriptions, 147–148
  members of, 146–147
  need for, 145–146
  writing scripts for potential members, 148
  See also Committees
Tasks, 29, 47
  developing, 35
Taxes

employment reporting, 221
  forms, 221
Term limits, for board of directors, 159
Title page, of a report, 17
Title VII (of the 1964 Civil Rights Act), 188, 201
Top-down communication, 128
  methods, 135
Training, board members, 161
Trustees, 157. *See also* Board of directors

Underfunding, 4
Universities, recruiting and, 184

Values, 44, 84–85
  core, 34
  defined, 33
  See also VIBES
Values, interests, beliefs, ethics, and slants. *See* VIBES
VIBES (values, interests, beliefs, ethics, and slants), 84–88
  categorizing groups by, 87–88
  summary of, 85
  using to structure strategy, 87–88
Victim-Offender Mediation of Madison County (VOMMC) financial management example, 215–221. *See also* Financial management
Vision, 30, 44
  defined, 33–34
Vision statements, 34, 45
Voices for Social Services (VSS), 51
Volunteer goals, for fundraising, 257–258
VSS. *See* Voices for Social Services

Work groups, creating, 10–11, 20, 31–33, 41, 52–53
Writing
  classified advertising tips, 177
  contingency plans, 58–59
  strategic plans, 36–37, 48
  written communication, 132–133
  See also Foundations; Fundraising letters; Government grants
Written communication, 132–133

Zero-based budgeting, 213